Governance in Ancient India

Reconstructing Indian History & Culture

(ISSN 0971-3824)

1. Society in Ancient India; by Sures Chandra Banerji
2. Political Thought in Ancient India; by G.P. Singh
3. Early Indian Historical Tradition and Archaeology; by G.P. Singh
4. Vasantotsava: The Spring Festivals of India; by Leona M. Anderson
5. Ecological Readings in the Veda; by M. Vannucci
6. Vṛndāvana in Vaiṣṇava Literature; by Maura Corcoran
7. Social History of the Tamils (1707–1947); by P. Subramanian
8. Ancient Indian Coinage; by Rekha Jain
9. Buddhism and Socio-Economic Life of Eastern India; by Bimal Chandra Mohapatra
10. Chandragupta Maurya; by P.L. Bhargava
11. Mṛtyu: Concept of Death in Indian Traditions; by Gian Giuseppe Filippi
12. Yama: The Glorious Lord of the Other World; by Kusum P. Merh
13. Sacred Complex of Ujjain; by D.K. Samanta
14. Vedic View of the Earth; by S.R.N. Murthy
15. Society in the Atharvaveda; by B.S. Kharade
16. Orissan History, Culture and Archaeology; by S. Pradhan
17. Education in Ancient India; by Mitali Chatterjee
18. Surā: The Liquor and the Vedic Sacrifice; by M.B. Kolhatkar
19. Human Ecology in the Vedas; by Marta Vannucci
20. Governance in Ancient India; by Anup Chandra Pandey
21. The Cultural Glory of Ancient India: A Literary Overview; by Sures Chandra Banerji
22. Kauṭilya's Arthaśāstra in the Light of Modern Science & Technology; by Sunil Sen Sarma
23. History of Jainism: With Special Reference to Mathurā; by V.K. Sharma
25. Ancient Indian Historiography: Sources and Interpretations; by G.P. Singh
26. Republics, Kingdoms, Towns and Cities in Ancient India; by G.P. Singh
27. Facets of Ancient Indian History and Culture: New Perception; by G.P. Singh
28. Kamakhya: A Socio-cultural Study; by Nihar Ranjan Mishra
29. History and Culture of Tamil Nadu as Gleaned from the Sanskrit Inscriptions (vol. 1: up to c. AD 1310); by Chithra Madhavan
30. Lifestyle of the Vedic People; by Pranati Ghosal
31. History and Culture of Tamil Nadu as Gleaned from the Sanskrit Inscriptions (vol. 2: up to c. AD 1310 - c. AD 1885); by Chithra Madhavan
32. Matrimonial Alliances and Ancient Indian Polity (c. 600 BCE to CE 650); by Preeti Prabhat
33. Artisans and Craftsmen of Northern India; by Kuldeep Singh Thind
34. The Evolution of Historiographical Tradition in Ancient and Medieval India; by G.P. Singh
35. Warfare in Ancient India: Theory and Practice; by Soma Basu
36. Sanskrit Education and Literature in Ancient and Medieval Tamil Nadu; by Chithra Madhavan
37. Rājadharma in Mahābhārata; by Priyanka Pandey
38. Interstate Relations in Northern India – Circa 800–1200 CE; by Shiva Gopal Bajpai

Reconstructing Indian History & Culture, no. 20

Governance in Ancient India

(From the Ṛgvedic Period to *c*.650 CE)

Anup Chandra Pandey

DK PRINTWORLD
Publishers of Indian Traditions

Cataloging in Publication Data — DK
[Courtesy: D.K. Agencies (P) Ltd. <docinfo@dkagencies.com>]

Pandey, Anup Chandra, 1959 –
Governance in Ancient India.
(Reconstructing Indian history & culture; no. 20)
Includes bibliographical references (p.).
Includes index.

1. India – Politics and government – To 997.
2. Political Science – India – History. 3. State, The.
I. Title. II. Series: Reconstructing Indian history & culture; no. 20.

ISBN: 978-81-246-0135-8
First published in India in 2000
Second revised edition published in 2024

Printed and published by:
D.K. Printworld (P) Ltd.
Regd. Office: "Vedaśrī", F-395, Sudarshan Park
ESI Hospital Metro Station, New Delhi - 110015
Phones: (011) 4172 2626, 98713 94815
e-mail: indology@dkprintworld.com
Website: www.dkprintworld.com

Dedicated to

My Father

Dr Vimal Chandra Pandey

Preface to the Second Edition

India is one of the most ancient civilizations. The governance structures that existed in ancient India were one of the most developed in the contemporary world. Long before the advent of modern-world thinkers, ancient India had a very well-organized administrative machinery run on scientific lines. It is interesting to note that a number of our modern-day administrative institutions are rooted deep in our ancient past.

I am happy to note that my description of ancient Indian governance structures and processes elaborated in the first edition of this book has been duly appreciated both by the academicians and administrators.

I sincerely hope that this book will be useful for researchers working in this field, and also provide the readers a peep in our glorious past.

Buddha Pūrṇimā **Anup Chandra Pandey**
Lucknow, 23 May 2024

Preface to the First Edition

THE ancient Indian word for the civil service, as used in literature and inscriptions, is generally *amātyas*. While words like *saciva* and *mantrī* denote particular posts and offices, the word *amātya* is generic in nature and stands for the whole lot of high functionaries comprising the central and provincial bureaucracy. It is a pool like our present-day All India and Provincial Civil Services from which are drawn various types of officials manning numerous departments. Thus, a *saciva*, a *mantrī*, a *senāpati*, a *sāndhivigrahika*, to name only a few, will all be *amātyas*. But, an *amātya* may not necessarily be a *saciva* or a *mantrī* only.

The perusal of our literary sources makes it amply clear that *amātyas* were carefully recruited, trained, appointed, maintained, promoted and demoted in accordance with well-set norms. Later, they were put in charge of different offices according to their qualifications, aptitudes and proven calibre and capabilities.

There was a well-organized hierarchy of bureaucrats with seniors supervising the work of their juniors; in most cases, with a view to avoiding red-tapism, the seniors were empowered to reward, punish and transfer their juniors without reference to the central authorities. Besides seniors' supervision, periodical auditing, counter-checking and the inspectional tours of the king and the high functionaries, the well-organized espionage, keeping a watchful eye on the activities of the officials, kept the bureaucracy on its toes. As gleaned from foreign testimony, the standard of public life was ethically high, yet corruption and exploitation, especially in the departments of revenue and police, always caused concern to the state. It was probably for this reason that some of the law-givers had advised the king to keep *kośa* and *bala* under his direct control.

As early as the Brāhmaṇas, it was commonly realized that the vigour and energy of the state was the result of the vigour and energy of its functionaries. Kauṭilya went to the extent of recording that the king and the bureaucracy were like the two wheels of the cart that was the state. In the absence of a written constitution, a parliament and the budgetary control, as we understand them today, it was the civil service, which, inter alia, constituted a powerful check on royal power in ancient India.

Ancient India abhorred one-man rule. This is why the *rājāyatta* state was decried. Jinasena only gave expression to the popular sentiments when he wrote that the noble would not reside in the kingdom of an arbitraty ruler. But equally bad was considered the *sacivāyatta* state where the bureaucracy was dominant. Ancient political thinkers sought to strike a balance between the powers of the king and the powers of the bureaucracy, and emphasized the political dictum that and *ubhayāyatta* state was the best where the powers of the king and the civil service held each other in check.

With the passage of time, ancient Indian Civil Service tended to be hereditary. Its hereditary character was probably derived from a general feeling that ancestral traditions and training, accumulated wisdom and virtue; loyalty and bravery of a set of families will automatically be imbibed by new entrants into the civil service, drawn from those families.

While it is understandable that in those days of frequent warfare even civil officers were usually trained in soldierly art; it is an additional feature of ancient Indian Civil Servants that very often they held more than one office. It was either done in recognition of their extraordinary merit or was occasioned by dearth of adequate number of talented men to man a large number of departments.

It is untrue that the śūdras were totally excluded from all responsible jobs. Nevertheless, the process of appointment of officers was very often vitiated by caste considerations. The brāhmaṇas, kṣatriyas and vaiśyas, among themselves, grabbed majority of the prestigious posts, mainly because the śūdras, on account of their social disabilities and lack of educational facilities, would hardly be expected to compete successfully with higher classes.

Perhaps, by far the most important feature of the ancient Indian Civil Service was its secular character. Since ancient India had no state religion or church and the ancient Indian king was never called upon to play the defender of faith, religion was never the criterion of recruitment. This explains why Brāhmanists, Buddhists, Jainas, Śaivas, Vaiṣṇavas and adherents of other faiths could freely enter the civil service solely on the basis of their merit.

The ancient Indian Civil Service had to perform manifold functions – deliberative, legislative, executive, police, judicial, military and financial – to name only the most important, and its performance was under constant vigil of the king through a number of devices.

It appears that the central government, for most of the period, maintained a secretariat and housed at least the most important civil servants at its capital. The civil servants, besides being handsomely paid, were given various amenities and privileges. If they died in harness, their families were taken care of by the state.

The designations of ancient Indian Civil Servants, their requisite qualifications, the process of their appointments, their functions and other allied subjects find mention, sometimes in a scattered manner, in our ancient literature, inscriptions and foreign accounts. Unfortunately, a critical, comparative and compact study of the available data on the subject has not been made so far in its entirety. We, therefore, propose to take up this very fascinating subject for our research and highlight the evolution, nature, scope, functions, importance and allied issues of the ancient Indian governance in a comprehensive manner.

Anup Chandra Pandey

Contents

List of Abbreviations

ĀcāSū	:	*Ācārāṅgasūtra*
AitBrā	:	*Aitareya Bhāhmaṇa*
AI	:	*Ancient India*
AmarK	:	*Amarakośa*
AṅguN	:	*Aṅguttara Nikāya*
API	:	Allahabad Pillar Inscription
Arth	:	*Arthaśāstra*
ASI, AR	:	*Archaeological Survery of India: Annual Reports*
Aṣṭ	:	*Aṣṭādhyāyī*
AV	:	*Atharvaveda*
ĀvaNir	:	*Āvaśyaka Niryukti*
BhagSū	:	*Bhagavatīsūtra*
CHB	:	*Comprehensive History of Bihar*
CHI	:	*Cambridge History of India*
CICAI	:	*Catalogue of Indian Coins in British Museum: Ancient India*
CII	:	*Corpus Inscriptionum Indicarum*
DīghaN	:	*Dīgha Nikāya*
Divyā	:	*Divyāvadāna*
EI	:	*Epigraphia Indica*
HC	:	*Harṣacarita*
HK	:	*History of Kanauj*
HP	:	*Hindu Polity*

HPS	:	*Harṣa: A Political Study*
IA	:	*Indian Antiquary*
IC	:	*Indian Culture*
IHQ	:	*Indian Historical Quarterly*
JASB	:	*Journal of Asiatic Society of Bengal*
JBORS	:	*Journal of Bihar and Orissa Research Society*
JBRS	:	*Journal of Bihar Research Society*
JRAS	:	*Journal of Royal Asiatic Society*
JUPHS	:	*Journal of U.P. Historical Society*
KA	:	*The Kauṭilīya Arthaśāstra*
Kād	:	*Kādambarī*
KalpaSū	:	*Kalpasūtra*
KāmN	:	*Kāmandakīya Nītisāra*
KāṭhSaṁ	:	*Kāṭhaka Saṁhitā*
KRE	:	Kaliṅga Rock Edict
Kumāra	:	*Kumārasambhava*
MaitrSaṁ	:	*Maitrāyaṇī Saṁhitā*
MajjhN	:	*Majjhima Nikāya*
Mālavikā	:	*Mālavikāgnimitra*
Manu	:	*Manusmṛti*
Mbh	:	*Mahābhārata*
McCrindle	:	*India as Described by Megasthenes and Arrian*
Mṛccha	:	*Mṛcchakaṭika*
MRE	:	Minor Rock Edict
Mudrā	:	*Mudrārākṣasa*
PañcaBrā	:	*Pañcaviṁśa Brāhmaṇa*
Pari	:	Pariśiṣṭa-Parva
PE	:	Pillar Edict

PHAI	:	*Political History of Ancient India*
PIHC	:	*Proceedings of the Indian History Congress*
Raghu	:	*Raghuvaṁśa*
Rāj	:	*Rājataraṅgiṇī*
Rām	:	*Rāmāyaṇa*
RE	:	Rock Edict
R̥V	:	*R̥gveda*
Sabhā	:	Sabhā-Parva
Śāk	:	*Abhijñānaśākuntalam*
SaṁN	:	*Saṁyutta Nikāya*
Śānti	:	Śānti-Parva
ŚatBrā	:	*Śatapatha Brāhmaṇa*
SBE	:	Sacred Books of the East
SI	:	*Select Inscriptions*
Sūtra	:	*Sūtrakr̥tānta*
SV	:	*Sāmaveda*
TaitBrā	:	*Taittirīya Brāhmaṇa*
VājSaṁ	:	*Vājasaneyī Saṁhitā*
Vana	:	Vana-Parva
Vik	:	*Vikramorvaśīyam*
VinP	:	*Vinaya Piṭaka*
Virāṭa	:	Vitrāṭa-Parva
Yājña	:	*Yājñavalkyasmr̥ti*
YV	:	*Yajurveda*

Transliteration Chart

a	ā	i	ī	u	ū	ṛ	ṝ
अ	आ	इ	ई	उ	ऊ	ऋ	ॠ

e	ai	o	au	ṁ	ḥ	m̐
ए	ऐ	ओ	औ	अं	अः	ँ

ka	kha	ga	gha	ṅa
क	ख	ग	घ	ङ
ca	cha	ja	jha	ña
च	छ	ज	झ	ञ
ṭa	ṭha	ḍa	ḍha	ṇa
ट	ठ	ड	ढ	ण
ta	tha	da	dha	na
त	थ	द	ध	न
pa	pha	ba	bha	ma
प	फ	ब	भ	म

ya	ra	la	va
य	र	ल	व
śa	ṣa	sa	ha
श	ष	स	ह
kṣa	tra	jña	śra
क्ष	त्र	ज्ञ	श्र

1

Framework Sources

FORTUNATELY for us we have a variety of sources at our disposal which shed light on the subject of our study. Of the ancient sources the Brāhmanical works constitute the earliest ones. Though a vast majority of them are religio-social in character, they do contain allusions to some or the other aspects of Indian polity.

On the apex stand the four Vedas – the *Ṛgveda*, *Yajurveda*, *Sāmaveda* and *Atharvaveda*. They "give us abundant information respecting all that is most interesting in the contemplation of antiquity".[1] The Veda formed of *ṛcā*s (hymns couched in *chanda*s and *caraṇa*s) came to be known as the *Ṛgveda*.

It appears that for quite sometime the hymns lay scattered and disjointed. But as their number grew and as the Aryans realized the need of keeping them free from tempering under the impact of non-Aryan ideas, they collected and arranged them in a systematic manner. Thereafter the *Ṛgveda* also came to be known as the *Ṛgveda Saṁhitā* (collection). It has ten *maṇḍala*s comprising 1,028 *sūkta*s.

The *Yajurveda* is so called because it deals with *yajuḥ* (sacrifice). It is ritualistic in character.

The *Sāmaveda* derived its name from the word *sāma* which means "song". Its hymns were sung in praise of gods and goddesses at the time of sacrifices. Barring seventy-five original hymns, all its hymns have been lifted from the *Ṛgveda*.

---

1 Radhakrishnan, S., *Indian Philosophy*, vol. I, p. 64.

> While the *Ṛgveda* describes the period of conflict between the fair-skinned Aryans and the dark *dasyus*, which the Indian mythology makes into a strife of *devas* and *rākṣasas*, the *Atharvaveda* speaks to us of the period when the conflict is settled and the two are trying to live in harmony by mutual give and take.[2]

With the passage of time sacrificial cult became more and more complicated. Hence, there arose the necessity of composing a new type of work which may spell out clearly the form and content of each sacrifice. This sacerdotal literature is known as Brāhmaṇas. They interpret the sacrificial Vedic hymns and are mostly in prose, though we occasionally come across certain verses in them. Each Veda came to have its own Brāhmaṇa. For instance, the *Aitareya Brāhmaṇa* and the *Kauṣītaki Brāhmaṇa* are related to the *Ṛgveda*. The *Śatapatha Brāhmaṇa* belongs to the *Yajurveda*. The *Sāmaveda* has the *Pañcaviṁśa Brāhmaṇa* and the *Atharvaveda* the *Gopatha Brāhmaṇa*.

In the course of time the Vedic religion started being more contemplative than ritualistic. This tendency is first noticed in the Āraṇyakas which constitute a new form of literature to be studied and contemplated upon in seclusion (*Araṇya* – forest).

The new comtemplative mood of the philosophers found fuller expression in the Upaniṣads. Being the last leg of the Vedic literature, they are known as Vedāṅgas as well. "There is no important form of Hindu thought, heterodox Buddhism included, which is not rooted in the Upaniṣad".[3] Some of the most important Upaniṣads are: *Īśāvāsya, Kena, Kaṭha, Aitareya, Chāndogya, Bṛhadāraṇyaka, Muṇḍaka, Praśna, Taittirīya, Kauṣītaki, Śvetāśvatara*, etc. They are neither the creation of one man nor of one time. The brāhmaṇas, kṣatriyas, vaiśyas and even ladies such as Gārgī and Maitreyī, made significant contribution to the growth of the Upaniṣadic thought.

The Vedic literature is predominantly religio-philosophical. However, it contains some very important, though casual, references

---

2 Radhakrishnan, S., *Indian Philosophy*, vol. I, p. 118.

3 Bloomfield, M., *The Religion of the Vedas*, p. 51.

to ancient Indian polity including bureaucracy.

Among the works on grammar, Pāṇini's *Aṣṭādhyāyī* is the most notable. Attributed to the fourth century BCE, some of its *sūtra*s allude to several aspects of ancient Indian administration. They are more vividly explained by Patañjali, the grammarian of the second century BCE in his famous *Mahābhāṣya*.

Amid the Sūtra literature, the Kalpasūtra consisting of the Śrautasūtras, Gṛhyasūtras and the Dharmasūtras are noteworthy. Though they mainly dwell upon the ritualistic, social and religio-ethical life of people, occasionally we come across some political ideas of their times as well. Of the *dharmasūtrakāra*s Gautama seems to be the most ancient. He has been quoted in the *Baudhāyana Dharmasūtra*. He may be placed somewhere between 600 BCE and 400 BCE.

Most of the Dharmasūtras were posterior to the Buddha and betray an anxiety to reorganize the Brāhmanical socio-political set-up which was greatly shaken by the onslaught of Buddhist ideas and ideals. Among other *dharmasūtrakāra*s mention may be made of Āpastamba and Vasiṣṭha. The latter has been mentioned by Manu for the first time as a law-giver and can be placed between 300 BCE and 100 BCE. From the linguistic point of view Āpastamba appears to be anterior to Vasiṣṭha and may be placed somewhere between 600 BCE and 300 BCE. All these *dhrama-sūtrakāra*s are only marginally relevent to our study because of their very stray references to ancient Indian governance.

The *Arthaśāstra* of Kauṭilya, however, enjoys a unique importance as a source-book of ancient Indian polity and civil service. That the *Arthaśāstra* was the work of Kauṭilya is borne out by its internal evidence.[4] Kāmandaka,[5] who regards Kauṭilya as his model, ascribes the *Arthaśāstra* to him. Later, Daṇḍin[6] tells us the same thing. That

---

4 *Arth* 15.13.

5 *Nītisāra* 1.7.

6 *Daśakumāracarita* 2.8.

Viṣṇugupta, Cāṇakya and Kauṭilya were one and the same person is clearly attested by Śaṅkarācārya. Scholars such as A.B. Keith have doubted Kauṭilya's authorship of the *Arthaśāstra* mainly on the ground that it does not mention Candragupta Maurya. But the non-occurrence of his emperor's name might be due to royal etiquette. It is further asserted that the *Arthaśāstra* contains such phrases as *iti kauṭilyaḥ* and *neti kauṭilyaḥ* no fewer than seventy-two times which may suggest it to be the work of a school and not Kauṭilya himself. But a number of examples from Sanskrit literature can be cited to show that many authors have used their names in third person in their works. The terminology and style used by Kauṭilya are more akin to those of Baudhāyana and Āpastamba than of Manu and Yājñavalkya. Moreover, the comparison of the contents of the *Arthaśāstra*, Megasthenes' accounts and the Aśokan inscriptions put the three sources in one and the same chronological bracket. Over and above everything the ancient Indian tradition invariably describes Kauṭilya as Candragupta Maurya's contemporary.[7] The mention of the Licchavis, Vajjis and Mallas in the *Arthaśāstra* – the republics mentioned in early Buddhist literature – may also point to its date around fourth century BCE.

The *Arthaśāstra* has fifteen *adhikaraṇas*, 150 *adhyāyas* and 180 *prakaraṇas*. Mainly written in prose, it has a meagre scattering of verses also. It is a unique source of study of the socio-economic, ethico-religious, political and diplomatic institutions in ancient India. For the first time in ancient India, it deals with a variety of subjects concerning ancient Indian governance in an exhaustive manner.

The two epics of India – the *Rāmāyaṇa* and the *Mahābhārata* – also provide us with useful information on the subject. The former is anterior to the latter. Veda Vyāsa, the author of the *Mahābhārata*[8] is familiar with Vālmīki, the author of the *Rāmāyaṇa*. He cites a

---

7 Law, N.N., *Studies in Ancient Hindu Polity*, Introductory Essay, pp. 35-43.

8 *Mbh* 1.143.66.

śloka from the *Rāmāyaṇa* in his work.[9] Not only that, the *Mahābhārata* contains *Rāmopākhyāna* also. On the other hand, the *Rāmāyaṇa* is not at all familiar with the heroes and events of the *Mahābhārata*. Since the *Rāmāyaṇa* does not mention the Buddha, it is natural to presume that it was the creation of the pre-Buddhist age. This presumption is further supported by the fact that whereas the capital of Kosala has always been called Sāketa in the Buddhist works, the *Rāmāyaṇa* calls it Ayodhyā. Its language is also pre-Pāṇinian and archaic in nature and may not be far removed from the Vedic language. Thus, the kernel of the *Rāmāyaṇa* might have come into existence in the second millennium BCE. Its present form has come much later.

The *Mahābhārata* has been mentioned for the first time in the *Āśvalāyana Gṛhyasūtra* (600 BCE). An inscription of Cambodia (600 BCE) also mentions the *Mahābhārata* as a religious work. However, the Mahābhārata war seems to have been fought around 1200 BCE.[10] Its historicity is confirmed by persistent traditional allusion to it in Brāhmanical, Buddhist and Jaina works as also in foreign accounts, inscriptions and sculptures through the ages. The Painted Grey Ware found at all important sites of the *Mahābhārata* period by archaeologists, provides additional archaeological evidence of its historicity.

But what is most important for us is the great value of the two epics as a source of information regarding numerous aspects of ancient Indian people. They shed profuse light on administrative and bureaucratic set-up of states.

Like the Sūtra literature, the Smṛti literature is also very vital tool of historical research. While the Sūtra literature is mostly in prose, the Smṛti literature is in verse. Unlike the Dharmasūtras, the Smṛtis are regarded as divine in character.

Of all the Smṛtis, the *Manusmṛti* is the oldest and the most important. It is very difficult to ascertain the authorship of this *smṛti*

---

9 *Rām* 6.81.28.

10 *The Mahābhārata: Myth or Reality,* p. 254.

for the simple reason that many Manus find mention in our ancient literature right from the *Ṛgveda* onward.

The *Nāradasmṛti* informs us that the *Manusmṛti* was finally composed by Sumati, the son of Bhṛgu. The *Bṛhaspatismṛti* is also familiar with the *Manusmṛti*. It accepts the *Manusmṛti* as the final authority on law when it says that

> the *Manusmṛti* contains the gist of the Vedas and therefore a Smṛti contrary to Manu's does not obtain force.

The *Mahābhārata* refers to it.[11] Both Baudhāyana[12] and Āpastamba[13] knew it. The *Rāmāyaṇa* contains an allusion to it.[14] The *Chāndogya Upaniṣad* VIII.15 observes that Manu transmitted knowledge from Prajāpati to the mankind. Manu figures in the *Taittirīya Saṁhitā* II.2.10.2 and the *Maitrāyaṇī Saṁhitā* I.1.5.

Though it is intimately familiar with the geography of the Madhyadeśa – the territory extending from the Himalayas to the Vindhyas and from the Sarasvatī to Prayāga – it contains references to Gauḍadeśa (XI.94), the ocean (VIII.100) and the Coḷas and the Draviḍas (X.44). It refers to the Yavanas, the Śakas and the Pahlavas (X.44).

All these facts put together go to denote that the core of the *Manusmṛti* is very ancient, but subsequent ages witnessed the incorporation of later material into it.

The *Manusmṛti* comprises twelve *adhyāya*s consisting of 2,694 *śloka*s. Apart from its socio-religious data, it contains much that is relevant to our study.

Of the other Smṛtis, *Yājñavalkyasmṛti*, *Bṛhaspatismṛti*, *Nāradasmṛti* and *Kātyāyanasmṛti* occasionally allude to civil service. More than anything else they throw vivid light on the ancient Indian judiciary and the officers manning it.

---

11 *Mbh*, Anu., 47.34.

12 *Baudhāyana* IV.1.14.

13 *Āpastamba* II.16.1.

14 *Rām*, Kis, 18.30.

The Purāṇas have much that is important for the construction of ancient Indian history. Generally speaking, the majority of them can chronologically be placed between the Gupta period and the early medieval period. Though important otherwise, they are remotedly concerned with the civil service. Of all the Purāṇas the *Agni Purāṇa* needs special mention, because it alludes to several aspects of ancient Indian polity.

However, the *Nītisāra* of Kāmandaka is a serious work on Hindu polity and, therefore, dwells upon manifold aspects of ancient Indian governance. It has bodily lifted much of its material from the *Arthaśāstra* of Kauṭilya. To that extent, it is not original. But its description clearly shows all the same that many of the Kauṭilyan ideas and ideals had outlived him as late as the Gupta period or even the post-Gupta period. The *Nītisāra* of Kāmandaka is placed variously between 600 and 800 CE.

Of the Brāhmanical works belonging to the category of secular literature the following are important for our purpose:

1. Works of Kālidāsa, especially the *Raghuvaṁśa*.
2. The *Mudrārākṣasa* of Viśākhadatta.
3. The *Amarakośa* of Amarasiṁha.
4. The *Mr̥cchakaṭika* of Śūdraka.
5. The *Harṣacarita* and *Kādambarī* of Bāṇa.
6. The *Nāgānanda*, the *Priyadarśikā* and the *Ratnāvalī* of Harṣa.

Some of the Buddhist works give valuable, though sketchy, information about ancient Indian bureaucracy. The Jātakas contain stray references to *amātyas*. The Ceylonese chronicles contain stray references to the subject. The *Mahāvastua* which was composed between the first and third centuries CE[15] is a good source of history. The word *mahāmātra* occurs in the *Mahāvastu Avadāna*. Like the *tīrthas*, the *mahāmātras*, therein eighteen in number of whom

15 Keith's, A.B., Foreword to N.N. Law's, *A Study of the Mahāvastu*.

daṇḍapāla was one.[16] The *Milindapañha* which belonged to the first century CE[17] is familiar with *śulkādhyakṣa*.[18] It also informs us that King Milinda had a council of ministers.[19] The *Lalitavistara* (first century CE) mentions the chief of the army. The *Saṁyukta-Ratnapiṭakasūtra* has it that Aśvaghoṣa was Kaniṣka's courtier. The *Divyāvadāna* which may be placed anywhere between the second and the fourth centuries, speaks of evil ministers advising the king to levy oppressive taxes on the people.[20] The ministers were called *pāriṣadya*.[21] It also speaks of a councillor as *tulaka*. The *Saddharmapuṇḍarīka* (second century) speaks of the civil servants as *rājapuruṣas*, *rājaputras* and *rājamahāmātras* as well as *rājāmātya*.[22]

The foreign accounts too give us some valuable information regarding ancient Indian polity. Herodotus was probably the earliest writer on India. But his *Historica* hardly contains anything about polity. Ktesias who was the royal physician of Artazerxes, the Persian emperor, wrote on the basis of hearsay and gave a highly unrealistic account of India. The accounts of Nearchus, Onesicritus and Arisrobulos who accompanied Alexander on his military expedition, though true, are sketchy and do not tell us anything regarding the ancient civil service.

The first foreign writer to supply us valuable information regarding our subject was Megasthenes, the Greek ambassador, sent to Candragupta Maurya's court by Seleucus. Though his original book named *Indica* is lost, its extracts are preserved in the writings of later writers such as Strabo and Arrian. The charge that Megasthenes was a liar is unjustifiable, though many of his statements based on hearsay or his poor understanding of Indian customs and language

---

16 Basak, R.G., *A Study of the Mahāvastu Avadāna*, pp. 3-4.

17 Winternitz, M., *History of Indian Literature*, vol. II, p. 171.

18 *Milinda*, p. 365.

19 Ibid., pp. 4, 19-20.

20 *Divyā*, p. 562.

21 Puri, 1965, *India Under the Kuṣāṇas*, p. 85.

22 *Saddharmapuṇḍarīka*, pp. 180, 288.

are incorrect. All that he wrote on the basis of his personal knowledge and experience is invaluable for students of history. He belonged to the fourth century BCE. The account of Megasthenes corroborates, in many respects, several pieces of information provided to us by the *Arthaśāstra* of Kauṭilya. His caste numbers V, VI and VII comprise the vast Mauryan bureaucracy. His accounts of the Municipal Board of Pāṭaliputra and of the Military Board cover many of the functions of the *nāgaraka*, the *senāpati* and their subordinates. His overseers are the *cara*s of Kauṭilya. His councillors are the *mantrī*s of Kauṭilya. The similarities between the descriptions of the two contemporary writers can be examined and made use of in our study.

Of other classical works the *Periplus of the Erythrean Sea*, written by an anonymous author of the first century CE, *Geography* of Ptolemy of the second century CE and *Natural History* of Pliny of nearly the same period are noteworthy. However, they shed information mainly about Indian trade and commerce and contain little that is important for the study of ancient civil service.

Among Chinese travellers who visited India from time to time and wrote about her, Fa-hien, Yuan Chwang and I-tsing are the most important. But they were Buddhists; their main interest centred round Buddhism in and outside India. Even so, their accounts contain several significant references to the Indian state and government of their times.

Inscriptions too constitute a very important source of ancient Indian polity. The Aśokan inscriptions engraved on rocks and pillars, which are found all over India, are extremely comprehensive for constructing the history of the Mauryan period. When studied in the light of the contents of the *Arthaśāstra* of Kauṭilya and Megasthenes' account, they present a very reliable picture of India of their times. Significantly, all the three sources, which have much in common, contain much that is relevant to the study of ancient Indian governance.

The Aśokan inscriptions, inter alia, refer to the *pariṣad*, the *puruṣa*s, the *rājuka*s, the *mahāmātra*s, the *dharma-mahāmātra*s, the *prādeśikas*, the *paura-vyavahārikas*, the *yuktas* as some of the important constituents of Mauryan civil service.

Besides the Aśokan inscriptions some other inscriptions are also very useful. One of these is the Hāthīgumphā Inscription of Khāravela, which, inter alia, tells us how the *yuvarāja* was groomed for his future role as the king. The Ayodhyā Inscription of Puṣyamitra Śuṅga confirms that he was previously a *senāpati* but continued to hold that designation even when he became the king.

The Greek Inscriptions speak of their Strategoses and Meridarkhs ruling over their provinces and districts. Such one is the Swāt Relic Vase Inscription.

The Vidiśā Pillar Inscription has reference to the institution of *dūta*.

The Śakas have left behind them a large number of inscriptions giving us designations of several officers. For instance, the Takṣaśilā Copper Plate Inscription of the year 78 informs us that under Maues ruled Kṣatrapa Liaka Kusulika and his son Mahādānapati Patika. This is an example of the Satrapal system which prevailed in Indo-Greek and Śaka dynasties. The Mathurā Stone Inscription of the time of Soḍāsa calls the treasurer as *gañjavara*. The *grāmika* finds mention in a Mathurā Jaina Image Inscription of the year 41.

Inscriptions of the Śakas refer to a comprehensive civil service comprising *amātya*, *rājāmātya*, *senāpati*, *mati-saciva*, *karma-saciva* and *mahādaṇḍanāyaka*. Among their inscriptions found in western India, the Jūnāgaṛh Inscription of Rudradāman I is the most important.

Sātavāhana inscriptions also refer to the *senāpati*, the *mahārāṣṭrī*, the *mahāmātra*, the *amātya*, the *pratihārarakṣī*, the *navakarmika*, etc. The Nāsik Cave Inscription of Gautamīputra Śātakarṇī of the year 24 contains words *rājan*, *mahādevī*, *amātya* and *pratihārarakṣī*. Another inscription found at the same place belonging to the twenty-second year of Vāsiṣṭhīputra Pulumāvī refers to the *amātya* and *mahāsenāpati*.

Kuṣāṇa inscriptions are no less important from our point of view.

They contain designations of several state functionaries. The Sārnāth Inscription of the third year of Kaniṣka speaks of *mahākṣatrapa* Kharapallāna and *kṣatrapa* Vanaspara ruling over eastern provinces with their headquarters at Varanasi. The Surkh Koṭal Inscription informs us that Kaniṣka Nikaṭor had got a sanctuary built by one of his high officials, Nokonzoko. A Māṭ Inscription mentions a *mahādaṇḍanāyaka* under Huviṣka. A Mathurā Jaina Inscription of the days of Vāsudeva refers to a *grāmika*, signifying thereby that the village autonomy was still in tact. The famous relic tower at Puruṣapura was built by Kaniṣka's *navakarmika* (engineer) Agesilaos. Kaniṣka had other councillors in Aśvaghoṣa, Pārśva, Māṭhara and Caraka. These are some of the references to show that the Kuṣāṇas had a well- organized civil service.

Gupta inscriptions have preserved the memory of a vast bureaucracy of their times. They throw profuse light on central, provincial, district and village administration carried on by a host of officers. Some of the most important inscriptions are Allāhābād Pillar Inscription of Samudragupta, the Udayagiri Cave Inscription of Candragupta II, the Karamadāṇḍā Inscription of Kumāragupta I and the Jūnāgaṛh Inscription of Skandagupta. Several copper-plate inscriptions, especially those found at Dāmodarpur, provide us details of the local administration.

Among the inscriptions of Harṣa, the Bānskheṛā Inscription is the most important for our purpose containing the names of such officers as *dūtaka, mahāpramātāra, mahāsāmanta* and *mahākṣapaṭalādhikṛta*, as also those of territorial divisions, such as *grāma, pāṭhaka, viṣaya* and *bhukti*. The Madhuban Inscription corroborates some of these details.

Coins constitute another important source of our information regarding the civil service. Our knowledge of the Satrapal system or joint rule prevalent among Indo-Greeks, Śakas, Pārthians and probably Kuṣāṇas is derived mainly from coins. To quote, on one category of coins the name of the Śaka ruler Azes is inscribed on the obverse in Greek, whereas the name of Azilises occurs on the reverse of those coins in Kharoṣṭhi. It becomes clear that Azes I was the ruler and that he had associated Azilises as his subordinate. Now, in the second category of coins the name of Azilises appears on the obverse in Greek and the name of Azes II occurs on their reverse in Kharoṣṭhi, leaving us in no doubt that after the death of Azes I, his subordinate was elevated to the regal position and another Azes II was made his subordinate.

Many Kuṣāṇa as also the Gupta kings are portrayed on their coins in military dress suggesting them to be the supreme commanders of their armies who led them personally on the battlefield. The absence of city-deities on Kuṣāṇa coins have led some scholars to believe that towns and villages had lost their autonomy under the Kuṣāṇas. But this may not be correct. The practice of portraying city-deities on the coins had a foreign origin. And Kuṣāṇas were totally Indianized in course of time. So they might have discontinued the un-Indian practice of portraying city-deities. However, they preserved the traditional post of the *grāmika*, who must have maintained the village autonomy.

Coins also contain the titles of rulers such as *rājan*, *mahārāja*, *rājādhirāja* and *mahārājādhirāja*, showing their imperial status. Among the Gupta coins the Candragupta–Kumāradevī type of coin is unique insofar as it suggests the joint rule of an Indian king and his queen for the first and the last time.

2

Evolution of Civil Service during the Vedic Period

THE Vedas, being predominantly religious in character, are no works on polity. Their seers have expressed their ideas in symbols and images which, very often, are hard to comprehend.[1] In fact, the *mantras* admit of different interpretations. This explains why there is so divergence of opinion with regard to various aspects of Vedic studies.

As regards Vedic polity, its origin and evolution during the vast span of time were influenced by a variety of factors. The internal evidence of the Vedic literature testifies to the vast expanse to territory which gradually came under the control of Aryans. They were familiar with the Himalayas[2] in the Ṛgvedic period. However, the Vindhyas do not find mention in it. Afghanistan seems to have been under their sway. For its rivers the Kubhā (Kabul) and the Suvāstu (Swāt) are mentioned in the *Ṛgveda* (Nadīstuti, X.75). Punjab was, of course, the cradle of their civilization as is attested by the allusion to its seven rivers[3] – the Sindhu, Sarasvatī, Vitastā (Jhelum), Śutudrī (Sataluj), Vipāśā (Vyās), Asiknī (Cenāb) and Paruṣṇī (Rāvī).

---

1 *ta ete vakturabhiprāyavaśādarthānyatvamapi bhajante mantrāḥ* ।
na hyeteṣvarthasyeyattāvadhāraṇamasti ।
mahārthā hyete duṣparijñānāśca । – Durgā on *Nirukta* II.8

2 *yasyeme himavanto mahitvā* । – *ṚV* X.121.4

3 Ibid., X.75.

The other two rivers of Afghanistan are Krumu (Kurum) and Gomatī (Gomal) *saptasindhavaḥ*: *Ṛ̥V* VIII.24.27. They also suggest that the Aryans were very much familiar with the country.

Two of the most important rivers of Haryana, the Dṛ̥ṣadvatī[4] and the Āpayā,[5] have also been spoken of in the *Ṛ̥gveda*. The Gaṅgā and the Yamunā are also known to the Ṛ̥gvedic Aryans. Thus, the land occupied by the Ṛ̥gvedic Aryans extended from Afghanistan to the Gaṅgā and from the Himalayas to the Vindhyas.

By the time of the *Atharvaveda* it extended up to Aṅga and Magadha, including Gāndhāra as well.[6] It is natural to suppose that such a vast territory comprising several states could not have been ruled without some sort of a bureaucratic set-up. The functional organization must have been necessitated by political and socio-economic exigencies. The Aryans were constantly engaged in a tribal warfare among themselves as also against the non-Aryans. For instance, the Dāśarājña war was fought on the bank of the Paruṣṇī between Sudās, one of the greatest kings of the Ṛ̥gvedic period, on one hand and the kings of ten other Aryan tribes.[7] The *Ṛ̥gveda* contains numerous allusions to the armed clashes between the Aryans and the non-Aryans.[8]

The Vedic period also witnessed the emergence of extensive kingdoms ruled by such powerful kings as Divodāsa, Sudās,

---

4 *Ṛ̥V* III.23.4.

5 Ibid.

6 *gandhāribhyo mūjavadbhyogebhyo magadhebhyaḥ* । – *AV* V.22.14

7 *puroḷā itturvaśo yakṣurāsīdrāye matsyāso niśitā apīva* ।
sruṣṭim cakrarubhṛ̥gavo druhyavaśca sakhā sakhāyamataradviṣūcoḥ ॥

ā pakthāso bhalānaso bhanantālināso viṣāṇinaḥ śivāsaḥ ।
ā yo 'nayatsadhamā āryasya gavyā tṛ̥tsubhyo ajāganyudhā nṝn ॥
– *Ṛ̥V* VII.18.6-7

8 *ubhe punāmi rodasī ṛ̥tena druho dahāmi saṁ mahīranindrāḥ* ।
abhivlagya yatra hatā amitrā vailasthānaṁ pari tṛ̥ḷhā aśeran ॥
– *Ṛ̥V* I.133.1

uta dāsasya varcinaḥ sahaśrāṇi śatāvadhīḥ ।
adhi pañca pradhīm̐riva ॥ – *Ṛ̥V* IV.30.15

Purukutsu, Trasadasyu, Parīkṣit, Purūravā and Āyu. The rulers came to be graded according to their power and pelf. The royal gradation is indicated by their titles such as *rājā, jyeṣṭha, adhirāja, mahārāja, svarāṭ, ekarāṭ, virāṭ* and *samrāṭ*.[9] The *viśvasya bhuvanasya rājā* would herald his overlordship by the performance of such sacrifices as the Aśvamedha,[10] the Vājapeya[11] and the Rājasūya.[12] It is impossible to believe that these powerful states have not evolved a well-organized administrative and military system manned by specialized functionaries. They must have raised a financial and fiscal structure to meet the needs of standing armies with their equipment, the civil service with its expanding areas of administration and of public welfare, and of the law enforcing agencies. The earliest of the R̥gvedic kings might have depended upon irregular tributes and gifts for state revenue. But with the passage of time, the state started collecting regular and compulsory taxes, as would be indicated by the use of the words like *bali, bhāga, kara, saṁgr̥hīta* and *bhāgadugha*.

The growing complexities of the economic life of the Vedic

---

9 *samrāḷanyaḥ svarāḷanya ucyste vāṁ* । – *R̥V* VII.82.2

indraśca samrāṭ varuṇaśca rājā ।। – *YV* VIII.37

mahāntaṁ tvā mahīnāṁ samrājaṁ । –*R̥V* X.134.1

tvam rājā janānām । – *R̥V* VIII.64.3

indro adhirājo rājasu । – *AV* VI.98.1

jyeṣṭharājam । – *AV* XX.44.3

vyaciṣṭhe bahupāyye yatemahi svarājye । – *R̥V* V.66.6

ekarāḷasya bhuvanasya rājasi । – *R̥V* VIII.37.3

somo virājamanu rājati – *R̥V* IX.96.18

tatsomarājāya vidmahe mahārājāya dhāmahi । – *MaitSaṁ* II.9.1

tena viśvasya bhuvanasya rājā । – *R̥V* V.85.3

10 *R̥V* V.27.4-6.

11 *ammam vai vājo evam vidvānammamanti vājayatyenam somam vājapeyo ya evamvidvān somam pivati vājameva gacchati* । – *KāṭhSaṁ* XIV.4.5

12 *adhivīro abhiṣatvā sahojijjaitrāyaṇo rathamātiṣṭha govit* । – Ibid. XVIII.5

period is attested by a large number of vocational groups of *rathakāras*, *takṣans*, *maṇikāras*, *karmāras*, *kulālas*, *karṣakas* and the *vaṇikas*, etc. There was no dearth of anti-social elements, committing a variety of crimes.[13] The state was bound to organize a police force to apprehend them and forge some sort of a judicial system to punish them.

Thus, the existence of a civil service in the Vedic age can well be presumed in the political, military, economic and social compulsions of the state. We come across a number of words in Vedic literature which are generic in nature and denote a cadre of officers. The one which became the most important in later times and came to be used for the central civil service is *amātya* which finds its first reference in the *Ṛgveda*.[14] The other two words are *rājanya* and *kṣatra*. They are generally taken to mean kṣatriya and political power respectively. Sometimes the word *kṣatra* is used for a kṣatriya as well. But some of the Vedic allusions to them do not rule out the possibility of their being used as the civil service. The Vedic literature emphasizes a close cooperation between the *brahma-śakti* and the *kṣatra-śakti*.[15] While the *purohita* represented the former, the majority of civil servants seem to have been recruited from the kṣatriya class. Thus, the words *rājanya* and *kṣatra*, even when meaning the kṣatriya class, would automatically encompass within its orbit, the civil service whose primary motto was the service of the people.[16] The *Atharvaveda*[17] also uses words *rājā* and *rājanya* to signify the chief executive power and the administration respectively.

---

13 *yejaneṣu malimlava stenasastaskareravane ye va kṣeṣvaghāyavastān dadhāmi jambhayoḥ* । – *VājSaṁ* XI.79

ṛṇāvā bibhayaddhanamicchamāno 'nyeṣāmastamupa naktametī । – *ṚV* X.34.10

yuṣmākamastu taviṣī panīyasī mā martyasya māyinaḥ । – *ṚV* I.39.2

14 *ṚV* VII.15.3.

15 *yatra brahma ca kṣatram ca samyan vau carataḥ saha tam lokam puṇyam praśeṣam yatra devāḥ sahāgnihā* । – *VājSaṁ* XX.25

16 *kṣatraya rājanyam* । – *YV* XXX.5

17 *saṁśitam kṣatramajaramastu* । – *AV* III.19.1

The *Ṛgveda*[18] contains the following important hymn:

asapatnaḥ sapatnahābhirāṣṭro viṣāsahiḥ ।
yathāhameṣāṁ bhūtānāṁ virājāni janasya ca ॥

Here, the king aspires to keep under his control the *jana* which Sāyaṇa rightly interprets as the civil servants (*amātyas*) of the state.

The word *jana* seems to have been used in this sense in the following hymn of the *Atharvaveda*[19]:

ye dhīvāno rathakārāḥ karmāra ye maniṣiṇaḥ ।
upastīnparṇa mahyam tvam sarvānkṛṇvabhito janān ॥

A very prominent characteristic of the Vedic bureaucracy was to denote the authority of its functionaries by the use of the suffix *pati* to a number of words. Thus, there were *gṛhapatis, gaṇapatis, vrātapatis, vrājapatis, sabhāpatis, sthapatis*, etc. wielding considerable power. Another suffix *pa* served the same purpose of signifying official position. The words *hastipa, aśvapa, gṛhapa, vanapa, dāvapa*, etc. came under this category. It is interesting to note that even the word *adhyakṣa*, which became so common in later times to signify a departmental head, occurs in the *Ṛgveda*[20]:

viśāṁ rājānamadbhutamadhyakṣaṁ dharmaṇāmimam ।

The *Ṛgveda* mentions some of the functionaries of the state in no uncertain terms. The most important of them all was, of course, the *purohita*.[21] The *Nirukta*[22] explains it as *pura enam dadhāti* – one who is kept ahead in all matters. He was the Paragon of virtues. He ensured the spiritual and material development of the state.[23] He

---

18 *ṚV* X.174.5.

19 *AV* III.5.6-7.

20 *ṚV* VIII.43.24.

21 *sa saṁnayaḥ sa vinayaḥ purohitaḥ* । – *ṚV* II.24.9

22 *Nirukta* II.2.12.

23 *saṁśitam ma idam brahma saṁśitam vīryam balam, saṁśitam kṣatramajiramastu jiṣṇoryeṣāmasmipurohitaḥ* । – *AV* III.19.1

invoked divine powers for the victory of his king[24] as well as for the destruction of anti-social elements.[25] An Atharvavedic hymn speaks of Aṅgiras, the priest, as destroying the rival army, while wading through it.[26] It may suggest that some of the priests were adept in the martial art as well. The *Ṛgveda*[27] is the testimony of the great responsibility enjoyed by the *purohita*:

> That king, indeed, overpowers all opposing forces with his valour and might who maintains Bṛhaspati (the brāhmaṇa priest) well attended and praises and honours him as (a deity) deserving the first share (of the due homage). It was with the help of Aṅgiras, the priest, that Indra had destroyed *vala*.[28]

Sometimes, the words *brāhmaṇa* and *purohita* became interchangeable. The *Atharvaveda* observes that just as a leaky boat capsises, so also the nation where the brāhmaṇa is slain or tortured.[29] Thus, the *purohita* wielded immense influence on the king and was his chief guide in temporal as well as spiritual matters. It is generally believed that he was the forerunner of the future prime minister. It is interesting to note that the word *mantrī* is found in the Vedic literature. The *Yajurveda*[30] describes Rudra as *mantrī*. But we are not sure whether the Vedic king had a council of ministers which is invariably associated with his counterparts in later times. In this context the following hymn of the *Ṛgveda*[31] is noteworthy:

---

24 *nīcaiḥ padyantāmadhare bhavantu ye naḥ sūrim maghavānam śṛtamyām kṣiṇāmi brahmaṇāmitrāmunvayāmi svānaham* । – *AV* III.19.3

25 *ye janeṣu malimlava stenāsastaskarā vane ye va kṣeṣvaghāyavastānste dadhāmi jambhayoḥ* । – *VājSaṁ* XI.79

26 *madhyeha dhvanto yantu senāmamgiraso mahīm* । – *AV* VIII.8.30

27 *ṚV* IV.50.7.

28 *bhinad-valamindro aṅgirasvān* । – *ṚV* II.11.20

29 *tad vai rāṣṭramā sravatī nāvam bhimmamivodakam brahmāṇam yatra hinsanti tad rāṣṭram hanti ducchunā* । – *AV* V.19.8

30 *YV* XVI.19.

31 *ṚV* X.173.1.

tvāhārṣamantaredhi dhruvastiṣṭhāvicācaliḥ ।

Sāyaṇa thinks that it contains a reference to the *pradhānāmātya* (*rājapurohita*) as also to the council of ministers:

1. *pradhānāmātyo vā rājapurohito ... iti sāyaṇaḥ* ।
2. *antaredhītvenena mantrimaṇḍalāntarbhavati iti sāyaṇaḥ* ।

However, it is interesting to note that the *Ṛgveda* speaks of the *pariṣad*.[32] But we are not sure of the nature and composition of the Ṛgvedic *pariṣad*. From the above-quoted reference it appears that it was a war council.

The Vedic period was characterized by constant warfare. So the armies of the kings find frequent mention in the Vedas. The most popular words used for army were *senā* and *anikini*. The commander-in-chief of the army was called *senānī*[33] or *senāpati*. There are indications that the smaller units of the army in which it was divided had also its commanders. One of the Ṛgvedic hymns[34] speaks of *kulapa* and *vrājapati*. It appears that the former was the protector of the family and might have been the head of a number of *gṛhapati*s constituting the *kula*. His power and authority over the *gṛhapati*s might have had the sanction of the state. In normal circumstances, he would have been expected to enforce the *kula-dharma* and settled minor disputes among the members of the *kula*. The *vrājapati* appears to have been the leader of the village militia whose first duty was to ensure the safety of the life and property of villagers. That the *kulapa* enjoyed status and respectability is suggested by the use of the word *rājan* for him.[35]

Both these officers must have worked under the overall supervision and direction of the *grāmaṇī* who was yet another functionary at the village level. He has been eloquently spoken of in a number of hymns

---

32 *vi vajreṇa pariṣado jaghānā* । – *ṚV* III.33.7

33 *hiraṇyavāgave senānye* । – *YV* XVI.17

34 *pari tvāsate nidhibhiḥ sakhāyaḥ kulapā na vrājapatiṁ carantam* ।
– *ṚV* X.179.2

35 *eṣā te kulapā rājan* । – *AV* I.14.3

of the *Ṛgveda*.[36] As he is called Manu, his attitude towards his villagers was paternal. He has been called *dakṣiṇāvān*[37] suggesting thereby that the prosperity of the village was much dependent upon how he managed the affairs of his village. In the *Atharvaveda* also he has been alluded to along with some other important functionaries.[38]

At the bottom of the village hierarchy stood the *gṛhapati*.[39] He was not an ordinary head of the family, but wielded absolute powers over the members of his unit as would appear from the story of Śunaḥṣepa.[40] As the *Ṛgveda* contains evidence of the existence of personal property,[41] the *gṛhapati* must have played an important role in the preservation, division and management of the property in the family. Thus, the *grāmya*s lived under the protection of the *gṛhapati*s, *kulapati*s, *vrātapati*s, *grāmaṇī* and finally the *sabhāpati*. The latter was the head of the *sabhā*[42] which, on all accounts, was the village assembly, responsible for the overall management of the village affairs.

In the age of incessant warfare, the people's anxiety for general security is quite understandable. The *Ṛgveda* betrays this popular anxiety in a number of hymns.[43] So it is very likely that the state had

---

36 *sahasradā grāmaṇīrmā riṣanmanuḥ sūryeṇāsya yatamānaitu dakṣiṇā* ।
sāvarṇerdevāḥ pratirantvāyuryasminn śrāntā asanāma vājam ॥
– *ṚV* X.62.11

37 *dakṣiṇāvān prathamo hūta eti dakṣiṇāvān grāmaṇīragrameti* ।
– *ṚV* X.107.5
tameva manye nṛpatiṁ janānāṁ yaḥ prathamo dakṣiṇāmā vivāya ॥
– *ṚV* X.107.5

38 *ye rājāno rājakṛtaḥ sūtā grāmaṇyaśca ye* । – *AV* III.7

39 *agnirhotā gṛhapatiḥ sa rājā* । – *ṚV* VI.15.13

40 *śunaḥśepo yamahvadgṛbhītaḥ so asmān rājā varuṇo mumoktu* ॥
– *ṚV* I.24.12

41 *tvyā jeṣma hitaṁ dhanam* । – *ṚV* VI.45.12

42 *namaḥ sabhābhyaḥ sabhāpatibhyaśca vo namaḥ* । – *YV* XVI.24

43 *tvāṁ viprebhirvi paṇīm̐raśāyaḥ (viruddham dharmamaryādāto viparītaṁ paṇanta iti vipaṇayaḥ kuvyavahāriṇaḥ taniti sāyaṇaḥ* । – *ṚV* VI.33.2
pāhi no agne rakṣasaḥ pāhi dhūrterarāvṇaḥ ।
pāhi rīṣata uta vā jighāṅsato bṛhad bhāno yaviṣṭhya ॥ – *ṚV* I.36.15

organized police force at different levels. In the *Ṛgveda*[44] Agni has been described as the *gopā* (protector) of *ṛta*:

gopāmṛtasya dīdivim ।

Similarly, *gopā*s might have been appointed by the government for ensuring security of the people in various spheres. The *Ṛgveda,* speaks of the *jīvagṛbhaḥ*.[45] R. Roth seems to be correct in taking the word *jīvagṛbhaḥ* to mean the police. They might be doing some useful work in apprehending the criminals such as *durevaḥ* (vicious), *vṛkatiḥ* (thieves) and *dabhitiḥ* (violent) referred to in the *Ṛgveda*.[46] The following hymns of the *Atharvaveda*[47] is noteworthy:

na bhūmim vāto ati vāti nāti paśyati kaścana ।
striyeśca sarvāḥ svāpaya śunaścendrasakhā caraṇa ॥

Roughly, it means that, while Indra-*sakhā* moves around, it does not blow violently, and nobody looks towards anybody's house. Under these conditions women and dogs may continue sleeping (without disturbance for fear), Indra-*sakhā* may suggest the night-watchmen.

The existence of the police during the Vedic period is further attested by the references to the catching of the wicked, to their chaining and putting them behind the bars.

ayodaṁṣṭro arciṣā yātudhānānup spṛśa jātavedaḥ samiddhaḥ ।
ā jihvayā mūradevān rabhasva kravyādo vṛktvyapi dhatvāsan ॥
– *ṚV* X.87.2

asyanteparādhino 'sminnityāsyam kārāgāraḥ । – *Nirukta* 1.8

---

44 *ṚV* I.1-8.

45 *ātmā yakṣmasya naśyati purā jīvagṛbho yathā* । – *ṚV* X.97.11

46 *ṚV* IV.41.4.

47 *AV* IV.5.2.

tvamagne yātudhānānupabaddhān ihā vaha ।। – *AV* 1.7.7

The Vedic period had witnessed the emergence of a modest type of military service. Under the overall command of the *senānī* there worked a number of other functionaries also. There are references[48] to the commanders of the *gaṇa*s. The latter might have been a small military unit. Similarly another military unit has been spoken of as *varūtha*.[49] It must have had its own commander. At any rate, the infantry was put under the charge of a military officer.[50] *Anīka* was another smaller unit of the army.[51]

The *dūta* (envoy) seems to have played a very important diplomatic role during the Vedic period. This explains why he has been frequently referred to in the Vedic literature. On many occasions *agni* has been described as *dūta*.[52] He is desired to go to the enemies.[53]

The spies were different from the envoys. The former have been alluded to as *spaśa* in the Vedic literature. It appears that many of them assisted the *dūta* in collecting required information. This explains why *agni* has been prayed to send his spies on mission. If *agni* could apprehend the thieves and the burglars, it was probably on information[54] collected by his spies.[55] The latter might have informed *agni* of tax-evaders. This is why a prayer has been made to *agni* to make all people pay taxes.[56] In another reference Varuṇa

---

48 *yo vaḥ senārmahato gaṇasya* । – *ṚV* X.3.4
senānīrnahato gaṇasya । – *AV* VI.118.1

49 *mahi varūtham* । – *ṚV* II.34.14

50 *pattīnām pataye* । – *YV* X.6.19

51 *yairindraḥ prakīḍate padghoṣaiśchāyayā saha tairamitrāstrasantu no 'mī ye yantyanīkaśaḥ* । – *AV* V.21.8

52 *agne dūto viśāmapi* । – *ṚV* I.26.5
agniṁ dūtaṁ vṛṇāmahe । – *ṚV* I.12.1

53 *agnirno dūtaḥ pratyetu ... arātim* । – *AV* III.2.1

54 *prati spaśo vi sṛja* । – *ṚV* IV.4.3

55 *yāḥ senā abhītvarīrāvyādhinīrugaṇā* ।
uta ye stenā ye ca ... agnepi ... । – *YV* XI.77

56 *agnirviśaścakre balihṛtaḥ sahobhiḥ* । – *ṚV* VII.6.5

is said to have been surrounded by the spies.[57]

The Vedic literature speaks of *sthapati*[58] who might have looked after the department of creative arts. His high status can be gauged from his association with the king.[59] It can be presumed that, like some of the later *ratnin*s, a few officers mentioned in the Vedas, represented certain vocational classes. Besides the *sthapati*, the *sūta* was another officer belonging to that category. He was the charioteer and his importance was occasioned by frequent warfare in which the chariots played a significant role. He has been mentioned several times in the Vedas. In the *Atharvaveda* he has been mentioned as one of the king-makers.[60] Put in the company of the *grāmaṇī*, he was, undoubtedly, a functionary of the state. The *Yajurveda* also refers to him.[61] The *Atharvaveda*[62] also speaks of the *rathakāra*s (chariot-makers) and *karmāra*s (smiths) whom the king would like to bring under his control. They too might have been represented in the Vedic bureaucracy.

It appears that certain departments had their own administrative heads called *adhyakṣa*s. At least, the head of the department of justice or the chief justice has been referred to in the *Ṛgveda*.[63] The same source alludes to criminal cases[64] which might have fallen under his jurisdiction. The cases seem to have been decided on the evidence of the witnesses. Zeimer rightly thinks that the word *jñātṛ* in the

---

57 *varuṇo vasta nirṇijam parispaśo niṣedire* ॥ – *ṚV* I.25.13

58 *sthāpataye* । – *YV* XIV.19

59 *hato rājā krimīṇāmuteṣām sthapatirhataḥ* । – *AV* II.32.5

60 *ye rājāno rājakṛtaḥ sūtāḥ grāmaṇyaśca ye* ।
upastīn parṇa mahyam tvam sarvān kṛṇvamito janam ॥ – *AV* III.7

61 *sūtāya* । – *YV* XVI.18

62 *ye dhīvāno rathakārāḥ karmārā ye manīṣiṇaḥ* । –
upastīn parṇa mahyam tvam sarvān kṛṇvamito janān ॥ – *AV* III.5.6

63 *viśāṁ rājānamadbhutamadhyakṣam dharmaṇāmimam* ।
– *ṚV* VIII.43.24

64 *uta ghā nemo astutaḥ pumāṁ iti bruve paṇiḥ* ।
sa vairadeya itsamaḥ ॥ – *ṚV* V.61.8

Atharvaveda means a witness.[65]

The Vedas contain numerous references to taxes and their payment. The two most commonly used words for the tax are *bali* and *bhāga*. The taxpayer was called *balihṛt*.[66] A reference in the *Atharvaveda* expresses a wish that the people pay *bali* to Indra day after day.[67] Here the word *bali* may mean voluntary tributes paid as often as the payer desired. The taxpayers came from far and wide to deposit their taxes.[68] The emphasis was on the profusion of taxes with regard to their quantum and frequency.[69] But in the *Ṛgveda* and the *Atharvaveda* the word *bhāga* as Indra's share has been used.[70] It is, therefore, natural to suppose that the state would surely have appointed tax-collectors, though we do not explicitly hear of them till the period of the Brāhmaṇas.

Even as early as the *Ṛgveda*, the aim of the state was to give to the people good and clean administration.[71] According to Sāyaṇa, the word *praśiṣa* means *prakṛṣṭa śāsana*. To this end, the civil service during the Vedic period appears to have been well galvanized, as is attested by great emphasis on an all-round ethical approach and a self-imposed code of conduct. The whole administrative set-up was brought about for the protection of the people.[72] The ruler needs discipline to govern the people.[73] It is truth that sustains the

---

65 *mā jñātāram mā pratiṣṭhām vidanta* । – *AV* VI.32.3

66 *agnirviśaścakre balihṛtaḥ sahobhiḥ (balihṛtaḥ-arthakarasya pradātrīḥ iti sāyaṇaḥ)* । – *ṚV* VII.6.5

67 *tvamindrā puruhūta viśvamāyurvyaśnavat* । *aharaharbalibhinte harantāyeva tiṣṭha* ।। – *AV* XIX.55.6

68 *tubhyaṁ bharanti kṣitayo yaviṣṭha balimagne antita ota dūrāt* । – *ṚV* V.1.10

69 *bahum balim prati paśyāsā ugraḥ* । – *AV* III.4.3

70 *yamindra dadhiṣe tvamaśvaṁ gāṁ bhāgamavyayam* । – *ṚV* VIII.97.2
indrāya bhāgam pari tvā nayāmi । – *AV* IX.5.2

71 *yasya viśva upāsate praśiṣaṁ yasya devāḥ* । – *ṚV* X.121.2

72 *pāhi no agne rakṣasaḥ pāhi dhūrterarāvṇaḥ* । – *ṚV* I.36.5
kṣatrāya rājanyam । – *YV* XXX.5

73 *brahmacaryeṇa rājā rāṣṭram virakṣati* । – *AV* III.5.16

earth.[74] The people abhorred the idea of being governed by sinful administrators.[75] The Ṛgvedic maxim that one who eats alone eats sin points to a humanitarian approach of all concerned.[76] If the deities could not transgress the eternal code of conduct,[77] how could the mortals administering the state do it? The *Atharvaveda* had indirectly advocated the principle of coexistence of diverse races, languages and religions and had wished them all to prosper side by side.[78]

Later, the number of functionaries during the Vedic period multiplied to meet the requirements of an expanding state and society. An exhaustive additional list of these functionaries is found in the Puruṣamedha of the *Vājasaneyī Saṁhitā*[79] which runs as follows:

1. *takṣan* (carpenter)
2. *praśnavivāka* (judge)
3. *hastipa* (commander of the elephant division)
4. *aśvapa* (commander of the cavalry)
5. *prakarita* (distributor)
6. *kṣattā* (chamberlain)
7. *bhāgadugha* (collector of taxes)
8. *vanapa* (forest officer)
9. *dāvapa* (officer of the forest fire brigade)

---

74 *satyenottabhitā bhūmiḥ* । – *AV* XVI.1.1

75 *pūṣā naḥ pātu duritādṛtāvṛdho* ।
rakṣā mākirno aghaśaṁsa īśata ।। – *ṚV* VI.75.10

76 *kevalāgho bhavati kevalādī* । – *ṚV* VI.117.6

77 *ṛtasya devā anuvratāḥ* । – *ṚV* I.62.2

78 *janam vibhratī bahudhā vivācasam* ।
nānādharmāṇam pṛthivīyathaukasam ।।

sahasram dhārā draviṇasya me ।
duhām dhruveva dhenuranapasphurantī ।। – *AV* XII.1.45

79 *VājSaṁ* XXX.

The name of the *saṁgṛhītṛ* occurs in chapter 16 of the same Saṁhitā. He seems to have been the treasurer. This officer finds mention in the *Yajurveda*[80] also.

Thus, with the addition of the *takṣan* to the civil service, the representation of vocational groups was sought to be expanded. The later Smṛtis speak of the *prāḍvivāka* who was the chief justice, next only to the king with regard to the judicial authority. The *praśnavivāka* seems to be his earlier counterpart in the Vedic age. The *hastipa* and the *aśvapa* were obviously military officers whose task was primarily the procurement, training and maintenance of elephants and horses respectively, the two most important constituents of the army. *Prakarita*'s nature of work is not clear. He might have been entrusted with the task of distributing royal bounties. The *kṣattā* seems to have been the doorkeeper to regulate the entries of the seekers of audience with the king. The *vanapa* and the *dāvapa* come into existence with the growing realization of the importance of forests as a source of state revenue. The officers called *bhāgadugha* and *saṁgṛhitṛ* undoubtedly prove that taxation had become a regular feature of the government and it required exclusive services of a tax-collector and a treasurer.

The Brāhmaṇas shed further light on the functionaries of the state. While describing the coronation ceremony of the king, they vividly spell out the role and importance of these officers who were technically known as *ratnins*.[81] The coronation ceremony was called the Rājasūya sacrifice on the occasion of which the king-elect was to go to each one of the *ratnins* and offer his oblations to them. The king-elect used to say that he was coronated for the *ratnins* whom he wished to follow him.[82] The personal visit of the king to the *ratnins* at their residences was probably aimed at enlisting their cooperation in the task of running administration. Thereafter, the king was anointed with sacred water brought from rivers of the country. After the anointment was over, the king used to utter the

---

80 *YV* XVI.26.

81 *ŚatBrā* V.3.1, *TaitBrā* I.7.3, *MaitSaṁ* II.6.5, *KāṭhSaṁ* XV.4.

82 *ŚatBrā* V.3.1.1.

following words to the priest:

> From my birth to my death, my sacrifices, my good deeds, my life and my offsprings must thou take if I play thee foul.[83]

The *Aitareya Brāhmaṇa* adds that this assurance was to be given to the priest by the rulers of all types of states – *sāmrājya, bhaujya, vairājya, rājya, mahārājya, ādhipatya* and *sārvabhauma*. The whole context would suggest that the assurance was not given to the priest as an individual but as the representative of the people. To that extent, the coronation oath had a constitutional significance whereby the king gave assurance of a responsible and responsive rule.

But we are more concerned with the *ratnins* whose number varies in different Brāhmaṇas. Roughly speaking, the most important of them were the following:

Purohita: He was the royal priest and tops the list of *ratnins* in most of the Brāhmaṇas. It is significant that the *Aitareya Brāhmaṇa* calls him the *rāṣṭra-gopa* (protector of the nation). This designation would suggest that at the coronation ceremony, he spoke on behalf of the whole people. The precedence of the *purohita* over the *senānī* (commander-in-chief) points towards the fact that the civil and spiritual element dominated the military element in the Vedic polity.

Senānī[84]: He was the commander-in-chief of the state. In the *Śatapatha Brāhmaṇa* he has been given precedence over the *purohita* even. It may indicate that probably the two most important powers of the state – the *brāhmaṇa-śakti* and the *kṣatra-śakti* were contending for supremacy in the political domain. To present undesirable effects flowing from such a conflict, ancient Indian political thinkers had advocated their cooperation with one another.[85]

Rājamahiṣī: She was the chief queen. With her two other queens – *vāvātā* (favourite queen) and the *parivṛkti* (forsaken queen) – have been put on the list of *ratnins*. Jayaswal has rightly observed that the

---

83 *AitBrā* VIII.15.

84 *TaiSaṁ* I.8.9, *MaitSaṁ* II.6.5, 4.3, *KāṭhSaṁ* XV.4, *ŚatBrā* V.3.1.

85 *idam me brahma ca kṣatram cobhe śriyamaśnutatām* । – *YV* IX.30.216

queens were associated with the coronation ceremony to complete the spiritual self of the king-elect. The *parivṛkti* was also given the status of the *ratnin* with a view to disarming her of her opposition to the royal spouse.

Sūta: He was the charioteer and figures as an official in earlier literature also.

Takṣan: He was the carpenter and had already found place in the Vedic bureaucracy even before the Brāhmaṇas.

Rathakāra: He was the chariot-maker and figures in the *Ṛgveda* itself.

Saṁgṛhītṛ: He was the treasurer and came into existence as a functionary of the state when the collection of taxes became a regular and systematic activity of the state.

Bhāgadugha: He was the tax-collector and seems to have come into being along with the *saṁgṛhītṛ*. The *Śatapatha Brāhmaṇa* 5.3.1.9 makes an interesting observation that Pūṣā, the God of animals, was offered *bali* in the house of the *bhāgadugha*. This would probably indicate that he was drawn from the vaiśya class.

Pālāgala: He was the king's companion and was the forerunner of the *vidūṣaka* of later times.

Grāmaṇī: He was the village headman and was one of the earliest members of the Vedic bureaucracy. Sometimes, he is referred to as the vaiśya *grāmaṇī*.[86]

Kṣattā: He was the royal chamberlain. However, Ghoshal would make us believe that he was the food-distributor.

Akṣavāpa: He was the king's companion in games. Some have taken him to be the minister of sports.

Govikartan: He was probably the officer-in-charge of the cattle.

It would, thus, appear that the *ratnins* were representatives of different segments of society. The *purohita* represented the

---

86 *KāṭhSaṁ* XV.4.

brāhmaṇa class, while the *senānī* represented the kṣatriya class.[87] The *grāmaṇī* was generally a vaiśya. The three queens could speak for the womenfolk. The *sūta*, the *takṣan* and the *rathakāra* came from vocational groups. The *saṁgṛhītṛ*, the *bhāgadugha*, the *kṣattā*, the *pālāgala*, the *akṣavāpa* and the *govikartan* were drawn from the upper bureaucracy. Jayaswal is very pertinent in his observations that the *ratnins* were high functionaries of the state selected on the principle of class and caste representation. They enjoyed immense respectability and have been termed as givers of the kingdom (*rāṣṭrasya pradātāraḥ*).[88] They were also known as *rājakartāraḥ*. In one of the Brāhmaṇa texts, they were described as limbs of the ruling power[89] constituting the first stage in the evolution of the *saptāṅga* theory of the state. The *Maitrāyaṇī Saṁhitā* has gone to the extent of saying that

> if the *ratnins* become powerful and energetic, the state also becomes powerful and energetic.

They have also been designated as *vīra*.[90] They seem to have constituted the council of ministers in the Vedic period.[91] Their presentation of the sword[92] to the king after the coronation ceremony was symbolic of the fact that the king without them was powerless. He derived his strength from his functionaries. This is the reason why the *Śatapatha Brāhmaṇa* includes king also in the list of *ratnins*. This inclusion suggests that he was the first among the equals.

It is interesting to note that the *Aitareya Brāhmaṇa*[93] refers to the *saciva*. However, we do not know how he stood in relations to the *ratnins*. It is just possible that the king employed certain *sacivas*

---

87 *ŚatBrā* V.3.1.9.

88 *ete vai rāṣṭrasya pradātāraḥ* । – *TaitBrā* I.8.3

89 *kṣatrasya vai etāni aṅgāni* । – *MaitSaṁ* IV.3.8

90 *PañcaBrā* XIX.1.4.

91 Ibid., XIX.1.4.

92 *ŚatBrā* V.4.4.15-20.

93 *AitBrā* XII.9.

(ministers) for daily considerations. The *ratnins* might have been given audience on specific issues.

3

Civil Service in the Rāmāyaṇa

THE *Rāmāyaṇa* polity is centred round four main states of the time, namely, the Ikṣvāku state of Ayodhyā, the tribal states of the Niṣādas and Vānaras headed by Guha and Sugrīva respectively and the *rākṣasa* state of Laṅkā ruled by Rāvaṇa. Excepting regional and historical peculiarities, the form, nature and functioning of the governments and of the political institutions of all these states betray close similarities. They were so firmly established that even the upheaval caused by the issue of succession in Ayodhyā, the fratricidal animosity between Bāli and Sugrīva, ultimately resulting in the former's killing at the hands of the latter's protector Rāma in Kiṣkindhā as also the banishment of Vibhīṣaṇa by his ruling brother Rāvaṇa in Laṅkā and the former's joining hands with his borther's enemy Rāma did not effect their basic character.

The most prominent constituent of the governements of all the four states was a well-organized civil service. The *Rāmāyaṇa* uses the commonly accepted word *amātya*[1] for it, though there are also some less commonly known words used for it; they are: *tīrthas*,[2] *mahāmātras*,[3] *adhikr̥tāḥ narāḥ*,[4] *bhr̥tyas*,[5] and *rāja-bhāra-*

1 *amātyā balamukhyāśca mukhyā ye nirgamasya ca ।*
rāghavasyābhiṣekārthe prīyamāṇāḥ susaṅgatāḥ ॥ – *Rām* II.15.2

2 *tribhistribhiravijñātairvetsi tīrthāni cārakaiḥ* । – *Rām* II.100.36

3 *matimadbhirmahāmātrairanuraktairadhiṣṭhitam* । – *Rām* VI.10.3

4 *ājñāpyātha yathājñapti yuktāste 'dhikr̥tā narāḥ* । – *Rām* II.80.15

5 *kaccinmukhyā mahatsveva madhyameṣu ca madhyamā* ।
jaghanyāśca jaghanyeṣu bhr̥tyāste tāta yojitāḥ ॥ – *Rām* II.100.25

niyuktāḥ.[6] There are two other words, *mantrī* and *saciva* which were frequently used in the Epic. They very clearly denote the "minister" who belongs to the civil service (*amātya*). So when the *Rāmāyaṇa*[7] calls Sumantra both as *amātya* and *mantrī*, it simply suggests that the latter were drawn from the pool of the former. Similarly, Rāvaṇa's main functionaries Śuka and Sāraṇa, have been termed as *amātya*s as well as *mantrī*s.[8] That the words *mantrī* and *saciva* are synonyms is amply clear from the fact that Sumantra, the *mantrī*, has also been called as *saciva*.[9]

Ancient Indian thinkers were invariably opposed to one-man rule. They could not think of monarchy sans civil service or ministry. It was why the king was told again and again that he must hold deliberations with others before taking to a particular course of action. The king's victory was rooted in deliberations.[10] Deliberations with a variety of functionaries and people preceded all important actions concerning the state. When Daśaratha wanted to perform the Aśvamedha, he shared his thoughts with his ministers.[11] Later, he got approval of the royal priest, brāhmaṇas and the *amātyas*.[12] Before going to Mithilā to celebrate his sons' marriages, he sought the approval of his counsellors.[13] The decision to declare Rāma as the *yuvarāja* of the kingdom also bore the stamp of prior approval of

---

6 *rājyabhāraniyuktānāmeṣa dharmaḥ sanātanaḥ* । – *Rām* I.25.19

7 *tato 'bravīnmahātejāḥ sumantraṁ mantrisattama* । – *Rām* I.8.4
tasyāmātyā guṇairāsannikṣvākoḥ sumahātmanaḥ । – *Rām* I.7.1
akopo dharmapālaśca sumantraścāṣṭamor 'thavit ॥ – *Rām* I.7.3

8 *amātyau rāvaṇaḥ śrīmānabravīcchukasāraṇau* । – *Rām* VI.25.1
tasyaitau rākṣasendrasya mantriṇau śukasāraṇau । – *Rām* VI.25.14

9 *sa tvapaśyad viniṣkrāntaṁ sumantraṁ nāma sārathim* ।
dvāre manujasiṁhasya sacivaṁ priyadarśanam ॥ – *Rām* II.14.32

10 *mantro vijayamūlaṁ hi rājñāṁ bhavati rāghava* । – *Rām* II.100.16
mantramūlaṁ ca vijayaṁ pravadanti manasvinaḥ । – *Rām* VI.6.5

11 *mantribhiḥ saha* । – *Rām* I.8.3

12 *amātyānabravīd rājā harṣavyākula locanaḥ* । – *Rām* I.8.13

13 *yadi vo rocate vṛttam janakasya mahātmanaḥ* ।
purīṁ gacchāmahe śīghraṁ mā bhūt kālasya paryayaḥ ॥
mantriṇo bāḍhamityāhuḥ saha sarvairmaharṣibhiḥ ॥ – *Rām* I.68.17-18

ministers.[14] Examples of the king's consultations with his functionaries can be easily multiplied. Even Rāvaṇa discussed all matters, good and bad, with the functionaries of his kingdom.[15] Very often he convened the meeting of his *sabhā* to advise him on the future course of action.[16] Even the Niṣādarāja is seen as holding discussions with his ministers.[17] On meeting Bharata at Citrakūṭa, Rāma pointedly desired of him to keep consulting his ministers on important matters of the state.[18]

The *Rāmāyaṇa* describes of three kinds of counsel. The best of them is marked by unanimity among the counsellors. The middle type of counsels admits of difference of opinion at the outset which are later resolved through discussions. In the worst of them, differences persist, notwithstanding the damage that they will do to the state.[19]

Like all ancient Indian political thinkers, the author of the *Rāmāyaṇa* also lays great stress on the secrecy of the deliberations. Rāma did not miss to enquire from Bharata whether or not his counsels are kept secret.[20] Rāma, the ideal king, has been called *guptamantraḥ*.[21] If deliberations of the king are kept confidential, he is

---

14 *niścitya sacivaiḥ sārdhaṁ yauvarājyamamanyata* । – *Rām* II.1.42

15 *priyāpriye sukhe duḥkhe lābhālābhe hitāhite* ।
dharmakāmārthakṛcchreṣu yūyamarhatha veditum ॥
sarvakṛtyāni yuṣmābhiḥ samārbdhāni sarvadā ।
mantrakarmaṇīyuktāni na jātu viphalāni me ॥ – *Rām* VI.12.7-8

16 *bhavadbhirmantryatāṁ mantraḥ sunītaṁ cābhidhīyatām* । – *Rām* VI.12.25

17 *sthapatistūrṇamāhūya sacivānidamabravīt* ॥ – *Rām* II.52.5

18 *mantribhistvaṁ yathoddiṣṭaṁ caturbhistribhireva vā* ।
kaccit samastairvyastaiśca mantraṁ mantrayase budha ॥ – *Rām* II.100.71
kaccinmantrayase naikaḥ kaccinna bahubhiḥ saha । – *Rām* II.100.18

19 *ekamatyamupāgamya śāstradṛṣṭena cakṣuṣā* ।
mantriṇo yatra niratāstamāhurmantramuttamam ॥
bahvīrapi matīrgatvā mantriṇāmarthanirṇayaḥ ॥
punaryatraikatāṁ prāptaḥ sa mantro madhyamaḥ smṛtaḥ ॥
anyonyamatimāsthāya yatra sampratibhāṣyate ।
na 'caikamatye śreyo 'ti mantraḥ so 'dhamaḥ ucyate ॥ – *Rām* VI.6.12-14

20 *kaccit te mantrito mantro rāṣṭraṁ na paridhāvati* । – *Rām* II.100.18

21 *Rām* II.1.23.

assured of victory.[22] With a view to guarding against the possibility of leakage of secrets, certain people, such as fools, the mentally retarded, the greedy and womenfolk are sought to be kept away from secret parleys.[23] The ministers were to be consulted, separately and collectively.[24]

Later writers on polity speak of four examinations which a candidate for the ministerial post had to pass. They were:

1. *dharmopadhā* (to test righteousness),
2. *arthopadhā* (to test resistance to monetary gains),
3. *kāmopadhā* (to test the capacity to control desires), and
4. *bhayopadhā* (to test fearlessness).

The *Rāmāyaṇa* does not explicitly mention these examinations. But at one place it speaks of the *amātyas* as *upadhātin* (those who have got through the examinations).[25] They must have been drawn from different sections of the society. Like monarchy, the ancient Indian Civil Service also tended to be hereditary. This explains why the *Rāmāyaṇa* calls *amātyas*, probably only some of them, as *pitṛpaitāmahaḥ*.[26] Exactly the same phrase, indicating succession coming down from the father and grandfather, has been used for the heir-apparent at Ayodhyā.[27]

The *Rāmāyaṇa* is full of scattered references to other qualifications of the *amātyas*. Even a single *amātya*, if brilliant, can bring prosperity to the king.[28] The *amātyas* were expected to comprehend policies and

---

22 *mantro vijayamūlaṁ hi rājñāṁ bhavati rāghava* ।
susaṁvṛto mantridhurairamātyaiḥ śāstrakovidaiḥ ॥ – *Rām* II.100.16

23 *Rām* III.145.43-5; *Rām* II.100.46.

24 *kaccinmantrayase naikaḥ kaccinna bahubhiḥ saha* । – *Rām* II.100.18

25 *amātyānupadhātītān pitṛpaitāmahāñśucīn* ।
śreṣṭhā śreṣṭheṣu kaccit tvaṁ niyojayasi harmasu ॥ – *Rām* II.100.26

26 *Rām* II.100.26.

27 *pitṛpaitāmahaṁ rājyamavāpsyati nararṣabhaḥ* । – *Rām* II.8.16

28 *eko 'pyamātyo medhāvī śūro dakṣo vicakṣaṇaḥ* ।
rājānaṁ rājaputraṁ vā prāpayenmahatīṁ śriyam ॥ – *Rām* II.100.24

interpret the symptoms, be devoted to the welfare of the people and be uncorruptible and loyal in the discharge of duties.[29] They should have mastery over Śāstras.[30] Even Rāvaṇa's *amātyas* were possessed of virtues, were thoroughly knowledgeable and intellectual.[31] They seem to have been ex-officio members of the *sabhā* which was convened to take decisions on all important issues of the state.[32] Laṅkan polity also emphasized intellect and loyalty as two important virtues of the civil service.[33]

The most important and best qualified among *amātyas* were appointed as ministers called *mantrīs* and *sacivas*. While *amātyas*, in general, manned various departments of the state and were the executive officers, the ministers were involved in the process of decision making. On all important matters the king held regular consultations with them. This is why they were regarded as supporters (*sahāya*) of the king on whom depended the well-being of the state.[34] The minister was just like a teacher to the king.[35] Even Kumbhakarṇa had observed that the king holding prior consultations with his ministers would follow the proper course of action.[36] In Supārśva and Mālyavān Rāvaṇa had two very capable ministers who gave their master the correct advice even at the risk of courting his displeasure.[37] But whereas Daśaratha gave utmost respect to the advice given by his ministries. Rāvaṇa, being autocratic by disposition behaved high-handedly and admonished his ministers, if they gave

---

29 *mantrajñāśceṅgitajñāśca nityaṁ priyahite ratāḥ* ||
aṣṭau babhūvurvīrasya tasyāmātyā yaśasvinaḥ |
śucayaścānuraktāśa rajakṛtyeṣu nityaśaḥ || – *Rām* I.7.1-2

30 *susaṁvṛto mantridhurairamātyaiḥ śāstrakovidaiḥ* || – *Rām* II.100.16

31 *amātyāśca guṇopetāḥ sarvajñā buddhidarśanā* | | – *Rām* VI.11.25

32 *brāhmaṇān kṣatriyān yodhānamātyān gaṇavallabhān* |
kṣipramānayatāvyagrāḥ kṛtyamātyayikaṁ hi naḥ | – *Rām* II.81.12

33 *matimadbhirmahāmātrairanuraktairadhiṣṭam* | – *Rām* VI.10.3

34 *Rām* V.98.15.

35 *gurorguṇagṛhītāśca* | – *Rām* I.7.17

36 *Rām* II.63.7.

37 *Rām* II.35.6, III.41.1-8.

him unpleasant, though correct advice.[38] Ultimately his dictatorial conduct, totally ignoring the wise counsels of his ministers, brought about his downfall. When Viśvāmitra asked Daśaratha to send Rāma and Lakṣmaṇa with him, he sought not only their father's permission but also his ministers'.[39] Daśaratha decided to proceed to Mithilā to celebrate his son's marriage only after his ministers gave him their approval.[40] Ministers were given precedence over the commander-in-chief and other officials in seating arrangements.[41] While in court, Rāvaṇa was also surrounded by his ministers.[42] When Kaikeyī asked Sumantra to bring in Rāma, he refused to obey her on the plea that he needed the king's order to do so.[43] Thus, ministers owed their allegiance to the king and to none else. Not only that, Sumantra had no hesitation in scolding queen Kaikeyī in the severest terms for her misdeed.[44] It appears that sons of ministers were associated with administration during the lifetime of their fathers with a view to grooming them for future assignments in the government. This is indicated by the fact that in their fight with Hanumān, the *rākṣasas*

---

38 *na tāvat sadṛśaṁ nāma sacivairupajīvibhiḥ* । – *Rām* VI.29.7
ācāryā guravo vṛddhā vṛthā vāṁ paryupāsitāḥ ।
sāraṁ yad rājaśāstrāṇāmanujīvyaṁ na gṛhyate ॥
gṛhīto vā na vijñāto bhāro 'jñānasya vāhyate ।
īdṛśaiḥ sacivairyukto mūrkhairdiṣṭya dharāmyaham ॥
kiṁ nu mṛtyorbhayaṁ nāsti māṁ vaktuṁ paruṣaṁ vacaḥ । – *Rām* VI.9.11

39 *sthiramicchāsi rājendra* ।
rāmam me dātu marhaṣi ।
yadyabhyanujñām kākutstha dadate tava mantriṇaḥ । – *Rām* VI.9-11

40 *mantriṇo bāḍhamityāhuḥ saha sarvairmaharṣibhiḥ* । – *Rām* I.68.18

41 *ānupūvyānniṣeduśca sarve mantripurohitāḥ* ।
tataḥ senāpatiḥ paścāt praśāstā ca nyaṣīdata । – *Rām* II.91.40

42 *iti svamantriṇāṁ madhye bhrātā bhrātaramūcivān* । – *Rām* VI.10.26

43 *aśrutvā rājavacanaṁ kathaṁ gacchāmi bhāmini* । – *Rām* II.14.64

44 *yasyāstava patistyakto rājā daśarathaḥ svayam* ।
bhartā sarvasya jagataḥ sthāvarasya carasya ca ॥
nahyakāryatamaṁ kiñcittava devīha vidyate ।
patighnīṁ tvāmahaṁ manye kulaghnīmapi cāntataḥ ॥ – *Rām* II.35.5-6

had lost five military commanders and seven sons of the ministers.[45] This fact also indicates that the ministers and their sons, even though brāhmaṇas received military training. Again, the fact that the ministers accompanied their masters on military expedition[46] and that they were also called *śāstrajñaḥ*[47] does not necessarily mean that all of them were kṣatriyas, because right from the *Ṛgveda* onwards, non-kṣatriya ministers too were adept in the art of war.

It appears that there were two bodies of ministers, one consisting of two to eight ministers for immediate and frequent consultations, and the other consisting of more members. The first was in the nature of the cabinet and the second the council of ministers. Rāma expects Bharata to hold consultations with three or four ministers who might have been the members of the cabinet.[48] Rāvaṇa is shown as holding parleys with four ministers.[49] Daśaratha, at one place, is depicted as having eight ministers around him.[50] But the *Rāmāyaṇa* does not throw any light on the composition of the council of ministers.

It is important to note that by the time of the *Rāmāyaṇa* the office of the chief minister had come into existence. He was called *mantrī-śreṣṭha*, and *mantrī-pati*. These terms[51] have been used for Sudāmana, the chief minister of Janaka. At Ayodhyā this office seems to have been held by Siddhārtha.[52] Rāvaṇa's chief minister

---

45 *pañca senāgragān hatvā sapta mantrisutānapi* । – *Rām* I.1.75

46 *Rām* IV.25.19.

47 *Rām* I.7.7.

48 *mantribhistvam yathoddiṣṭam caturbhistribhirevavā* । – *Rām* II.10.71
kaccit samastairbyastaiśca … ।
mantrastribhirhi saṁyuktaḥ samarthairmantranirṇaye । – VI.6.7

49 *Rām* II.100.7.

50 *mantrajñāśceṅgitajñāśca nityaṁ priyahite ṛtā* ।।
aṣṭau babhūvurvīrasya tasyāmātyā yaśasvinaḥ । – *Rām* I.7.1-2

51 *preṣayāmāsaturvīrau mantriśreṣṭhaṁ sudāmanam* ।
gaccha mantripate śīghramikṣvākumamitaprabham ।। – *Rām* 1.70.11

52 *Rām* II.39.18.

was called *mukhya-mantrī*.[53] The king of the Niṣādas too appears to have had a chief minister. He has been described as *mahān amātya* or *mahāmātya*.[54] When Hanumān was spoken of as *sacivottama*,[55] he gave the impression of having acted as chief minister.

The *Rāmāyaṇa* speaks of the eighteen *tīrtha*s or *amātya*s who were assigned important portfolios.[56] They constituted the core of the civil service of the *Rāmāyaṇa* age. However, the *Rāmāyaṇa* does not specifically mention designations of these *tīrtha*s. It is the *Tilaka-Ṭīkā* on the *Rāmāyaṇa* which mentions their designations. They were as follows:

MANTRĪ

Since the king has several ministers, the word *mantrī* may denote the chief minister or the whole lot of ministers collectively.

PUROHITA

He was the royal priest and commanded great respect for his purity and erudition. Vasiṣṭha was Daśaratha's royal priest.[57] There was hardly any event at Ayodhyā in which he did not take the leading part. He was regarded as the deity of the Ikṣvākus.[58] Whether it was the coronation of the *yuvarāja*[59] or the marriage of the princes[60] or the decision to enthrone Bharata[61] or the funeral of the king,[62] he played a dominant role. After the death of Daśaratha, the *sabhā*

---

53 *Rām* II.11.24-26.

54 *tam niśamya guhādeśam guhāmātyo gato mahān* ׀ – *Rām* II.2.7

55 *atha saṁskārasampanno hanumān sacivottamaḥ* ׀ – *Rām* VI.17.50

56 *kaccidaṣṭādaśānyeṣu svapakṣe daśa pañca ca* ׀
tribhistṛbhiravijñātairvetsi tīrthāni cārakaiḥ ׀׀ – *Rām* II.100.36

57 *Rām* II.88.20.

58 *Rām* I.66.14.

59 *Rām*, II.7.2.

60 *Rām* I.66.7.

61 *Rām* II.14.1.

62 *Rām* II.14.1.

was convened by Vasiṣṭha.[63] He was well known for his knowledge of hymns.[64] Similarly, Śatānanda enjoyed great respectability as the royal priest at Mithilā.[65]

However, it has to be re-examined as to whether he was regarded as a minister as well. There are certain points which mitigate against the assumption that he was also a minister. First, the list of the *tīrtha*s mentions *mantrī* and *purohita* separate. Second, such phrases as *purohitamamātyānśca* would indicate that technically speaking, he was not even an *amātya*.[66] Again, references to the *purohita* in the company of *amātya*s or separately from ministers[67] will also lead to the conclusion that he did not hold any ministerial or government post as such. But since *brahma-bala* was considered to be superior to *kṣatra-bala*, the *purohita*, representing the former, enjoyed tremendous power and esteem in the state. He was invariably consulted along with, nay, even before *amātya*s and other functionaries of the government. It was on account of his unique position as the king's constant guide and philosopher that he was sometimes termed as the minister par excellence.[68] It will be correct to regard him as the ex-officio member of the civil service.

YUVARĀJA

He was the crown-prince and was declared as such after the performance of a ceremony. He was the eldest son who was made the *yuvarāja*.[69] However, the eldest son could be superseded if he

---

63 *Rām* II.9.2.

64 *Rām* II.7.4.

65 *śatānandaṁ puraskṛtya purohitamananditaḥ* ॥ – *Rām* I.50.6

66 *purohitamamātyāñśca preṣayiṣyati satkṛtān* । – *Rām* I.9.15

67 *sahāmātyaḥ purohitaḥ* । – *Rām* I.10.2
agrataḥ prayayustasya sarve mantripurohitaḥ । – *Rām* II.83.2
abruvan mantriṇaḥ sarve vasiṣṭhaśca purohitaḥ ॥ – *Rām* II.115.4
purodhā ṛtvijaścaiva rājā ca sahamantribhiḥ । – *Rām* I.50.12

68 *vasiṣṭhaṁ mantriṇāṁ varam* । – *Rām* II.93.6

69 *rāmo rājasuto jyeṣṭho yauvarājyamato 'rhati* । – *Rām* II.8.14
asmin kule hi sarveṣāṁ jyeṣṭho rājye 'bhiṣicyate । – *Rām* II.73.20

had any physical or moral defect.[70] This explains why Daśaratha had observed that Rāma had no ailments whatsoever. And if all the princes were simultaneously made kings, there would be total confusion.[71] The *yuvarāja* was constitutionally approved by the *sabhā* consisting of the brāhmaṇas, military commanders and representatives of people.[72-73] Similarly, Vibhīṣaṇa[74] was the *yuvarāja* in Laṅkā and Sugrīva[75] in Kiṣkindhā. Later, Sugrīva associated Aṅgada as the *yuvarāja* with him.[76] Before a prince was made the *yuvarāja*, he was given thorough education and training to enable him to shoulder his future responsibilities. Daśaratha was well-versed in polity.[77] Rāma and Lakṣamaṇa had received special training in weaponry.[78] In fact, all Ikṣvāku princes had received thorough education. Even Rāvaṇa had given high education to his sons and brothers. The *yuvarāja* was associated with administrative and military activities during the reign of his father. He is described as disposing of public work assigned to him by Daśaratha.[79] During his absence from Laṅkā, Rāvaṇa had entrusted *yuvarāja* Vibhīṣaṇa with the task of administration.

---

70 *arogastaruṇo vāgmī vapuṣmān deśakālavit* । – *Rām* II.1.18

71 *nahi rājñaḥ sutāḥ sarve rājye tiṣṭhanti bhāmini* ।
sthāpyamāneṣu sarveṣu sumahānanayo bhavet ।। – *Rām* II.8.23

72 *tataḥ pariṣadaṁ sarvāmāmantrya vasudhādhipaḥ* । – *Rām* II.2.1

73 *brāhmaṇā balamukhyāśca paurajānapadaiḥ saha* ।।
sametya te mantrayituṁ samatāgatabuddhayaḥ । – *Rām* II.2.19-20

74 *Rām* V.90.32.

75 *tato'ham taiḥ samāgamya śametairabhiṣecitaḥ* ।
rājyam praśāsatastasya nyāyato mama rāghava ।। – *Rām* IX.4.21

76 *eṣa vānararājena sugrīveṇābhiṣecitaḥ* ।
yuvarājo 'ṅgado nāma tvāmāhvayati saṁyuge ।। – *Rām* VI.26.17

77 *pṛthivyāṁ rājasiṁhānāṁ mukhyasya viditātmanaḥ* ।
snuṣā daśarathasyāhaṁ śatrusainyapraṇāśinaḥ ।। – *Rām* V.33.15

78 *tāni divyāni bhadraṁ te dadāmyastrāṇi sarvaśaḥ* । – *Rām* I.27.4

79 *tvayā yataḥ prajāścemāḥ svaguṇairanurañjitāḥ* । – *Rām* II.3.40
amba pitrā niyukto 'smi prajāpālanakarmaṇi । – *Rām* II.4.35

SENĀPATI

He was the commander-in-chief of the army for which the *Rāmāyaṇa* uses words *senā, vāhinī* and *camū* as well as *anīkinī*. It was divided into units (*bhāgaśaḥ*), variously called as *yūthas*, *anīkas*, *balas*, *gaṇas*, etc. So there were *yūthapas*, *anīkapatis*, *balamukhyas*, *gaṇamukhyas*, etc. under the *senāpati*.[80] It appears that the *yūthapas* were put under *mahāyūthapas* and the latter under *mahāyūthapa-yūthapas*.[81] It is important to note that the army was also represented in the *sabhā* and associated with functions of the state.[82] Daring, bravery, forebearance, brilliance, purity, high birth, loyalty and proficiency were among the top qualities which the *senāpati* was expected to possess.[83] The government was very particular in making adequate payments of the salaries and allowances in time to him and his forces.[84] Sugrīva had a number of unit commanders under him, such as Hanumān, Aṅgada, Nala, Nīla, Kumada, Rambha, Śarabha, Panasa, Vinata, etc. In Prahasta Rāvaṇa had a very good commander.

DAUVĀRIKA

He was variously called as *pratihāra, dvāḥstha, dvārapāla* and

80 *senāpati* I – *Rām* VI.3.31, VI.4.10
vāhinīpati II – *Rām* VI.4.21
yūthapā yūthapaśreṣṭhaṁ yeṣāṁ yūthāni bhāgaśaḥ I
yastu bhīmāṁ pravalgantīṁ camūṁ tiṣṭhati śobhayan II – *Rām* VI.26.40-41
gaṇa I – *Rām* VI.8.17
svenānīkena I – *Rām* VI.26.46
anīkapāḥ II – *Rām* VI.19.4

81 *sa eṣa jāmbavān nāma mahāyūthapayūthapaḥ* I – *Rām* VI.27.11

82 *amātyā balamukhyāśca mukhyā ye nigamasya ca* I
rāghavasyābhiṣekārthe prīyamāṇāḥ susaṁgatāḥ II – *Rām* II.15.2
brāhmaṇān kṣatriyān yodhānamātyān gaṇavallabhān I
kṣipramānayatāvyagrāḥ kṛtyamātyayikaṁ hi naḥ II – *Rām* II.81.12

83 *kaccid dhṛṣṭaśca śūraśca dhṛtimān matimān śuciḥ* I
kulīnaścānuraktaśca dakṣaḥ senāpatiḥ kṛtaḥ II – *Rām* II.100.30

84 *kaccid balasya bhaktaṁ ca vetanaṁ ca yathocitam* I
samprāptakālaṁ dātavyaṁ tadāsi na vilambase II – *Rām* II.100.32

dvārādhyakṣa.[85] He was the chamberlain.[86] Precisely speaking, the *dauvārika* was the doorkeeper, the watchman at the entrances of the palace. Since there were several entrances, they were manned by many *dauvārikas*. Generally, they held *vetra* (staff) in their hands. The *pratihārī* is a female counterpart of the *pratihāra*. He was no mean servant, because he was expected to be well-versed in etiquette and protocol, so that he could usher visitors in the court and make proper seating arrangements according to their status. According to a later tradition, Lakṣmaṇa himself had worked as Rāma's *pratihāra*.

ANTAḤPURĀDHIKṚTA

He was designated as *antarvaṁśika*[87] also and was the chief of the guards of the harem. The *Rāmāyaṇa* speaks of the old *stryadhyakṣas*, holding *vetras* (staffs) in their hands, guarding the door.[88] They were probably working under the overall supervision of the *antaḥpurādhikṛta*. We are told elsewhere that the guarding of the entrances to the *antaḥpura* was entrusted to females, girls and old men.[89] The attendants of inner apartments wore special dress. The *Rāmāyaṇa* describes the attendants bringing Sītā out of Rāvaṇa's palace, as wearing *kañcuka* and *uṣṇīṣa* and holding cane-sticks in their hands.[90]

BANDHANĀGĀRĀDHIKṚTA

The word *bandhanāgāra* means a jail. Hence, the officer-in-charge of jails came to be known as *bandhanāgārādhikṛta*. However, Kauṭilya

---

85 *Rām* VI.3.1.

86 *sa rājño darśanākāṅkṣī dvārādhyakṣānuvāca ha* । – *Rām* I.18.39
kaḥ sthitaḥ pratihāro me ... । – *Rām* I.73.14
pratihārī tvathovāca saṁtrastā tu kṛtāñjaliḥ । – *Rām* II.10.20
dvāḥsthairutthāya vijayamuktastaiḥ sahito yayau ॥ – *Rām* II.71.33

87 *Arth* I.12.

88 *tatra kāṣāyiṇo vṛddhān vetrapāṇīn svalaṁkṛtān* ।
dadarśa viṣṭhitān dvāri stryadhyakṣān susamāhitān ॥ – *Rām* II.16.3

89 *striyo bālāśca vṛddhāśca dvārarakṣaṇatatparāḥ* । – *Rām* II.20.12

90 *kañcukoṣṇīṣiṇastatra vetrajharjharapāṇayaḥ* । – *Rām* VI.114.21

has used the word *praśāstā* for it according to some scholars.[91]

DHANĀDHYAKṢA

He was an officer responsible for revenue collection. Since the *Rāmāyaṇa* refers to many *dhanādhyakṣas*,[92] they seem to have been working under some supreme revenue officer, probably the *kośādhyakṣa*, who also finds mention in the Epic. The *Rāmāyaṇa* refers to the *kośa* several times, indicating the importance it had for the good running of administration.[93]

RĀJĀJÑĀ-VAKTĀ

It is not clear which officer this term indicates. But it seems that he was some sort of a judicial officer. It is just possible that he was Kauṭilya's *pradeṣṭā*.

PRĀḌVIVĀKA

According to Nilakantha,[94] *prāṭ* means one who questions and *vivāka* means one who understands the attitude of both parties in a legal dispute. This etymology will make *prāḍvivāka* appear as the chief justice. He was next to the king in judicial hierarchy.

DHARMĀSANĀDHIKR̥TA

He was also called *dharmādhyakṣa* and was one of the judges. It was for the judicial and police officers that Rāma gave a very pertinent advice to guard themselves against monetary temptations.[95]

---

91 *Arth* I.12.

92 *adya sarve dhanādhyakṣā dhanamādāya puṣkalam* । – *Rām* I.69.2

93 *kośasaṁgrahaṇe yuktā ...* । – *Rām* I.7.11

rājā satvaramāhūya vyāpr̥taṁ vittasañcaye । – *Rām* II.39.14

94 Commentary of the *Mahābhārata*, Śānti 121.46:
prāṭ sa cāso vivākaśca vivadamānayordvayor pr̥cchatītinimittāvettā ।

95 *gr̥hītaścaiva pr̥ṣṭhaśca kāle dr̥ṣṭaḥ sakāraṇaḥ* ।
kaccinna mucyate coro dhanalobhānnararṣabha ।। – *Rām* II.100.57

VYAVAHĀRANIRṆETĀ

According to the *Amarakośa*, *vyavahāra* also means *vivāda* (disputes). So *vyavahāranirṇetā* would be a civil judge. And if we assume that his jurisdiction was confined to a *pura* only, he may be identified with Kauṭilya's *paura-vyavahārika*.

SENĀBHṚTIDĀNĀDHYAKṢA

It is evident that he was a military personnel. But the nature of his job cannot be precisely determined.

KARMĀNTA VETANAGRĀHIṆAḤ

It is difficult to determine the nature and functions of this officer.

NAGARĀDHYAKṢA

He was the city magistrate wielding executive and judicial powers.

RĀṢṬRĀNTAPĀLA

He may be identified with Kauṭilya's *āṭavika* and officer-in-charge of the forest people.

DAṆḌĀDHIKĀRĪ

He is clearly Kauṭilya's *daṇḍapāla*. Since the word *daṇḍa* means both punishment and army, he may either be identified with head magistrate[96] or a commander of an unit of the army.[97]

DURGAPĀLA

He is included in the list of Kauṭilya's *mahāmātra*s and was clearly the officer-in-charge of the forts. The great importance was attached to the *durga*s is made clear by Rāma's reference to them in his advice to Bharata.[98]

---

96 Apte, V.M., *Students' Sanskrit English Dictionary*, p. 244.

97 *Arth* VI.1.

98 *kvacid durgāi sarvāṇi dhanadhānyāyudhodakaiḥ* । – *Rām* II.100.53

Besides these *tīrthas*, the *Rāmāyaṇa* refers to a number of other functionaries of the state. Its reference to *amātya-mukhyas* may mean the departmental heads of the state.[99] It is also interesting to note that the female *ratnins* who enjoyed great importance in the age of the Brāhmaṇas find mention in the *Rāmāyaṇa*.[100] They were *mahiṣī* (chief queen), *parivṛkti* (forsaken queen), and the *vāvātā* (favourite queen). But it is not clear whether they wielded the same influence as their counterparts in the later Vedic age.

However, the *Rāmāyaṇa* leaves us in no doubt about the important role of *dūtas* (envoys, messengers) in polity. They are shown as being sent with urgent messages to courts of the neighbouring kingdoms. Quick mobility was considered as their prime quality.[101] *Dūtas* on speedy horses were sent to bring back Bharata from his maternal uncle.[102] Rāma wants *dūtas* to be citizens of the *janapada*, scholarly, proficient, brilliant, precise conveyor of the message and erudite.[103] They enjoyed certain diplomatic immunities. Howsoever, bitter their message might be, they could not be killed.[104] But it appears they did not enjoy complete inviolability of their person. Vibhīṣaṇa tells Rāvaṇa that, though certain types of punishment can be given to the *dūta*, namely, mutilation of organs, whipping, shaving of the head and stamping by hot iron, but he cannot be slain.[105]

---

99 *svalaṁkṛtān sāśvarathān sakuñjarān amātyamukhyāṁśca dadarśa vallabhān* । – *Rām* II.15.47

100 *mahiṣyā parivṛttyātha vāvātāmaparāṁ tathā* ॥ – *Rām* I.14.35

101 *paureṣu preṣayāmāsa dūtān vai śīghragāminaḥ* । – *Rām* I.11.24

102 *evaṁ bhavatu yāsyanti dūtāḥ śīghrajavairhayaiḥ* ।
bharataṁ mātulakulādihāvartayituṁ narāḥ ॥ – *Rām* II.19.13

103 *kvaccijjānapado vidvān dakṣiṇaḥ pratibhānavān* ।
yathoktavādī dūtaste kṛto bharata paṇḍitaḥ ॥ – *Rām* II.100.35

104 *dūtā na vadhyāḥ samayeṣu rājan sarveṣu sarvatra vadanti santaḥ* ॥
– *Rām* V.52.13

105 *vairūpyamaṅgeṣu kaśābhighāto mauṇḍyaṁ tathā lakṣaṇa sannipātaḥ* ।
etān hi dūto pravadanti daṇḍān vadhastu dūtasya na naḥ śruto 'sti ॥
– *Rām* V.52.15

The *Rāmāyaṇa* makes a clear distinction between a *dūta* and a *cara*. While the former was an envoy enjoying great respectability, the latter was a spy and was looked down upon. This becomes clear from Aṅgada's impression about Śuka sent by Rāvaṇa to Rāma's camp. He told Rāma that the *rākṣasa* from Laṅkā seemed to him to be a spy and not an envoy and that he had come there to assess their strength.[106] Though Śuka and Sāraṇa, the ministers of Rāvaṇa, were in the guise of Vānaras, they were recognized by Vibhīṣaṇa.[107] Later, they themselves confessed that they were sent by Rāvaṇa to collect military information. The episode indicates that the spy's task, being very difficult, could even be undertaken by such big officers as ministers. It was very hazardous as is proved by the case of Śuka who, after being discovered, was belaboured by the Vānaras.[108] Though Śuka and Sāraṇa had acted as spies, they claimed the status of a *dūta* which was most generously granted by Rāma.[109] This is how they were spared.

Another important officer of the state was *sūta* who was one of the *ratnins* in the later Vedic period. He continued to enjoy great reputation during the age of the *Rāmāyaṇa*. Sumantra, a great functionary of that time, was both a *sūta* and a minister. The king and the *purohita* utilized his services for important matters. Vasiṣṭha asked him to invite all kings on the occasion of Rāma's proposed coronation ceremony.[110] Daśaratha also bade him to send for the *dhanādhyakṣas*.[111] He has been described as *mantra-kovida*.[112] He was

---

106 *nāyaṁ dūto mahārāja cārakaḥ pratibhāti me* ||
tulitaṁ hi balaṁ sarvamanena tava tiṣṭhatā | – *Rām* VI.20.29-30

107 *tasyaitau rākṣasendrasya mantriṇau śukasāraṇau* |
laṅkāyāḥ samanuprāptau cārau parapurañjaya || – *Rām* VI.25.40

108 *vānaraiḥ pīḍyamānastu śuko vacanamabravīt* ||
na dūtān ghnanti kākutstha vāryantāṁ sādhu vānarāḥ | – *Rām* VI.20.17-18

109 *nyastaśastrau gṛhītau ca na dūtau vadhamarhathaḥ* ||
pracchannau ca vimuñcemau cārau rātriṁ carāvubhau | – *Rām* VI.25.20-21

110 *tataḥ sumantramāhūya vasiṣṭho vākyamabravīt* ||
nimantrayasva nṛpatīn pṛthivyāṁ ye ca dhārmikāḥ | – *Rām* I.13.19

111 *adya sarve dhanādhyakṣā dhanamādāya puṣkalam* | – *Rām* I.69.2

112 *śūtaṁ sumantraṁ mantrakovidam* | – *Rām* II.15.24

so much respected that he could afford to administer a rebuke to Kaikeyī even.[113]

Sometimes the *sūtas* have been spoken of in the company of *māgadhas* when they were shown as singing and praying in praise of royal people.[114]

The *Rāmāyaṇa* refers to *sandhi-vigraha*[115] which mean peace and war. It is doubtful whether the office of the later *sāndhivigrahika* had come into existence during the age of the Epic. It is more likely that matters connected with peace and war were handled by the *senāpati* himself.

The *Rāmāyaṇa* describes how, at the instance of Bharata, a royal road, termed as Narendra-mārga[116] from Ayodhyā to the bank of the Ganges, was constructed. It was an uphill task involving levelling of the ground, digging, felling of trees and shrubs, laying out the road and beautifying it by planting trees, etc. Its construction harnessed the services of a large number of specialists in road-construction (*vartna-karmāṇi kovidāḥ*).[117] Since it has also been termed as the "military road", it may be assumed that it was constructed by the Public Works Department, more so because in its construction was involved the supervision of functionaries of the state (*adhikr̥tā narāḥ*).[118]

---

113 *patighnīṁ tvāmahaṁ manye kulaghnīmapi cāntataḥ* ।। – *Rām* II.35.6

114 *pradeyāṁśca dadau rājā sūtamāgadhavandinām* । – *Rām* I.18.20

115 *tatra śr̥ṇvan sukhā vācaḥ sūtamāgadhavaṁdinām* । – *Rām* II.6.6

puraḥ saraiḥ svastikasūtamāgadhaiḥ । – *Rām* II.17.46

sandhivigrahau । – *Rām* II.100.70

116 *Rām* II.80.22.

117 *atha bhūmipradeśajñāḥ sūtrakarmaviśāradāḥ* ।
svakarmābhiratā śūrāḥ khanakā yantrakāstathā ।।

karmāntikāḥ sthapatayaḥ puruṣā yantrakovidāḥ ।
tathā vardhakayaścaiva mārgiṇo vr̥kṣatakṣakāḥ ।।

sūpakārāḥ sudhākārā vaṁśacarmakr̥tastathā । – *Rām* II.80.1-3

... *vartmakarmaṇi kovidāḥ* । – *Rām* II.80.5

118 *bahvaśobhata senāyāḥ panthāḥ surapathopamaḥ* ।।
ājñāpyātha yathājñapti yuktāste 'dhikr̥tā narāḥ । – *Rām* II.80.14-15

Otherwise too, the march of the army was preceded by an advance party to make sure of topographical conditions of the region. Nala,[119] who was the engineer of the time and had constructed the *setu* on the ocean, was often the leader of the advance party.[120]

The *Rāmāyaṇa* mentions a class of officers as *yukta*s.[121] They seem to have been officers in general.[122] By the time of the Mauryas, they gained responsibility.

High principles of governance, which guided monarchy, must have been the guiding principles of the civil service also. They were to protect the life and property of the people who paid one-sixth of their produce to the king exactly for this purpose.[123] As Rāma, so also his functionaries, must have been engaged in ensuring the welfare of the people.[124] If people were like the children of the king, they could not be otherwise to his bureaucracy.[125] It seems to have been instructed to guard against red-tapism.[126] It was aware of the fact that excessive punishment very often proves counter-productive.[127] It was a commonly recognized principle of governance that one who governs justly has not to repent later.[128]

---

119 *Rām* II.3.8, II.15.14.

120 Sircar, D.C., *Indian Epigraphical Glossary*, p. 386.

121 *setuheturayaṁ nalaḥ* ॥ – *Rām* VI.26.21

122 *agre yātu balasyāsya nīlo mārgamavekṣitum* । – *Rām* VI.4.9

123 *baliṣaḍbhāgamuddhṛtya nṛpasyārakṣituḥ prajāḥ* । – *Rām* II.75.25

124 *sarvasya lokasya hite niviṣṭam* । – *Rām* II.2.54

125 *pūrvakairmama rājendraiḥ sutavat baripālitam* ॥ – *Rām* II.2.4

126 *kṣipramārabhase karma na dīrghayasi rāghava* ॥ – *Rām* II.100.19

127 *kaccinnogreṇa daṇḍena bhṛśamudvejitāḥ prajāḥ* । – *Rām* II.100.27

128 *nyāyena rājakāryāṇi yaḥ karoti daśānana* ।
na sa saṅtapyate paścāt niścitārthamatirnṛpaḥ ॥ – *Rām* VI.12.30

4

Civil Service in the Mahābhārata

THE political horizon of the *Mahābhārata* age was far larger than that of the *Rāmāyaṇa* age. It extended from Prāgjyotiṣa in the east to Gāndhāra in the west and from the Himalayas in the north to the kingdoms of the Pāṇḍyas, Coḷas and Keraḷas in the south. Of these, the kingdoms of Trigartas, Madras, Śālvas, Yādavas, Śūrasenas, Pāñcālas, Matsyas, Cedis, Māgadhas, Aṅgas, Andhaka-Vr̥ṣṇis, etc. were some of the most important. Many of them find mention in Buddhist literature, the *Aṣṭādhyāyī* of Pāṇini and the *Arthaśāstra* of Kauṭilya. These states had different types of government, though monarchy was, by far and large the most popular. Thus, the multitude of states, the differing forms of governments, the craze for the attainment of the *cakravartitva*, the frequent interstatal war, the maintenance of standing armies, the tapping of vast sources of revenue and the enormity of socio-economic problems all combined together to give new dimensions to the polity of the time, as also to the bureaucratic set-up of the government.

The most popular word for the civil service continued to be *amātya*.[1] Another word *puruṣa*, which seems to have been the abbreviation of *rājapuruṣa*, too denoted a civil servant.[2] From the authority that the officers wielded they earned the royal designation

---

1 *kaccit samvr̥tamantraistairamātyaiḥ sāstrakovidaiḥ* ।
rāṣṭram surakṣitam tāta śatrubhirna visupyate ॥ – Sabhā 5.28

2 *kaccit viditvā puruṣānuttamādhamamadhyamān* ।
tvamkarmasvanurūpeṣu niyojayasi bhārata ॥ – Sabhā 5.75

of *adhikṛtas*.[3] Being the assignees to a variety of government jobs, they were also known as *rājayuktas*.[4] Since all officers were in service during the pleasure of the king, they were sometimes modestly described as *bhṛtyas*[5] even. For the same reason, they were called *nṛpasevīs*,[6] *rājopasevīs*[7] and *rājopajīvīs*.[8] In general terms, the word *sahāya* too has been used for civil servants.[9]

It was universally held that it was impossible to run the government without bureaucracy. But it was equally impossible to run it with wicked bureaucrats.[10] The *Mahābhārata* was against one-man rule and regarded bureaucracy as an inseparable part of monarchy. This explains why it puts forth emphatically that the kingdom cannot be run single-handed.[11] The importance of the *amātyas* can be gauged from the fact that some of them were given the reverence deserved by a father.[12]

The *Mahābhārata* lays down qualifications of an *amātya* at several places. He should be expert in *jñāna* and *vijñāna*, the king's well-wisher, high-born and sweet-natured.[13] It appears that military training was a desideratum for all civil servants.[14] At another place the *Mahābhārata* states besides enjoying the confidence of the people

---

[3] *kāryeṣvadhikṛtāḥ* । – Śānti 85.16

[4] *sarveṣām rājayuktānām duṣkaram paridṛṣṭavān* । – Śānti 82.9

[5] Śānti 82.23.

[6] Śānti 82.24.

[7] Śānti 82.25.

[8] Śānti 82.26.

[9] *sahāyānanuraktāṁśca nayajñānupasaṁhitān* । – Śānti 111.23

[10] *na śakyam hyanamātyena mahatvamanuśāsitam* ।
duṣṭāmātyena vā vīra śarīraparīpanthinā ॥ – Śānti 111.22

[11] *na ca praśāstum rājyam hi śakyamekena bhārata* । – Śānti 115.13

[12] *amātyo me bhava prājña piteveha praśādhi mām* । – Śānti 138.133

[13] *yasya bhṛtyajanaḥ sarvo jñānavijñāna-kovidaḥ* ।
hitaiṣī kulajaḥ snigdhaḥ sa rājyaphalamaśnute ॥ – Śānti 115.14-15

[14] *nityayuktāśca tebhṛtyā bhavantu raṇakovidāḥ* ।
vājinām ca prayogeṣu vaiśāradyamiheṣyate ॥ – Śānti 119.18

and being a scholar, he should also be a warrior.[15] They were not only to be high-born, virtuous, patient, frank, truthful, scholar, beautiful and noble, but also brave.[16-17] The words[18] *suparīkṣitaiḥ* and *maulāḥ* used for *amātyas* clearly indicate two things: First, they were thoroughly tested before they were given appointments. Second, some of the *amātyas*, if not all, held hereditary posts. Generally, the *amātyas* had to get through the four tests: *dharmopadhā*, *arthopadhā*, *kāmopadhā* and *bhayopadhā*. But the *Mahābhārata* prescribes five tests for them.[19] Nilakantha, commenting on the *upadhās* in the *Mahābhārata*, wrongly interprets them as tricks, namely, *vācikī*, *kāyikī*, *mānasikī*, *kāyikī*-cum-*vācikī*-cum-*mānasikī*.

From the pool of *amātyas*, who were even called *rājavallabhas* (Sabhā 33.4), the most brilliant and successful were appointed as ministers technically called *mantrīs* or *sacivas*. There are many references in the *Mahābhārata* to show that the *mantrī* and the *saciva* were identical.[20] The king was forbidden to appoint ministers without putting to tests.[21] They were to be high-born, educated, wise, expert in *jñāna* and *vijñāna*, the right interpreter of all the Śāstras, tolerant, native of the country, familiar with *deśa* and *kāla*, expert in matters of peace and

---

15 *paurajānapadā yasmin viśvāsam dharmato gataḥ* ।
yoddhā nayavipaścicca sa mantram śrotumarhati ॥ – Śānti 83.46

16 *yaścāmātyān mānayitvā yathārtham* ।
mantro ca yuddhe ca nṛpo niyujyāt ॥ – Śānti 91.29

17 *kulīnaḥ śīlasampannastitikṣuravikatthanaḥ* ।
sūraścāryaśca vidvāṁśca pratipattiviśāradaḥ ॥
ete hyamātyāḥ kartavyā sarvakarmasvavasthitāḥ ।
pūjitāḥ samvibhaktāśca susahāyāḥ svaniṣṭhitāḥ ॥ – Śānti 80.28-29

18 Śānti 83.19.

19 *parīkṣya ca guṇān nityam prauḍhābhavān dhuraṁdherān* ।
pañcopadhāvyatītāṁśca kuryāt rājārthakāriṇaḥ ॥ – Śānti 82.22

nityam pañcopadhātītairmantrayet saha mantribhiḥ । – Śānti 83.52

20 *mayā sammantrya paścācca na hiṁsyā sacivāstvayā* । – Śānti 111.38

chidram tu tasya tad dṛṣṭvā procuste pūrvamantriṇaḥ । – Śānti 111.51

21 *nāparīkṣya mahīpālaḥ sacivam kartumarhati* । – Śānti 118.4

war, bold and brave.[22] Additionally, he should be truthful, virtuous, serene, apprehensive of calumny, soft-spoken and a member of the family which has been in royal service since the time of his father and grandfather.[23] Loyalty of the minister was regarded as his great asset. A disloyal minister might join hands with other treacherous ministers to create problems for the king.[24] Ministers were trained soldiers. Śālva's minister had accompanied his master's commander-in-chief and fought with Sāmba.[25] In other reference Duryodhana along with his *amātyas* is shown in military actions.[26] It appears that some of the ministers were retained in service even when old. Their experience was thought to be an asset to the king. The *Mahābhārata* speaks of such old *amātyas* of Duryodhana.[27] Time and again, the *Mahābhārata* uses the word *kulīna*[28] for a minister. It appears from it that they were mostly brāhmaṇas, but the possibility of some of them being kṣatriyas and vaiśyas cannot be ruled out. Even a wise and virtuous śūdra could be appointed as a minister. Vidura,[29] for instance, though a śūdra, always acted as a counsellor. Among the courtiers of Virāṭa were, inter alia, the *mantrī-dvijas*,[30] who were obviously his brāhmaṇa ministers.

---

22 *kulīnam śikṣitam prājñam jñānavijñānapāragam* ׀ *sarvaśāstrārthatattvajñam sahiṣṇum deśajam tathā ... sacivam deśakālajñam ... yuktacāram svaviṣaye saṅdhivigrahakovidam ... dhīram śūram* ׀ – Śānti 118.7-14

23 *satavāk śīlasampanno gambhīraḥ satrapo mṛduḥ* ׀
pitṛpaitāmahī yaḥ syāt sa mantram śrotumarhati ׀׀ – Śānti 83.43

24 *mantriṇyananurakte tuviśvāso nopapadyate* ׀
vyathayet hi sa rājānam mantribhiḥ sahitonṛjuḥ ׀׀ – Śānti 83. 30-31

25 *gṛhītvā kārmulam sāmbaḥ śālvasya sacivam raṇe* ׀
yodhayāmāsa samhṛṣṭaḥ kṣemavṛddhim camūpatim ׀׀ – Vana 16.11

26 *gaccha duryodhanam baddhvā sahāmātyamihānaya* ׀ – Vana 246.6

27 *vṛddhānduryodhanāmātyān* ׀ – Vana 242.14

28 *kulīnān śīlasampannāniṅgitajñānaniṣṭhurān* ׀
deśakālavīdhānajñān bhartṛkāryahitaiṣiṇaḥ ׀׀
nityamartheṣu sarveṣu rājā kurvīta mantriṇaḥ ׀ – Śānti 83.8-9

29 *mantre ca niścaye caiva ṣāḍguṇasya cacintane* ׀
viduram buddhisampannam prītimān sa samādiśat ׀׀ – Śānti 41.10

30 *mantrīdvijān sūtamukhān viśastathā* ׀ – Virāṭa 7.5

During the *Mahābhārata* period also there seem to have been two bodies of the *amātyas* – one the inner council, which served the purpose of the modern cabinet, and the other – a bigger one – was the *mantrī-pariṣad*. The cabinet, according to the *Mahābhārata*, had eight ministers[31] whom the king consulted on all important issues regularly and probably daily. They seem to have been *dhī-sacivas* (ministers for counsel) of the *Amarakośa* as against the *karma-sacivas* (executive officers).[32] The bigger council, which seems to have been the council of ministers, had thirty-seven *amātyas*, namely, four brāhmaṇas, well-versed in the Vedas, brilliant, *snātaka* and pure, eight kṣatriyas, strong and weapon-wielding, twenty-one vaiśyas, who may be moneyed, three śūdras, who should be humble and pure, and a *sūta*, who may be above fifty, non-backbiter, scholarly, balanced and well-versed in the ancient lore.[33] The composition of the *mantri-pariṣad* indicates that it was representative of all *varṇas* including the śūdras. The vaiśyas being most numerous got the highest representation. The *sūta* as a minister retained his position which he had continued to enjoy ever since the Ṛgvedic period.

The main task of the minister was to advise the king on all important matters. All kings in the *Mahābhārata* are shown as holding deliberations with their ministers.[34] The king whose deliberations are well-guarded from his enemies is safe in his kingdom.[35] Deliberations between the king and his ministers constitute the root of the

---

31 *aṣṭānām mantriṇām madhye mantram rājopadhārayet* । – Śānti 85.11

32 *mantrī dhīsacivo 'mātyo 'nye karmasacivāstataḥ* ।
– *AmaraK*, Kṣatriyavarga

33 *caturo brāhmaṇān vaidyān pragalbhān snātakān śucīn* ।
kṣatriyāśca tathā cāṣṭau balinaḥ śastrapāṇinaḥ ।
vaiśyān vittena sampannānekaviṁśatisaṁkhayā ।
trīṁśca śūdrān vinītāṁśca śucīn karmaṇi pūrvake ।
aṣṭābhiśca guṇairyuktam sūtam... ॥ – Śānti 85.7-11

34 *gate bhīṣme mahārāja dhārtarāṣṭro janeśvaraḥ* ।
punarāgamya tam deśamamantrayata mantribhiḥ ॥ – Vana 253.14

35 *yasya cārāśca mantrāśca nityam caiva kṛtākṛtā* ।
na jñāyante hi ripubhiḥ sa rājā rājymarhati ॥ – Śānti 58.39

kingdom.[36] The counsels of wise ministers are a top secret.[37] While the root of the kingdom is the spy, its essence is the counsel.[38] The main cause of the downfall of the republics was that they could not keep their deliberations confidential.[39] The need to guard the secret counsels sometimes led political thinkers to advise the king to keep them to themselves and not to share them even with ministers. Only when it is not possible for the king to take decisions by himself alone he should take others into confidence.[40] But this was the extreme view of only a few political thinkers. The majority of them always advised the king to hold consultations with his ministers. According to some, he was first to consult three ministers, each of them separately, assess their advice and finally discuss it with his *guru*.[41] At another place the *Mahābhārata* ordains that the king should always hold discussions with his ministers who have been thoroughly tested.[42] The brāhmaṇa *guru* was well-versed in *dharma, artha* and *kāma* and his decision should invariably be accepted by all.[43] The venue of holding consultations with the ministers should be a secluded place like the upper apartment of the palace to which certain categories of persons like the infirm,

36 *mantriṇāṁ mantramūlaṁ hi rājño rāṣṭram vivardhate* । – Śānti 83.48

37 *mantragūḍhā hi rājyasya mantriṇo ye manīṣiṇaḥ* । – Śānti 83.50

38 *rājyam praṇidhimūlam hi mantrasāram pracakṣate* । – Śānti 83.51

39 *bhedamūlo vināśo hi gaṇānāmupalakṣaye* ।
mantrasaṁvaraṇaṁ duḥkhaṁ bahūnāmitimematiḥ ।। – Śānti 107.8

40 *yadaivaikena śakyeta guhyam kartum tadā caret* ।
yacchanti sacivā guhyam mitho viśrāvayantyapi ।।
aśakyamiti kṛtvā vā tato 'nyaiḥ saṁvidham caret । – Śānti 103.26-27
naca mantram prakāśayet । – Śānti 71.7

41 *teṣām trayāṇām vividhaṁ vimarśaḥ* ।
vibuddhya cittam viniveśya tatra svaniścayam ।
tam paraniścyam ca nivedayeduttaramantrakāle ।। – Śānti 83.53

42 *nityam pañcopadhātītermantrayet sahamantribhiḥ* । – Śānti 83.52

43 *dharmārthakāmajñamupetya pṛcchet* ।
yukto gurum brāhmaṇamuttarārtham ।।
niṣṭhā kṛtā tena yadā sadaḥ syāt ।
tam mantramārgam praṇayedasaktaḥ ।। – Śānti 83.54

the disabled, the deformed, the abnormal, the womenfolk and the eunuchs should be debarred entry to ensure secrecy of deliberations.[44] According to yet another view, the king should consult that minister who shares his happiness and unhappiness.[45]

As a precautionary measure, the minister, whose father was previously dismissed, but later restored, shoud not be consulted on important issues.[46] Only a minister of proven wisdom and purity should be depended upon for secret parleys.[47] Highly qualified and conscientious ministers were revered like teachers and fathers.[48] That king enjoys the fruits of his kingdom whose ministers come from noble families, are not vulnerable to monetary temptations, have been living together, are knowledgeable of human relations, capable of improvising for the unseen eventualities, appreciative of the needs of the times and unshaken by the bygone events.[49] The *amātyas* were assigned different jobs according to their capabilities and aptitudes after ascertaining their work.[50] As a general rule, only one *amātya* was given a particular assignment, for it was feared that

44 *na vāmanāḥ kubjakṛṣā na khañjā* ।
nāndho jaḍaḥ strī ca napuṁsakam ca ।।
nordhvam na cādhaḥ pracareta kathañcit ।
āruhya vā veśma tathaiva śūnyam, sthalam prakāśam kuśakāśahīnam ।।
– Śānti 83.56-57

45 *samānaduḥkhasukham tam pṛcchedartheṣu mānavam* । – Śānti 83.34

46 *vidharmato viprakṛtaḥ pitā yasyābhavat purā* ।
satkṛtaḥ sthāpitaḥ so 'pi na mantram śrotumarhati ।। – Śānti 83.39

47 *kṛtaprajñaśca medhāvī budho jānapadaḥ śucaḥ* ।
sarvakarmasu yaḥ śuddhaḥ sa mantram śrotumarhati ।। – Śānti 83.41

48 *sahāyānanuraktāṁśca nayajñānutasaṁhitam parasparamasamsṛṣṭān* ।
vijigīṣūnalolupān atitopadhān prājñān hite yuktān manasvinaḥ pujayethā mahābhāga yathācāryān yathā pitṛn ।। – Śānti 111.23-24

49 *mantriṇo yasya kulajā asahāryā sahoṣitāḥ* ।
nṛpatermatidāḥ santaḥ sambandhajñānakovidāḥ ।
anāgatavidhātāraḥ kālajñānaviśāradāḥ ।
atikrāntamaśocantaḥ sa rājyaphalamaśnute ।। – Śānti 115.16-17

50 *anurūpāṇi karmāṇi bhṛtyebhyo yaḥ prayacchati* ।
sa bhṛtyaguṇasampanno rājāphalamupaśnute ।। – Śānti 119.4
ata ūrdhvamamātyānām parīkṣeta guṇāguṇam । – Śānti 83.18

if many persons were put on one and the same job, then functioning would be hampered by internal jealousies.[51]

The *Mahābhārata* speaks of the seven chief officials of the state.[52] Commenting on it, Nilakantha[53] states that these seven officials were as follows:

1. *durgādhyakṣa* (commandant of forts)
2. *balādhyakṣa* (commnader-in-chief of the army)
3. *dharmādhyakṣa* (chief justice)
4. *camūpati* (field commander of the army)
5. *purodhā* (priest)
6. *vaidya* (physician)
7. *daivajña* (astrologer)

The *Mahābhārata* contains scattered allusions to each one of them:

DURGĀDHYAKṢA

The Epic mentions six kinds of forts, viz., *dhanva durga*, *maṇī durga*, *giri durga*, *manuṣya durga*, *mṛd durga* and *vana durga*. They were under the overall charge of the *durgādhyakṣa*, also known as *durgapāla*. *Durga*s were well-protected by units of the army.[54]

---

51 *naivadvau na trayaḥ kāryā na mṛṣyeran parasparam* ।
ekārthe hyeva bhūtānām bhedo bhavati sarvadā ॥ – Śānti 80.25

52 *kaccit prakṛtayaḥ sapta naluptā bharatarṣabha* । – Sabhā 5.23

53 *tatra svābharūpa prakṛtiḥ saptavidhā durgādhyakṣo balādhyakṣo dharmādhyakṣaśca bhūpatipurodhā vaidyadevajñau sapta prakṛtayaḥ smṛtā iti proktāḥ* । – Nilakantha's commentray

54 *nyaset gulmān durgeṣu sandhau ca kurunandana* । – Śānti 69.6

BALĀDHYAKṢA

The *Mahābhārata* uses the word *bala* for the army.[55] Thus, the word *balādhyakṣa* would evidently mean the head of the army or the commander-in-chief. He was also called *senāpati*. Till the age of the *Mahābhārata* the separate post of the *sāndhivigrahika* had not come into existence. The matters of peace and war were looked after by the *senāpati* himself. He was drawn from the pool of the *amātyas* and was given this high office for his deep knowledge of the Dharmaśāstras, wisdom, perseverance, high birth and purity among other things.[56] Additionally, he should be an expert in military formations and use of weapons, as also brave, capable of bearing the extremities of weather and aware of the weak points of the enemies.[57] The *Mahābhārata* uses the word *senāgrya* also for him, because he was the leader of the army.[58] For the same reason, he was the *praṇetā* of the army.[59] It appears that the *senāpati* had a number of commandars under him. They were known as *bala-mukhyas*.[60]

The units of a ten hundred and a thousand soldiers were put under the charge of the *daśādhipati*, *śatādhipati* and *sahasrādhipati*.[61] Smaller units of the army were led by a number of *yūthapas*,[62] each comprising a special column such as the chariots or elephants.

---

55 *balasya parimāṇe ca bhaktavetanayostathā* ।
nakulam vyādiśat rājā karmaṇām canvavekṣaṇe ॥ – Śānti 41.42

56 *dharmaśāstrārthatattvajñaḥ sāndhivigrahiko bhavet* ।
matimān dhṛtimān hrīmān rahasyavinigūhitā ॥
kulīnaḥ sattvasampannaḥ śuklo 'mātyaḥ praśasyate ।
eteraiva guṇairyuktastathā senāpatirbhavet ॥ – Śānti 85.30-31

57 *vyūhayantrāyudhānām catattavajño vikramānvitaḥ* ।
varṣāśītoṣṇavātānām sahiṣṇuḥ pararandhrivit ॥ – Śānti 85.32

58 *senāgryam dhārtarāṣṭrasya prāptam dvaitavanam saraḥ* । – Vana 240.20

59 *praṇetā kīcakastasya balavānabhavat purā* । – Virāṭa 30.4

60 Śānti 69.39.

61 *daśādhipatayaḥ kāryāḥ śatādhipatayastathā* ।
tataḥ sahaśrapatim kuryāt śūramantandrītam ॥ – Śānti 100.31

62 *atha rājā trigartānām suśarmā rathayūthapaḥ* । – Virāṭa 30.1

When the *senāpati* meant an ordinary commandar, the word *adhi-senāpati* was used to denote the commander-in-chief, as would appear from the following verse:

> *bhīmasenastu taddṛṣṭvā tasya karma mahātmanaḥ* ।
> *adhisenāpatim cakre sudharmāṇam mahābalam* ॥
> – Sabhā 29.6

DHARMĀDHYAKṢA

Great importance was given to the dispensation of justice in ancient India, as it was generally held that the king stood for *dharma* and not for the fulfilment of his desires. He was essentially the protector of the people.[63]

The one-sixth part of the produce that the king collected from the people was in lieu of the protection that he gave to them.[64] Of all the duties of the king, three were the most important:

1. Punishing the wicked,
2. Protecting the noble, and
3. Not fleeing the battlefield.[65]

He was to treat people like his sons and grandsons, but was not to show any favour to anybody in the discharge of his judicial functions.[66] The existence of the kingdom was rooted in justice.[67] It was this set of high principles of justice which guided the functioning of the *dharmādhyakṣa* and the *dharmasthas* under him.

---

63 *dharmāya rājā bhavati na kāmakaraṇya tu* ।
māndhātā jānīhi rājā lokasya rakṣitā ॥ – Śānti 90.3

64 *ādadīta balim cāpi prajābhyaḥ kurunandana* ।
sa ṣaḍbhāgamapi prājñastāsāmevābhiguptaye ॥ – Śānti 69.25

65 *asatām pratiṣedhaśca satām ca paripālanam* ।
eṣa rājñām paro dharmaḥ samare cāpalāyanam ॥ – Śānti 14.16

66 *yathā putrā tathā pautrā dṛṣṭavyāste na saṁśayaḥ* ।
bhaktiścaiṣām na kartavyā vyavahāre pradarśite ॥ – Śānti 69.27

67 Śānti 69.28.

CAMŪPATI

Camūpati is a synonym of *senāpati*. Thus, it may be difficult to differentiate it from the word *balādhyakṣa*.

But looking into the references minutely, it may be said that the *balādhyakṣa* was the overall commander-in-chief of the army and the *camūpati* refers to a commander in action in the battlefield. For instance, Kṣemavṛddhi, who was the commander-in-chief of Śālva, has been called *camūpati*, when he was engaged in a fight with Sāmba.[68] It appears he was assisted by a number of junior military leaders whom the *Mahābhārata* refers to us as *senāgryāyiṇaḥ*.[69]

PURODHĀ

He was the royal priest and ever since the Vedic age enjoyed immense respect as the king's counsellor and spiritual guide. Evidently the words *purodhā* and *purohita* are synonyms.[70] The *Mahābhārata* enjoins upon the king to consult him in matters of *dharma* and *artha*, as he was generally a scholar and well-read person.[71] He was invariably consulted in religious and ritualistic matters.[72] He made the king protect the good and shun the evil.[73]

The king, whose priest is well-versed in hymns and is righteous, is always safe.[74] Like many posts of the state, that of the priest was

---

68 *gṛhītvā kārmukam sāmbaḥ śālvasya sacivam raṇe* ।
yodhayāmāsa samhṛṣṭaḥ kṣemavṛddhim camūpatim ॥ – Vana 16.11

69 *tasya tad vacanam śrutvā rājñaḥ senāgryāyinaḥ* । – Vana 240.25

70 *purodhāstu purohitaḥ* । – *AmaraK*, Kṣatriyavarga

71 *rājñā purohitaḥ kāryo bhaved vivdān bahuśrutaḥ* ।
ubhau samīkṣya dharmārthavaprameyāvanantaram ॥ – Śānti 73.1

72 *purohitam samānāyya vacanam cedamabravīt* ।
... na sa śakyaḥ kratuśreṣṭho jīvamāne yudhiṣṭhire ॥ – Vana 255.11-13

73 *dvijānām devakāryeṣu kāryeṣvanyeṣu caiva ha dhaumyam purodhasām* ।
śreṣṭham nityameva samābiśat ॥ – Śānti 41.14
purohito 'yamasmakamagnihotrāṇi rakṣatu । – Virāṭa 4.2

74 *ya eva tu sato rakṣedasataśca nivartayet* ।
sa eva rājñaḥ kartavyo rājan rājapurohitaḥ ॥ – Śānti 72.1

also, very often, hereditary. For instance, *ṛṣi* Kālakavṛkṣīya belonged to the hereditary priestly class.[75]

VAIDYA

He was the royal physician, responsible for the preparation of herbal medicines, *āsavas*, *ariṣṭas* and *rasas*. The health and well-being of the king was his special concern in an age when the administration of poison in foods and drinks was widely practised to get rid of one's enemy.[76] Commenting on the *Mahābhārata* (Sabhā 5.64), the *Bhārata-Kaumudī-Ṭīkā* speaks of the physicians in the army. The *Mahābhārata* (Sabhā 5.91) speaks of the royal physician in these terms:

> *kaccid vaidyāścikitsāyamaṣṭāṅgāyam viśāradāḥ* ।
> *suhṛdaścānuraktāśca śarīre te hitāḥ sada* ॥

DAIVAJÑA

He was the royal astrologer, expert in the knowledge of stars and physical phenomena. He was to forecast about the coming events and ward off evils. He determined auspicious days for big events. He enjoyed as much respect as a minister.[77] At another place, the *Mahābhārata* (Sabhā 5.42) describes him in the following manner:

> *kaccidaṅgeṣu niṣpāto jyotiṣaḥ pratipādakaḥ* ।

It is interesting to note that Nilakantha, while commenting on Śānti-Parva 57.17 has referred to the eighteen *tīrtha*s on the authority of some *Nītiśāstra* whose authenticity is far from certain. But these *tīrtha*s are almost the same as described in Tilaka commentary on the *Rāmāyaṇa* (Ayodhyā 100.36). However, the *Mahābhārata* alludes to a number of functionaries of the state here and there. The crown-prince, called the *yuvarāja*, played a significant role in the polity of

---

75 *dharmātmā mantravid yeṣām rājñām rājan purohitaḥ* । – Śānti 73.2

76 *tato rājakule nāndīsaṁjajñe bhūyasā punaḥ* ।
purohitakule caiva samprāpte brāmaṇarṣabhe ॥ – Śānti 82.68

77 *agnidairgaradaiścaiva pratitūpakārakaiḥ* । – Śānti 59.49

that period. As was common in earlier periods also, it was customary for the king to appoint his heir-apparent. For example, Yudhiṣṭhira had appointed Bhīmasena as his *yuvarāja*.[78] Simliarly, before going out for the fight, Jarāsandha had appointed Sahadeva, his son, as his heir-apparent.[79] The *yuvarāja* was associated with administrative and military activities of his father. Uttara, for instance, had led the army against the Kauravas in the absence of his father Virāṭa.[80]

The *Mahābhārata* alludes to the appointment of the prime minister as well. At certain places, the word *rājamukhya* stands for him. The word *pratyantara* also stands for him. He was to be well-renowned, never transgressing the limits, unenvious of others, resourceful, never doing the evil, steadfast in *dharma* in the face of desires, fear and anger, proficient and restrained in speech.[81-82] Additionally, he was expected to be of attractive features, complexion and voice, forgiving, non-backbiter, high-born and virtuous.[83] It is noteworthy that the *Mahābhārata* describes the *mantrī-mukhya*[84] in plural. From it, it would appear that the term *mantrī-mukhya* had not come to be used for the prime minister till then. It was obviously used for the senior ministers. Similarly, the word *mahāmātra* had not come to be used for a high officer, as was the case during the Mauryan period. In the age of the *Mahābhārata* it meant an overlord and was used for the king.[85]

---

78 *yauvarājyena kaunteyam bhīmasenamayojayat* । – Sabhā 41.9

79 *evamuktvā jarāsaṁdhaḥ sahadevābhiṣecanam* ।
ājñāpayao tadā rājā yuyutsurbhīmakarmabhiḥ ।। – Sabhā 22.31

80 *rājaputra hitaprepsuḥ kṣipram niryāhi ca svayam* । – Virāṭa 35.11

81 *kīrtipradhāno yastu syād yaśca syāt samaye sthitaḥ* ।
samarthān yaśca na dveṣṭi nānārthān kurute ca yaḥ ।।

yo na kāmād dhayāllobhāt krodhāt vā dharmamutsṛjet ।
dakṣaḥ paryāptavacanaḥ sa te syāt pratyantaraḥ ।। – Virāṭa 80.26-27

82 Ibid.

83 *rūpavarṇasvaropetastitikṣuranasūyakaḥ* ।
kulīnaḥ śīlasampannaḥ sa te syāt pratyantaraḥ ।। – Virāṭa 80.21

84 *provāca sarvānatha mantrīmukhyān* । – Virāṭa 68.9

85 *rājñe bhojakaṭasthāya mahāmātrāya dhīmane* । – Sabhā 31.63

The *Mahābhārata*[86] alludes to a number of territorial officers:

1. *grāmika*: He was in-charge of a village.
2. *daśika*: He was in-charge of ten villages.
3. *viṁśadhipa*: He looked after a group of twenty villages.
4. *śatapāla*: A group of a 100 villages was placed under his charge.
5. *sahasrapati*: He was in-charge of a thousand villages.

The *grāmika* had to remove the shortcomings of the village under him and report to his immediate boss, the *daśika*. Similarly, the other officers had to keep informed their superiors about the developments in their territories. Similarly, each town was entrusted to the care of a separate officer.

The king was called *cara-netra*,[87] because he saw through the eyes of his spies throughout his kingdom. Duryodhana had employed his spies for the purpose of tracing out the Pāṇḍavas.[88] They were *bahiścarāḥ* as against those who had their fixed headquarters of work. They frequented markets, gardens, social gatherings, ascetics, pleasure-resorts, academic meetings, road-crosses, assemblies, inns, etc. to gather information regarding spies of enemies.[89] The essential

---

[86] *grāmasyādhipatiḥ kāryo deśagrāmapatistathā।*
dviguṇāyaḥ śatasyaivam sahasrasya ca kāratyet॥

grāmīyān grāmadoṣāṁśca grāmikaḥ pratibhāvayet।
tānbrūyāt daśapāyāsau sa tu viṁśatipāyavai॥

so 'pi viṁśatyadhipatirvṛttam jānapade jane।
grāmāṇām śatapālāya sarvameva nivedayet॥

yānigrāmyāṇi bhojyāni grāmikastānyupāśriyāt।
daśapastena bhartavyastenāpi dviguṇādhipaḥ ...
nagare nagare vā syādekaḥ sarvārthacintakaḥ। – Śānti 87.2-11

[87] Śānti 180.22.

[88] *atha vai dhārtarāṣṭrena prayuktā ye bahiscarāḥ।*
mṛgayitvā bahūn grāmān rāṣṭrāṇi nagarāṇi ca॥ – Virāṭa 25.5

[89] *cārāṁśca vidyāt prahitān pareṇa bharatarṣabha।*
āpaṇeṣu vihāreṣu samājeṣu ca bhikṣuṣu॥
ārāmeṣu tathodyāne paṇḍitānām samāgame।
deśeṣu catvare caiva sambhāsvāsthesu ca॥ – Śānti 69.11-12

qualification of a spy was his devotion to his master.[90] Even the activities of civil servants, friends and sons were under their vigil.[91] They also kept a watch on the designs of the neutral, hostile and friendly kings and operated in the urban and rural areas.[92]

Another important institution of the government was the *dūta*s (envoys or messengers). The *Mahābhārata*[93] speaks of their three categories:

NISṚṢṬĀRTHA DŪTA

He was a high-powered envoy with the authority to negotiate with the king of the other states in whatever manner he deemed fit. Śrī Kṛṣṇa was such a *dūta* sent by the Pāṇḍavas to the court of the Kauravas.

PARIMITĀRTHA DŪTA

He was sent to other king's court to negotiate within the framework provided to him. He was to act in accordance with the specific instructions of his master.

ŚĀSANAHARA

He was only a messenger to deliver some message to the other party.

The most essential qualities of a *dūta* were:

1. Swift movement, and
2. Precision in conveying the message.[94] Additionally, he should have been high-born, virtuous, good speaker, proficient, sweet-

---

90 *nābhaktam cārayeccāram* । – Śānti 71.5

91 *amātyeṣu ca sarveṣu mitreṣu vividheṣu ca* ।
putreṣu ca mahārāja praṇidodhyāt samāhitaḥ । – Śānti 69.9

92 *udāsīnārimitrāṇām sarvaneva cikīrṣitam* ।
pure janapade caive jñātavyam cāracakṣuṣā । – Śānti 86.21

93 For discussion, see *Pāṇinikālīna Bhāratavarṣa*, pp. 402-03.

94 *vāgmī dakṣah priyaṁvadaḥ yathoktavādī smṛtivān ...* । – Śānti 86.28

tongued and possessed of good memory.[95] According to an ancient Indian tradition, he was not to be murdered.[96]

The *Mahābhārata* speaks of the *cara*s and *praṇidhi*s, separately:

caraśca praṇidhiścaiva – Śānti 58.5

But both were employed for intelligence purposes. The *praṇidhi*s, though well-tested, wise and capable of bearing the pangs of thirst and hunger as also fatigue, should look as if they were dumb, blind and deaf to conceal their detection:

praṇidhīśca tataḥ kuryājjaḍāndhavadhirākṛtīn ।
punsaḥ parīkṣitān prājñān kṣutpipāsāśramakṣāmān ॥

The *pratihāra* continued to be an important officer in the king's retinue. The *Mahābhārata* lays down that he should also be much possessed of the same qualities which are associated with a good *dūta*.[97] In many cases, his post had become hereditary. It appears, even the high functionaries of the state employed *pratihāra*s.[98] When a distinction was made between a *pratihāra* and a *dvārapāla*, the latter was placed under the former. The distinction between the two is clear from the fact that the *pratihāra* is spoken of in singular number, while the *dvārapāla*s manning the entrances of the royal palace were many.[99] While the *pratihāra* made seating arrangements for visitors in order of protocol, and brief them about the etiquette in the presence of the king, the *dvārapāla*s simply led visitors to the king.[100] The *dvārapāla*

---

95 *nimantraṇārtham dūtaśca preṣyāmasa śīgharagān* । – Vana 256.6
dūtaścāpai yathāvṛttam dhārtarāṣṭre nyavedayat । – Vana 256.18

96 *na tu hanyānnṛpo jātu dūtam kasyāñcidāpi* ।
dūtasya hantā nirayamāviṣet sacivaiḥ saha ॥ – Vana 85.26

97 *etaireva guṇairyuktaḥ pratihāro 'sya rakṣitā* । – Vana 85.29

98 *pāramparyāgate dvāre ye kecidanuvartinaḥ* ।
paricaryāvato dvāre ye ca kecana vargiṇaḥ ॥ – Vana 100.29

99 Ibid.

100 *tasyā dvāram samāsadya niḥśaṅkaḥ praviveśa ha* ।
tatrāpi dvārapālastamugravācā nyaṣedhayama ॥ – Śānti 325.25
pūjayitvā yathānyāyamabhivādya kṛtāñjaliḥ ।
prāveśayat tataḥ kakṣyām dvitīyām rājavesmanaḥ ॥ – Śānti 325.28-29

has been described as *dvāḥstha* as well.[101]

Whereas the officers in the police force have been denoted by a general term *rakṣābhyadhikṛtāḥ*,[102] those of the income tax department are suggested by yet another term *dhanadāna-prayojakāḥ*.[103] The *kośavṛddhikarāḥ* indicated the treasurers who used to be men of great reliability and resources.[104] Similarly, officers-in-charge of the *koṣṭhāgāra*s (godowns) were dependable, ungreedy and good dues collectors.[105]

The charioteer was known as *sārathī* or *sūta* and enjoyed a position of importance. If his master became unconscious, while fighting on his chariot, it was his duty to protect him by swiftly, taking him away from the battlefield.[106] In many cases, his office was also hereditary and he was very well familiar with conventions of war.[107]

In the age of the Brāhmaṇas, the *akṣavāpa* and the *govikartana* were two important *ratnin*s of the king. The former was the king's companion in sports and the latter was probably the officer-in-charge of the cattle. Yudhiṣṭhira worked as a *matākṣa* (expert in the game of *akṣa*) in the court of Virāṭa. Since the *Mahābhārata* calls him as a member of the king's *sabhā*, he seems to have been equivalent to the *akṣavāpa* of earlier times.[108] Again, the Epic refers to Bhīma as

---

101 *tato dvaḥsthaḥ praviśyaiva virāṭamidamabravīt* । – Virāṭa 68.52

102 Śānti 87.13.

103 *iqdaṇḍyāste ca mahārāja dhānādānaprayojakāḥ* । – Śānti 88.26

104 *kośākhyapaṭalam yasyakośavṛddhikarairnaraiḥ* ।
āptaistuṣṭaiśca satatam cīyate sanṛpottamaḥ ॥ – Śānti 115.20

105 *koṣṭhāgāramasahārairāptaiḥ sañcayatatparaiḥ* ।
pātrabhūtairalubdhaiśca pālyamānam guṇī bhavet ॥ – Śānti 115.21

106 *mohiṭasya raṇe śūro rakṣyaḥ sārathinā rathī* । – Vana 18.8

107 *tvam ca sūtakule jāto vinītaḥ sūta dharmajanaścāsi* ।
vṛṣṇīnānmāhaveṣvapi karmaṇi dāruṇe । – Vana 18.50

108 *sabhāstāro bhaviṣyāmi tasya rājño mahātmanaḥ* ।
keko nāma dvijo bhūtvā matākṣaḥ priyadevanaḥ ॥ – Virāṭa 1.24

govikartā in the court of Virāṭa.[109]

According to the *Mahābhārata*, *ākara* (mines), *lavaṇa* (salt), *śulka* (customs), *tara* (ferry tax) and *nāgabala* (elephants) constituted important sources of state revenue. The Epic advises the king to appoint trustworthy *amātyas* in-charge of these sources.[110]

The age of the *Mahābhārata* continued to have *sūtas* and *māgadhas* to sing in praise of the king.[111]

The *Mahābhārata* speaks of the *vetana* and *bhakta*[112] given to employees. The former means salary and the latter allowances. Incidently, the *Mahābhārata*[113] lays down the rules of conduct for the courtiers which might had been equally applicable to the smaller as well as high officers of the court. They were not to use the king's vehicle like the elephant and the chariot. They should refrain from giving him unwarranted advice. It is dangerous to be untruthful to the king. The employees, in general, should keep themselves away from the king's harem. They must take the king in the confidence before embarking upon any work, howsoever small. They should not take their seats until asked by the king. He should neither be taken for granted nor slighted. While in the king's service, one has to give up carelessness, conceit and anger. If it is in the interest of the king to tell him unpleasant things, one should never shirk from doing so. The functionaries of the state should never occupy a higher seat than that of the king. The falseful of the king should not be exposed before others. In the presence of the king, an employee should be restrained in his emotional reactions like pleasure and pain. The *amātya*, who tries to bring the king under his control, falls. His secret counsels should never be disclosed. The employees should be above monetary temptations. These and similar rules, propounded by the *Mahābhārata*, have an appeal and applicability even today.

---

109 *ākāliko govikartā sūpakartā niyodhakaḥ* । – Virāṭa 2.9

110 *ārāre lavaṇe śulke tare nāgabale tathā* ।
nyasedamātyān nṛpatis svāpatān vāpuruṣān hitam ।। – Śānti 69.29

111 *utpannau vandinau cāsya tatpūrvau sūtamāgadhau* । – Śānti 59.112

112 *balasya parimāṇe ca bhaktavetanayostathā* । – Śānti 41.12

113 Virāṭa 6.14-15.

5

Mauryan Civil Service

THE Mauryan period witnessed the culmination of several important trends set in motion during the earlier periods. The assertion of political supremacy of the Magadhan kingdom, which started during the days of Bimbisāra in the sixth century BCE, reached its complete fruition by the time of Candragupta Maurya who presided over an all-India empire. As a result of an expansionist policy, Magadha annexed to it the small republican and monarchical states to transform itself into a huge empire. Candragupta Maurya's victory over Seleucus led to the annexation of the greater part of Afghan istan and Baluchistan to the Mauryan empire which now touched the eastern boundary of the Syrian empire. The conterminous Indian and Syrian empires were bound to influence each other in many respects.

Economically also, the Mauryan period witnessed great changes. The greater use of iron in the manufacture of agricultural implements during the previous ages had already led to the clearing of the forests and the reclamation of more and more agricultural land. The attitude of the Brāhmanical religion towards marriage as a mandatory social institution and the insistence on numerous progeny led to the gradual growth of population, augmenting manpower of each family which was put to effective use in economic and vocational pursuits. The overpopulous families were bound to surge forth to occupy new areas of habitation. Greater manpower, better tools of agriculture, familiarity with new lands, commercial contact with the outside world, which were gradually developing more and more since the days of Persian and Greek invasions, the emergence of money economy as early as the sixth century BCE resulting in the appearance of numerous trade-centres and urban habitats, had all combined together to pose great socio-economic problems for the Mauryan state to solve. The widening gulf between the poor and the rich, between the employees and the employers, between the landlords and the labourers, and between the free men and the slaves must have brought about socio-economic tensions by the time of the establishment of the Mauryan empire. The Buddhist call to the people to renounce families and join the Buddhist Order for the sake of individual salvation must have threatened numerous families with the loss of their bread-earners, spelling social disorder all around. Thus, the growing cult of renunciation before the Mauryan period also called for state intervention to regulate the social behaviours of the people. Thus, the Mauryan state was confronted with unprecedented situation and the age-old political system, which had well-served the needs of earlier smaller kingdoms, betrayed its limitations and demanded innovations. It must be said to the credit of the Mauryas that they were appreciative of the requirements of their times and very completely gave a new orientation to their policies and a new dimention to Indian polity. This explains why the Mauryan state and government are very different from their counterparts in the past in matters of structural organization and implementation.

The Mauryas organized a bureaucracy which had no parallel in the preceding and following ages in northern India. Caste numbers V, VI and VII mentioned by Megasthenes, in fact, referred to Mauryan civil service consisting of all high civil and military officers.[1] Kauṭilya's[2] long list of officers also indicates its high number and power. As before, in the Mauryan period also, the word *amātya* denoted the whole civil service.

Though the word is as old as the *Ṛgveda;*[3] its nature, scope and

---

[1] McCrindle 1877: 5.

[2] *Arth* V.3.

[3] *ṚV* VII.15.3.

functions kept on steadily increasing. A *kārikā* on Pāṇini (4.2.104) explains the formation of the word *amātya* from the root *ama* with *tyap pratyaya* added to it. The root, *ama* is understood to mean "near" or "with".[4] Thus, the *amātya*s would be that body of officials which would always be near or with the king.

Though the word *amātya* is frequently used in the *Arthaśāstra* of Kauṭilya, it is conspicuous by its absence in the Aśokan inscriptions. Instead, they use the word *puruṣa* which may not designate a particular class of officers, as suggested by some scholars, but the whole civil service. This point of view is further supported by the fact that Aśoka had classified the *puruṣa*s in three groups – *ukasa* (superior), *majjhima* (middling) and *gevaya* (inferior) – in the way Kauṭilya had classified his *amātya*s in the three groups. It is again illogical to identify the *puruṣa*s of Aśoka with *gūḍhapuruṣa*s of Kauṭilya. In fact, the *puruṣa*s were the *rājapuruṣa*s who constituted the civil service since the days of the Epics.

Incidently, Kauṭilya[5] makes a difference between an *amātya* and *mantrī* when he makes following observations:

> Having divided the sphere of their powers and having definitely taken into consideration the place and time where and when they have to work, such persons shall be employed not as councillors (*mantrī*s), but as ministerial officers (*amātya*s).

Obviously, Kauṭilya held the *mantrī*s much more important than *amātya*s. However, most of the Indian works, including the *Amarakośa*, have used the words *mantrī* and *saciva* as synonyms. In the *Arthaśāstra* the word *saciva* stands for advisors, in general, ministers as well as non-ministers.

Kauṭilya was against one-man rule. Even a small kingdom, not to say of the huge Mauryan empire, could not be run singly by a king. Kauṭilya very clearly says that "Kingship is possible only with

---

4 *Mahābhāṣya*, vol. II, p. 291.

5 *Arth* I.8.

the aid of assistants; a single wheel cannot run the chariot".[6] He envisages the cooperation and coordination of the king and civil service in the management of the affairs of the state. Hence, he shall employ ministers (*saciva*) and hear their opinion. The word *sahāya* does not mean an ordinary assistant. It has been used for the *amātya* or *mantrī* in earlier literature as well.

All undertakings were rooted in the *amātyas*. To quote Kauṭilya,[7]

> *amātyamūlāḥ samārambhāḥ* ।

They were responsible for executing all schemes of the government and ensuring the safety and prosperity of the state. He regarded the king (*svāmī*) and civil service (*amātya*) as the first two of the seven limbs of the state.

Since the *amātyas* constituted the backbone of the administration, great care was taken to appoint only right type of persons as *amātyas*. According to Kauṭilya,[8] they should possess the following qualifications:

> A native of the soil, high-born, influential, well-trained in arts and crafts, far-sighted, wise, of retentive memory, intelligent, skilful, bold, eloquent, sweet in speech, good debator, full of enthusiasm and energy, self-controlled, of amiable nature, firm in royal devotion, free from qualities exciting hatred and enmity, of tested honesty, possessing an attractive personality.

It is clear from the above statement that, though high birth of a candidate was of consequence, no mention has been made of his heredity. It may indicate that the civil service in the Mauryan period had not become hereditary.

While the *Mahābhārata* speaks of five *upadhās* (tests), Kauṭilya mentions only four, namely, *dharmopadhā*, *arthopadhā*, *kāmopadhā*

---

6 *sahāyasādhyam rājatvam cakramekam na vartate* । – *Arth* I.7.9

7 *Arth* VIII.I.22-23.

8 *Arth* I.8.24-26, I.9.3.

and *bhayopadhā* which an *amātya* was subjected to. Generally, those who got through the *dharmopadhā* were appointed as judges. Those who passed the *arthopadhā* were appointed as high functionaries in the revenue department. The candidates who could not fail or falter in the face of desires or love (*kāmopadhā*) were put in charge of the king's pleasure gardens and harems. Those who proved their fearlessness in the *bhayopadhā* were recruited as the king's bodyguards. The candidates passing all the four tests were regarded as most suitable and were given posts of *mantrī*s (ministers). The candidates, who showed general fitness, but in one or all the tests, were absorbed in jobs away from the king or the capital, such as those of the superintendents of factories, mines, elephant-forests, etc. All these *amātya*s were classified under three grades: (1) the top one, (2) the middle one, and (3) the average one. The first one was endowed with all the good qualities required of an *amātya*. The other two were wanting in one-quarter or half of those qualities respectively.

Tīrthas

The top-ranking officers of the Mauryan government have been designated as *tīrtha*s by Kauṭilya.[9] They constituted the top brass of the Mauryan civil service:

MANTRĪ

The list of the eighteen *tīrtha*s is headed by the *mantrī*. This proves two things: First, the king depended heavily on his councillors. In fact, he could not take any important decision without holding consultations with them. All undertakings of the state were rooted in their counsels.[10] Second, the state was under the control of the civil authorities as represented by the *mantrī* and not by the military authorities led by the *senāpati* who has been given the third ranking in the list of the *tīrtha*s.

---

9 *mantripurohitasenāpatiyuvarājadauvārikāhtar-vaṁśikadaṇḍakārakapradeṣṭṛ ṇāyakapauravyavahārikakarmānti-kamantripariṣadādhyakṣadaṇḍadurgāntap ālātavikeṣu* । – *Arth* I.12.20

10 *mantrapūrvāḥ samārambhāḥ* । – *Arth* I.15.2

The *mantrī*, in this list, perhaps means the prime minister, who was assisted by his colleagues in the cabinet as well as in the council of ministers. His role during the illness and death of the king and in facilitating smooth take over by the heir-apparent has been described by Kauṭilya as follows:

> The minister (here the prime minister) shall thus avert the calamities in which the king is involved long before the apprehended death of the king, shall, in concert with his friends and followers, allow visitors to the king once in a month or two (and avoid their visits on other occasions) under the plea that the king is engaged in performing such rites as are calculated to avert national calamities or are destructive of enemies or capable of prolonging life or of procuring a son.
>
> ... having gradually placed the burden of administration on the shoulders of the heir-apparent, the minister may announce the death of the king to the public.[11]
>
> He had his headquarters at the capital to be always available to the king and other functionaries of the state on all times.[12]

Besides the prime minister, there were other ministers (*mantrīs*) as well. As stated earlier, those who got through all the tests (*upadhās*) were appointed as *mantrīs*.[13] Since the *mantrīs* were the most important part of the government structure, there had been going on a lively debate in ancient India as to who should be entrusted with the coveted job of a *mantrī*. Kauṭilya has quoted the opinions of his predecessors in this regard. One of them, namely, Bharadvāja had observed that

> [a] king should employ his classmates as his ministers, for they can be trusted by him inasmuch as he has personal knowledge of their honesty and capacity.

---

11 *Arth* V.6.

12 *Arth* II.4.8.

13 *sarvopadhāśuddhān mantriṇaḥ kuryāt* । – *Arth* I.10.14

However, Viśālākṣa differs from Bharadvāja saying that they had been his playmates also and, therefore, would despise him. He would, therefore, want the king to employ such persons as his ministers whose secrets he shared.[14] Piśuna had yet another point of view. He thinks that devotion alone was not enough, if a minister was wanting in intelligence. Kauṇapadanta laid down the principle of heredity in matters of appointment. One whose father and grandfather had held the ministerial posts deserved most to be appointed as a minister.

> Such persons by virtue of their knowledge of past events and of established relationship with the king will, though offended, but never desert him.[15]

Vātavyādhi tended to believe that hereditary persons in ministerial jobs developed vested interests. So new persons should be appointed as ministers on the basis of their proficiency in polity.

> He shall employ as ministers such new persons, who will regard the king as the real sceptre-bearer and dare not offend him.[16]

Bāhudantiputra makes his point in the following manner:

> A man possessed of only theoretical knowledge and having no experience of practical politics is likely to commit serious blunders when engaged in actual works. Hence, he (the king) shall employ as ministers such as are born of high family and are possessed of wisdom, integrity of purpose, bravery and loyal feelings inasmuch as ministerial appointments shall purely depend upon proper qualifications and merit for the job.

Kauṭilya[17] has endorsed the point of view of Bāhudantiputra when he avers that.

> This is satisfactory in all respects, for a man's ability is inferred from his capacity shown in that work.

---

14 *Arth* I.8.

15 *Arth* I.8.

16 *Arth* I.8.

17 *Arth* II.8.

Secrecy of deliberations was regarded as the root of success of the state undertakings. With a view to ensuring it, one of the political thinkers of ancient India, Bharadvāja, went to the extent of saying that the king should not deliberate with any minister, and the latter their own. This successive line of ministers, he believed, led to the leakage of secrets.

But Bharadvāja had few to support his gospel of despair. Almost all ancient Indian political thinkers had it that the king should never take a decision without consulting his ministers. To quote Viśālākṣa:

> No deliberation made by a single individual will be successful. The king should despise none and hear all. Piśuna also advised the king to consult capable persons. Kauṭilya was of the opinion that the king shall consult three or four ministers. ... A single minister proceeds wilfully and without restraint. In deliberating with two ministers, the king may be overpowered by their combined action. But with three or four ministers he will arrive at satisfactory results. With ministers more than four in number, he will have to come to a decision after a good deal of struggle, nor will the secrecy of counsel be maintained without much trouble.[18]

These three or four ministers were in the utmost confidence of the king and constituted his inner cabinet. It were these ministers whom the king met daily in the morning in the fourth hall of his palace for deliberations.[19] They also accompanied the king to the battlefield and infused the army with greater enthusiasm.[20] They also chose spies for specific purposes.[21] They were the highest deliberative body and formulated the policies of the government. The king could consult all, even one of them, as per need, or even took decision by himself. To quote Kauṭilya,

---

18 *mantribhistribhiścaturbhirvā saha mantrayet* । – *Arth* I.15.34

19 *Arth* I.5.52.

20 *Arth* X.3.32.

21 *Arth* I.11.1.

deśakālakāryavaśena tvekena saha dvābhyāmeko vā yathā-sāmarthyam mantrayet ।

The ministers were expected to be honest in expressing their opinion freely even if it was not to the liking of the king. This explains why the king was enjoined upon not to lose his temper while deliberating with his ministers.[22] Though the king was free to accept or reject the opinion of his ministers, generally, he went by the majority decision (*bhūyiṣṭham*[23]).

There was another body to execute these policies. This was the *mantrī-pariṣad*[24] (council of ministers) which was different from the *mantrīs* referred to above. Kauṭilya[25] makes a clear distinction between the two. While the *mantrīs* held consultations with the king daily (1.15.58), the council of ministers was convened only in emergency (*ātyāyika kārya*). The number of the *mantrīs* was three or four, but the council of ministers could have any number in accordance with the requirements (*yathā sāmarthyam*). While the salary of each minister was 48,000 *paṇa*s per annum, that of the member of the council of ministers was 12,000 *paṇa*s.

The *mantrī-pariṣad* seems to have been an old institution. The *Jātaka*s mention it as *paritha*.[26] Later, it finds mention in the Aśokan inscriptions as *pariṣā*.[27] The Aśokan RE III informs us that the council instructed *yukta*s, in particular, in regard to the inspection of personal accounts of the people. It seems that the king was constrained to pass oral orders at times. But they too had to be debated by the council of ministers and its opinion known to him before the king took final decision about their implementation. This explains why in RE VI, Aśoka wants debates of the *pariṣad* to be known to him immediately at all places and at all times.

22 *mantrakāle na kopayet* ।

23 *Arth* I.15.59.

24 *Arth* I.50.

25 *Arth* I.15.58.

26 *Jātakas*, vol. VI, pp. 403, 431.

27 RE III and VI.

It can safely be inferred from these allusions to the *pariṣad* that the king consulted it even, when in emergency, sometimes he could not attend its meetings, so its resolutions were conveyed to him. In case a member of the *pariṣad* was not in a position to attend, he could send his opinion to it in writing.

Thus, whereas the *mantrīs* were a policy-making body, the *mantrī-pariṣad* was the implementing body. It was its responsibility to start the work decided upon, to complete the work which was in progress, to improve the completed work and to see that the orders were strictly followed.[28] Though inferior to the cabinet, it played an important role in the governance of the kingdom. It was, in nature, the Mauryan counterpart of our modern secretariat.

PUROHITA

During the Vedic period, the *purohita* was also the king's councillor in political matters as well. Thus, it would appear that the office of the prime minister had branched off from that of the *purohita* in later times. But even after the prime minister had come into existence, the *purohita* continued to enjoy considerable respectability. He was consulted not only in religious, spiritual and ritualistic matters, but also in political affairs. According to Kauṭilya,[29] he was one whose family and character are highly spoken over, who is well-versed in Vedas and the six *aṅgas*, is skilful in reading portents, providential or accidental, is expert in the science of government, is obedient and can prevent calamities, providential or human, by performing such expiatory rites as are prescribed in the *Atharvaveda*. Kauṭilya advises the king to follow him as a student would follow his teacher, as son his father and a servant his master. This advice is indicative of the fact that the *purohita* was consulted by the king in both personal and political matters. Though different from the *mantrī*, he possessed

---

28 *Arth* I.15.12.

29 *Arth* I.9.10.

all the qualifications of the latter (*amātya*[30] *-sampat*). Like the prime minister, he too had his headquarters at the capital.[31]

SENĀPATI

He was the commander-in-chief of the Mauryan army. Like the *mantrī*, the *senāpati* too was the highest paid officer of the bureaucracy, drawing 48,000 *paṇa*s per annum. Though the king very often led the army in person, the *senāpati* was officially responsible for recruitment, training, equipment, ration for men and animals, war plans, espionage in the enemy country, etc.

For functional purposes the army was divided into smaller units. The commander[32] of the biggest unit had ten generals under him. One general commanded ten lieutenants, and lieutenants, had smallest units under him. The army had its own professors[33] to train elephants and horses, and its own physicians to render medical and surgical services and first aid to its men and animals. This they did with herbal medicines, medicinal oils, surgical instruments and bandages. The army had under it, probably, a separate department whose staff marched with the army to make routes and bridges, clear damps, roads and wells and carry the weapons of war to the battlefield and the sick and the wounded away from it. Thus, this department was multi-functional insofar as it handled construction, transport, engineering and nursing.[34] It would appear that females were not only posted in the harem and as bodyguards of the king, but were kept trained to accompany the army also to supply it foods and drinks and also to enthuse soldiers on battlefields.[35] It is not clear whether the

---

30 *purohitamuditoditakulaśīlām ṣaḍaṅge veda daive nimitte daṇḍanītyām cābhivinītamāpadām daivamānu ṣīnām atharva-bhirupāyaiśca pratikartāram kurvīt*। *tamācāryam śiṣyam pitaram putro bhr̥tyaḥ svāminamiva cānuvarteta*॥ – *Arth* I.10

31 *Arth* II.48.

32 *Arth* X.6.45.

33 *Arth* II.33.1.5-6.

34 *Arth* X.4.17.

35 *Arth* X.3.47.

non-regulars like physicians, engineers and women accompanying the army had some sort of military training as well.

The army was divided into infantry, cavalry, elephantry, and chariotry with one superintendent and one commander over each one of them. They were paid 4,000 and 8,000 *paṇa*s each annually. Kauṭilya[36] speaks of a superintendent of shipping which must have included warships also, because Megasthenes mentions the Admiral.

It were only the specially employed artisans who could manufacture weapons of war for the state. They belonged to two categories, those used for aggression and those for defence. There was a military storehouse under the supervision of the superintendent of armoury where the manufactured war-material including weapons, was preserved and wherefrom it was issued to the army in times of need. All types of war-material was under close scrutiny from time to time.[37]

Similarly, the superintendent of chariots got war chariots manufactured and selected and trained horses to draw them. He recruited a number of attendants to meet the needs of chariotry.[38]

Elephants and horses, according to Megasthenes, could not be owned by private persons. They were the monopoly of the state. They were kept in royal stables and were issued to soldiers in times of need who brought them back to stables after the need was over.[39] Kauṭilya informs us that there were superintendents of elephants as well as horses for their procurement, training, equipment, feeding, nursing and general upkeep. Elephant forests were securely guarded. There were physicians to treat ailing elephants.[40] The superintendent of horses maintained a register in which he had to make entries, as how a horse was procured, to which breed he belonged and the degree of his fitness.

---

[36] *Arth* II.28.

[37] *Arth* II.18.1-4.

[38] *Arth* II.33.1.5-6.

[39] McCrindle 1877: 88-90.

[40] *Arth* II.31.13-15, II.31.1, II.32.16.

Megasthenes[41] speaks of a Military Board of thirty members divided into six commands. The first command, in-charge of warships, was headed by an Admiral of the Fleet.

The second command looked after the transport of war material and supply of food, drink and fodder.

The third command had under it the infantry.

Horses, war chariots and elephants were put under the fourth, fifth and sixth commands.

Megasthenes says that "the fifth caste among the Indians consists of warriors who are second in point of number to the husbandmen". He was all praise for the discipline of the Mauryan army.

Thefts in the military camp were rarety.[42] Even so Kauṭilya has advised the king to keep the army and the treasury under his direct control to eliminate any possibility of a military coup against him.[43]

YUVARĀJA

He was the crown-prince, being generally the eldest son of the king. However, Kauṭilya has clearly ordained that an indisciplined son, even though the eldest, could be superseded in the matter of succession. He was associated with administrative and military activities during the reign of his father. Aśoka was appointed as a governor first at Ujjayinī and second at Takṣaśilā by his father. He was also commissioned to quell a rebellion at Takṣaśilā in the reign of Bindusāra according to the *Divyāvadāna*. The same source[44] tells us that Aśoka had appointed Śamprati, his grandson, as his *yuvarāja*. The *Arthaśāstra* of Kauṭilya refers to the *yuvarāja* at some places.[45] The *kumāras*, including the *yuvarāja*, had their own councils

41 McCrindle 1877: 88-89.

42 McCrindle 1877: 68.

43 *Arth* 8.2.3-4.

44 *Divyā*, p. 430.

45 *Arth* V.6, I.12.8, V.2.91.

of ministers as governors.[46] Being a *tīrtha*, the *yuvarāja* was a member of the council of ministers, though he was not in the king's cabinet.[47]

DAUVĀRIKA

He was variously called a *pratihāra, dvārapāla, dvāḥstha, vetradhara* and *daṇḍin*. The latter two names were given to him on account of the fact that he held a cane or stick in his hand. He is mentioned in earlier literature also. From all accounts, it becomes clear that he was not an ordinary doorkeeper, but an officer of great responsibility, entrusted with the task of making seating arrangements for the visitors in order of protocol, briefing them on etiquette to be observed in the presence of the king and attesting their bonafides. This explains why he was paid the salary of such high officers as *samāhartā* and *sannidhātā*. Every morning he would receive the king in the company of the ministers and the royal kinsmen. Kangle[48] calls him the chief of palace attendants, while N.K. Sastri translates the word as "doorkeepers". It is true that a number of palace attendants were put under his charge. But his duties were more than merely supervising the functions of the palace attendants. Sastri has ignored the point that the *dauvārika* was one of the *tīrtha*s. Therefore, he was an officer and cannot be taken to mean a doorkeeper.

ANTARVAṀŚIKA

He was the officer-in-charge of the inner apartments of the king. Rather than the chief of the king's guard as thought by R.P. Kangle[49] he was one of the most trustworthy fuctionaries of the king's household. Since he had always accessibility to the king, his treachery could be more dangerous than that of any high official of

---

46 Jaugaḍa and Dhauli, RE.

47 HP, vol. II, p. 133.

48 *KA*, vol. III, p. 194, Sastri, p. 20.

49 *KA*, vol. IX on *tīrtha*s.

the state.[50] Ancient India had two types of *amātyas* – the *bahirāmātyas* and the *antarāmātyas*. The *dauvārika* and the *antarvaṁśika* belonged to the latter category. He must have been one who had passed the *kāmopadhā*. It is not certain whether he was, in any way, a functionary connected with the *stryadhyakṣamahāmātra*[51] of Aśoka. Kauṭilya ordains that eighty men and fifty women under the guise of fathers and mothers and aged persons and eunuchs shall not only ascertain purity and impurity in the life of the inmates of the harem, but also regulate the affairs as to be conducive to the happiness of the king.[52] It is likely that these spies worked in concert with, if not under, the guidance of the *dauvārika* and *antarvaṁśika*.

PRAŚĀSTṚ

He finds mention in the *Arthaśāstra* at two places only – in the list of the *tīrthas* and in Book X. Kangle observes that it seems that the *praśāstṛ* of the *tīrtha* list is distinguished from the *praśāstṛ* of Book X. The former, it may be suggested, was probably a sort of an administrator-in-charge of the management of the king's household. He is mentioned immediately after the *dauvārika* and *antarvaṁśika* who are palace officials and before the *samāhartā* with whom the list of administrative officers of the state may be supposed to begin. It is hardly possible to suppose that the *praśāstṛ* of an earlier theory lost his status and was given only minor duties in a later theory, and that both these stages in the development of the same officers are prescribed in the same text. It is more likely that the two *praśāstṛ* are unrelated to each other, being derived by the author from two different sources. But Kangle's theory suffers from two serious limitations: First, it is not at all necessary that an officer enlisted immediately after two or three household officers should also be an household officer, much less in a list of *tīrthas* which comprises all types of officers. Second, it is very unusual to presume that there

---

50 *Arth* X.3.20, VIII.2.3.

51 RE XII.

52 *Arth* 1.20.

were two totally different kinds of functionaries with one and the same designation in the service of the same king.

The fact of the matter is that the *praśāstṛ* of the *Arthaśāstra* was endowed with punitive powers, being included in the chapter on the *saṁgrāmika*. It is tempting to identify him with the *bandhanāgārādhikṛta* of the *Rāmāyaṇa* and the *kārāgārādhikārī* of the *Mahābhārata*. However, from the description of his functions in the *Arthaśāstra*, he seems to be a military officer.

SAMĀHARTĀ

In the *Arthaśāstra*[53] he is the counterpart of the *bhāgadugha* of the later Vedic period and the *dravyasañcayakartā* of the *Mahābhārata*. He was, in fact, the collector of revenue. He had to supervise the collection of revenue from the seven well-known sources of the state income, namely, *durga* (forts), *rāṣṭra* (countryside), *khanī* (mines), *setu* (buildings and gardens), *vana* (forests), *vraja* (cattle) and *vaṇika-patha* (roads for merchants). His main concern was the *samudāya prasthāpanam* (increase in the revenue of the state). Kauṭilya adds that,

> A wise collector-general of revenue shall conduct the work of revenue collection, increasing the income and decreasing the expenditure.

Though such officers as the *sthānika* and the *gopa* under him, he maintained a complete record of deaths and births, irrigational land, its produce and other sources of income of inhabitants. The whole countryside was directly under his charge where he undertook classification of villages, their census and preparation of the budget. He had the authority to levy new taxes. Along with the financial responsibilities, he was also entrusted with the task of maintaining peace and order in his area.

The census of the villages was very thorough insofar as it registered the total number of population, caste-wise, sex-wise, age-wise and occupation-wise in each village along with details of cultivated and wastelands. For determining the state revenue it

---

53 *Arth* II.6.

found out the number of taxpayers and non-taxpayers.[54] More than once Kauṭilya had pointed towards the tendency of revenue officers to misappropriate government money. To quote him,

> It is possible to know even the path of birds flying in the sky, but not the ways of officers moving with their intentions concealed.[55]

He speaks of no fewer than forty ways of embezzlement.[56] Therefore, the administration had worked hard to pluck loopholes in its revenue department. Revenue records were periodically checked by the *gopa*, the *sthānika*, the *pradeṣṭā* and finally the *samāhartā*.[57] So far as the superintendents were concerned, they were asked to check the accounts everyday, every five days, every fifteen days, every month, every four months and every year.[58] A large number of spies kept confidential vigil over them and their detection of embezzlement was suitably rewarded.[59]

To contain high-handedness of overzealous staff of *samāhartā*, Kauṭilya has asked them to bear in mind that:

> Just as fruits are gathered from a garden as often as they become ripe, so revenue shall be collected as often as it becomes ripe. Collection of revenue or fruits, when unripe, shall never be carried on lest their source should be injured causing immense trouble.[60]

SANNIDHĀTĀ

Along with the *bhāgadugha* the brāhmaṇas speak of the *saṅgṛhītā* as one of the *ratnins*. The latter's work during the Mauryan period was taken over by the *sannidhātā*, who was evidently the treasury officer. According to the *Arthaśāstra*, his job was to get constructed

---

54 *Arth* II.35.2-6.

55 *Arth* II.9.32-36.

56 *Arth* II.8.20.

57 *Arth* II.35.7.

58 *Arth* II.7.24, 30, 34.

59 *Arth* II.8.29-39.

60 *Arth* V.2.7.

the treasury, the chamber of commerce, the granary, the godown, the armoury and the jail. Additionally, he had to supervise the construction of the courts and the secretariat buildings. He was responsible for keeping accounts of all cash payments and valuables. While the *samāhartā* was in-charge of the collection of revenues, the *sannidhātā* was responsible for their safe custody. Kauṭilya has advised the king to keep treasury under his direct control.

PRADEṢṬĀ

Thomas would make us believe that he was the chief of the intelligence department. According to R.G. Basak, he was the Executive-cum-Magisterial Officer of the Criminal Department. But he seems to have performed multifarious functions. Kauṭilya tells us that he was to check the work of superintendents (*adhyakṣas*) and their subordinates. This implies that his position was higher than that of a superintendent.[61] He was assisted by *gopas* and *sthānikas* in apprehending thieves outside the fort.[62] This statement makes him superior to the *gopa* and the *sthānika* and reveals that he had to perform police functions as well. He is also shown as presiding over the *kaṇṭakaśodhana* courts,[63] betraying the judicial nature of his post. Thus, he was a magistrate, performing the functions of a police officer, a revenue officer and a judge. He had the rank of an *amātya*. N.K. Shamasastry[64] has taken him to mean a "commissioner".

NĀYAKA

He has been separately spoken of from the *senāpati* by Kauṭilya. Whereas the *senāpati* drew an annual salary of 48,000 *paṇas*, the *nāyaka* was paid 12,000 *paṇas* per annum.[65] He, and not the *senāpati*,

---

61 *Arth* V.9.1.

62 *Arth* IV.6.20.

63 *Arth* IV.1.

64 *AK*, p. 20.

65 *Arth* V.2.

was entrusted with the task of getting the *skandhāvāra* (cantonment) constructed in collaboration with the carpenter and the astrologer.[66] It had separate headquarters for the *senāpati* and the *nāyaka*. The marching army had the *nāyaka* in the front and the *senāpati* in the rear.[67] At another place, Kauṭilya informs us that the commandant of ten units was called the *padika*, that of ten *padika*s was called the *senāpati* and that of ten *senāpati*s was called the *nāyaka*.[68]

At the same time, *senāpati* is placed prior to the *nāyaka* in the list of eighteen top ranking officers.[69] He is in the company of *yuvarāja* at another place.[70] In the *puruṣāntara-sandhi*, he figures with *kumāra* (prince).[71] Elsewhere, he is commanding the army and enthusing soldiers by making lucrative promises.[72]

From all this, it would appear that both *senāpati* and *nāyaka* were military leaders and that the *senāpati* was placed higher than the *nāyaka* in terms of salary, upper ranking and his coupling with *yuvarāja* and *kumāra*. Then why does Kauṭilya say that the *nāyaka* was a commander of the unit of ten *senāpati*s? This question is not answered even if we assume that both of them were the commanders-in-chief with the difference that the *senāpati* was the member of the *mantrī-pariṣad*, while the *nāyaka* was the supreme field commander. It appears that Kauṭilya has used the word *senāpati* in two different ways: When he is spoken of in singular number, he is the commander-in-chief of the army. But when he refers to more than one *senāpati*, he means a commandant of some military unit.

---

66 *vāstukapraśaste vāstuni nāyakavardhakimauhūrtikaḥ ...āpayeyuḥ* ।
– *Arth* X.1

67 *purastānnāyakaḥ ... paścatsenāpatiḥ* । – *Arth* X.2

68 *Arth* X.2.

69 *Arth* I.11.

70 *dūṣyadaṇḍopanaṭeṣu tu yuvarājaḥ senāpatirvā* ।
kiñcidupakṛtyāpakrānto vikramet ॥ – *Arth* V.1

71 *senāpatikumārabhyāmupasthatavyamityayam puruṣāntarasandhiḥ syāt* ।
– *Arth* VIII.3

72 *senāpatiḥ ... anīkamābhāṣet śatasahasro rājabadhaḥ* । – *Arth* X.3

There were many such units and their commandants (*senāpatis*). *Nāyaka* was the commandant of ten such *senāpatis* working under the overall guidance of the commander-in-chief, also known by the same designation – *senāpati*.

PAURA-VYĀVAHĀRIKA[73]

N.K. Shamasastry has taken it to be a *dvandvasamāsa*, *paura* being the officer-in-charge of the city and *vyāvahārika* being the superintendent of transaction. But he is silent about the nature of the transaction. The fact is that the *paura-vyāvahārika* is a *tatpuruṣa samāsa* and means one single officer, the city-judge. He was the equivalent of the *nagara-vyāvahārika* of Aśoka.[74]

KARMĀNTIKA

He was the superintendent of state-owned manufactories and can easily be identified with *kāryanirmāṇakṛta* of the *Mahābhārata* list.

MANTRĪ-PARIṢADĀDHYAKṢA

Shamasastry has split this compound into two *tīrthas* – *mantrī-pariṣad* (assembly of councillors) and *adhyakṣas* (superintendents of departments). But *mantrī-pariṣad* (council of ministers) cannot be designated as an officer. So our conclusion is that the *mantrī-pariṣadādhyakṣa* denotes one *tīrtha* – the president of the council of ministers. Caturdhara rightly calls him as *sabhādhyakṣa* in his commentary on the *Mahābhārata*.

DAṆḌAPĀLA

There seems to be divergent views regarding his nature of work. He might have been a chief magistrate enjoying executive and judicial powers.[75] Since *daṇḍa* means both punishment as well as army, he

---

73 *Arth* I.12.6, I.2.3, I.2.6.

74 KRE II (Dhauli).

75 Apte, V.M., *Students' Sanskrit English Dictionary*, p. 244.

was either a police officer or a commander of a group of soldiers.

DURGAPĀLA

He was chief officer-in-charge of forts. Under him must have been working officers of numerous forts.

ANTAPĀLA

He was the warden of frontiers. He looked after the preservation of routes and collected road-tolls. His salary was 12,000 *paṇa*s per annum. He is the same as *rāṣṭrāntapāla* of Caturdhara.

Since Kauṭilya has referred to the *antapāladurga*, a fort on the common boundary of two *janapada*s, some scholars have translated the term *antapāla* as the officer-in-charge of a border-fort. According to Kauṭilya (2.1):

> There shall be constructed in the extremities of the kingdom, forts manned by *antapāla*s whose duty shall be to guard entrances into the kingdom.

He may be identified with *antamahāmātra* of the Aśokan inscriptions. Besides guarding the frontiers, Aśoka utilized their services in propagating *dhamma* in buffer states (PE I).

ĀṬAVIKAS

There were a number of forest kingdoms, especially in central India. They were inhabited by aboriginals and were very often turbulent and troublesome. Aśoka had threatened them to behave and Samudragupta had subdued them. It is not clear what Kauṭilya meant by including *āṭavika*s as his *tīrtha*s. Probably they were officers to keep vigil over forest kingdoms or were officers recruited from among aboriginals. Instead, Caturdhara uses the word *aṭavīpāla*.

This list has left out many civil servants who are known to us from the *Arthaśāstra* of Kauṭilya itself as also from the Aśokan inscriptions.

MAHĀMĀTRA

The *Arthaśāstra* speaks of the *mahāmātras*.[76] Aśoka had instructed them to go on tours of inspection to see that nobody was unduly tortured in jail or police custody.[77] It appears in certain provinces like Kaliṅga, the *mahāmātra* and the governor (*kumāra*) were jointly responsible for orderly functioning of the government. This explains why Aśoka used to send his instructions to both of them independently.[78] They were of the *amātya* rank and were kept reserved for handling important non-ministerial functions which attracted the attention of the central government from time to time.

PRĀDEŚIKAS

They are mentioned only in the Aśokan inscriptions and not in the *Arthaśāstra* of Kauṭilya. In one of his inscriptions Aśoka asks them to go on tour every five year for preaching *dhamma*.[79] But on the face of it, it was their additional responsibility. Therein they appear to be higher in position than the *rājukas*. It is very likely that they were the *pradeṣṭās* of Kauṭilya. In that case, they were magistrates performing police, revenue and judicial functions.

DHAMMAMAHĀMĀTRAS

Aśoka tells us in his RE V that these officers were created by him for the first time in the thirteenth year of his reign. In the words of Aśoka,

> They are employed among all sects and for the establishment of *dhamma*, promotion of *dhamma* and for the welfare and happiness of those devoted to *dhamma*. They are engaged ... among the brāhmaṇas and *gṛhapatis* who have become hirelings and among the helpless and the aged, for (their) welfare and happiness and the aged. They concern themselves with grant, the unfettering or

---

[76] *Arth* II.5.5.

[77] KRE II.

[78] KRE I, MRE I.

[79] RE, III, KRE, II.

> release of (anyone) who is bound with fetters, accordingly, as he is encumbered with progeny, is subjected to oppression, or is aged. ...

It would, thus, appear that their main task was to promote religious concord and ameliorate the conditions of the needy and the oppressed.

Even the Kauṭilyan state had recognized that, "The king shall maintain the orphans, the aged, the infirm, the afflicted and the helpless."[80] But it was left to Aśoka to create a special class of officers for accomplishing that objective.

AKṢAPAṬALĀDHYAKṢA

Kauṭilya has described him as *adhyakṣa* in the context of *akṣapaṭala*. So we may safely infer that the abbreviated form *adhyakṣa* stood for *akṣapaṭalādhyakṣa*. Since *akṣapaṭala* was a depository of royal documents and account books, the *akṣapaṭalādhyakṣa* may be equated with the accountant-general of our times. On the basis of reports submitted to him by heads of different departments, he had to make different entries in his own books with regard to the following:[81]

1. The work that has been accomplished.
2. The quantum of cash balances.
3. The amounts of income and expenditure.
4. The statements of accounts.
5. The dates and time of the submission of work reports by the scribes.
6. The locality where work was undertaken, the customs and systems.

He was also to provide suitable office accommodation to different departments and residential accommodation to their heads.

---

80 *Arth* II.1.26-29, III.8.6-9.

81 *Arth* II.7.

STRYADHYAKṢA-MAHĀMĀTRA

Aśoka had created this office to ensure welfare of the women. Referring to them the RE XII states that, to further "a growth of essentials among all sects and also mutual appreciation" are engaged the *dhamma-mahāmātra*s and the *stryadhyakṣa-mahāmātra*s. Thus, they were the superintendents of women. The identification of the *stryadhyakṣa-mahāmātra* with the *antarvaṁśika* is misplaced, for the former looked after the welfare of the womenfolk as a whole, the latter were concerned with the ladies of the harem only.

DŪTAS

Kauṭilya mentions them as diplomatic envoys and classifies them as follows: (1) *nisr̥ṣṭārtha*, (2) *parimitārtha* and (3) *śāsạnahara*. The first was of the *amātya* rank and was the highest among *dūta*s, the second and the third were endowed with the three-fourth and the half of the *amātya-sampat* respectively. They were to operate in foreign countries. Having befriended the forest-guards, the frontier-guards and people of urban and rural areas there, he was to collect information with regard to the enemy's army, forts, revenue, defence, etc. However, they were to enter the foreign territory only with the permission of its king. Even at the risk of his life, a *dūta* was to convey his master's message to the enemy exactly as it was delivered to him.

Kauṭilya terms the envoy as the mouth of the king through whom the interstate parleys were carried. It appears from the *Arthaśāstra* that the post of a *dūta* was generally given to a brāhmaṇa, but non-brāhmaṇas, even the low-castes, could be appointed as *dūta*s. Their person was inviolate and they could not be slain. They were not only the errand-carriers, but were entrusted with the task of maintaining peace, weakening the enemy by sowing seeds of dissension in his kingdom and winning over his friends to his master's side.[82]

---

[82] *amātyasampadopeto nisr̥ṣṭārthaḥ pādaguṇahīnaḥ parimitārthaḥ ardhaguṇahīnaḥ śāsanaharaḥ ... śāsanamca yathoktam brūyāt prāṇabādhepi dr̥ṣṭe ... dūtamukhā vai rājānaḥ ... teṣāmantāvasāyinopyabadhyāḥ kimaṅga punarbrāhmaṇaḥ। preṣaṇam sandhipālatvam pratāpu mitrasaṁgrahaḥ upajāpaḥ suhr̥dbhedo daṇḍagūhātisāraṇam।* – *Arth* 1.15

Aśoka utilized the services of the *dūtas* in propagating *dhamma* in foreign countries. In his RE XIII he says:

> Even where the envoys of the beloved of the gods do not go, they, hearing the utterances of *dhamma* ... practice *dhamma*.

ESPIONAGE

The institution of *espionage* was very thoroughly organized under the Mauryan rule. Generally, the spies were known as *gūḍhapuruṣas*,[83] *gūḍhas*, *caras* and *satrins* and operated in the guise of false students, apostate monks, householders, traders and ascetics, and worked in their own respective sections of the society. Kauṭilya has broadly divided them in two categories: (1) *sañcārāḥ* (those who kept on moving from place to place), and (2) *samsthāḥ* (stationary). They were, inter alia, set on the eighteen top ranking officers to ascertain their loyalty. They sent their information to the king in their code language. For cross-checking the veracity of the information at times, three spies were set on the same job to work independently and without knowing each other. Some of the spies entered into the service of the foreign kings to gather information. Others shadowed the chief minister. Some of the spies frequented the places of worship, meeting places and gatherings to know the mind of the people and current rumours. Spies were entrusted with different jobs by the king, ministers, envoys, *samāhartā*, *nāyaka*, and so on.[84]

---

83 *gūḍhapuruṣāṇutpādayat saṁjñālipibhiścārasañcāram kuryuḥ* । *ubhayavetanāḥ kr̥tamāhāmātyāpasarpaḥ paurajānapadānapasarpayet ... tīrthasabhāśālāpūga-janasamavāyeṣu ...* । – *Arth* I.10-12

84 *Arth* I.11.1-3, I.11.20, I.16.24-26, II.35, X.1.

Megasthenes was also familiar with the Indian institution of espionage. He calls spies as overseers. To quote him,

> the sixth caste consists of overseers. It is their province to enquire into all that goes in India and make report to the king.[85]

This statement would make us believe that there was a central agency of intelligence directly under the king. Spies of different sorts were recruited by the central government and sent to different wings of administration to cater to their specific needs. Some of them were directly working under the king whom they met everyday[86] and through whom he ascertained the loyalty of *mantrīs*, *purohita*, *senāpati* and other officers.[87] Those who worked in towns and villages must have supplied information to *nāgaraka*s, *rājuka*s and *samāhartā*.[88]

PRATIVEDAKAS

They are mentioned in the Aśokan inscriptions as reporters. Their function was to carry errands and not to operate as spies. Referring to them, RE VI informs us thus: Thus saith King Priyadarśī, Beloved of gods –

> For a long time, there was no dispatch of business and no reporting at all hours. This, therefore, I have done namely, that at all hours and in all places, – where I am eating or am in the female apartments, in the inner chamber, in the royal rancho or horseback, or in pleasure orchards, the *prativedaka*s may report people's business to me.

PRAŚĀSTĀ

According to Kauṭilya, the *praśāstā*, like *dauvārika*, *antarvaṁśika*,

---

85 McCrindle 1877: 41.

86 *Arth* I.19. 13, 18.

87 *Arth* I.12.6, V.1.1-36.

88 *Arth* I.13.1.

samāhartā and *sannidhātā* received an annual salary of 24,000 *paṇa*s. Thus,

> he was a pretty highly paid civil servant and his salary was even more than that of a member of the council of ministers. He too had his headquarters in the Skandhāvāra in the neighbourhood of elephants and *śreṇīs* (probably of the soldiers and artisans rendering help to the standing army).

The *praśāstā* was expected to march ahead of the king's military expedition along with his artisans and labour for military purposes to ensure the security and water supply for the marching army. Thus, he was a military officer commanding the engineering and supply department of the army.

Adhyakṣas

The Mauryan civil service provided *adhyakṣa*s (heads) to various departments of the government. Those *adhyakṣa*s were endowed with the qualifications of the *amātya*s (*amātya-sampat*).[89] The *Arthaśāstra* contains a long list of *adhyakṣa*s, some of whom were as follows:

SUVARṆĀDHYAKṢA[90]

He was in-charge of the *smithy* and jewellery. It was under his supervision that the *akṣaśālā* (manufactory) manned by accomplished goldsmiths and jewellers, purified gold, silver, other metals, pearls and diamonds. The entry into the manufactory was strictly regulated. It manufactured a variety of ornaments and jewellery under the supervision of the royal chief goldsmith called the *sauvarṇika*. Goldsmiths working under him were to use only authentic weights and measurements, brought from the *pautavādhyakṣa* (superintendent of weights and measurements).

KOṢṬHĀGĀRĀDHYAKṢA[91]

He was the superintendent of granaries. The *sītā* (tax in the form

---

89 *Arth* II.9.1.

90 *Arth* II.13-14.

91 *Arth* II.15-18.

of grains) collected by the *sītādhyakṣa* was deposited with him.[92] It was manned by a number of attendants who have been mentioned by Kauṭilya under the category of *viṣṭi*.[93] They were:

1. *mārjaka* (sweeper),
2. *ārakṣaka* (guard),
3. *dhāraka* (weigher),
4. *māpaka* (measurer),
5. *dāyaka* (distributor),
6. *dāpaka* (load carrier),
7. *śalākāpratigrāhaka* (assistants in the work of measuring and weighing),
8. *dāsakarmakāra* (slaves and servants).

That the Mauryan state maintained granaries is borne out by the Mahāsthān and Sohagaura inscriptions.[94] The royal kitchen which daily cooked huge amount of food, probably for distribution among the poor and the destitute, must have been supplied grains from the state granaries. Kauṭilya also recommends that during famines, cultivators were supplied grains and seeds by the government. They must have come from royal granaries.[95]

PAṆYĀDHYAKṢA[96]

He was the superintendent of markets, who assessed the quality and cost of various types of things coming in for sale by sea-routes and land-routes. While state products were sold at one specific place, those coming from outside were sold at different places. All traders were required to sell state products at fixed prices. Foreign trade was encouraged by giving loans to foreign traders and tax-concessions

---

92 *sītādhyakṣopanītaḥ sasyavarṇakaḥ sītā* । – *Arth* I

93 Ibid.

94 *SI*, vol. I, nos 45 and 47, pp. 79, 82.

95 *Arth* II.1.13-15.

96 *Arth* II.16.

to their exports. Sellers of state products were instructed to report to the *paṇyādhyakṣa* daily at the close of their business, with details regarding their sales, cash and unused articles and deposit their weights and measurements with him.

The *paṇyādhyakṣa* should always keep in view the sale prices of things in the country and their corresponding prices in foreign countries. He should calculate the profits after taking into consideration the sales tax, toll tax, road tax, forest tax, ferry tax and cost of production. This was necessary to maintain the price-index and the flow of supplies as also to facilitate just taxation on inland and foreign goods.

ĀYUDHĀGĀRĀDHYAKṢA[97]

He was the superintendent of the royal armoury. He employed expert artisans to manufacture several types of weapons of war. He was to take preventive measures to see that the stored weaponry did not get rusted, or dampened. In case some of them were there, they were to be separated from the good ones.

PAUTAVĀDHYAKṢA[98]

He was the superintendent of weights and measurements. He got the weights, scales and measuring instruments manufactured strictly in accordance with the rules. They should be made of such material as does not lose their original weight, shape and size under the impact of changing weather. They were inspected every four months by the *pautavādhyakṣa*. Such traders as evaded the official inspection were fined. For getting their weights, scales and instruments of measurement, traders had to pay a special tax.

ŚULKĀDHYAKṢA[99]

He was the superintendent of customs, who was responsible for getting a customs house (*śulkaśālā*) constructed. Its staff comprised

---

97 *Arth* II.18.

98 *Arth* II.19.

99 *Arth* II.21.

four or five officials, who entered in registers names, castes, addresses and goods of traders. If their goods did not bear the official seal of attestation, they were fined. If their seals were found to be spurious or defective, the fines were bigger.

Traders auctioned their goods in front of the customs house to the highest bidder. The replacement of superior goods by inferior ones to pay less duties was fined. Similarly, traders were penalized for overcosts. If the superintendent was found guilty of partisanship or bribery, he was heavily fined. Traders bypassing the customs house had to pay penalty.

However, Kauṭilya has enlisted following duty-free articles:

1. Articles required in marriage.
2. Donations made for free distribution.
3. Articles used in sacrifices and worship.
4. Articles required for certain sacraments.
5. Articles used in religious offerings and *vrata*s.

Those who falsely declared their articles as coming under these categories were treated as thieves. Transporting of prohibited articles led to their confiscation.

It was the function of the *antapāla* to charge duties from each vehicle of transport as also to restore to the trader his lost articles. Articles of import were sealed by him and passed on to the *śulkādhyakṣa* after realizing his dues. Such imports as were considered injurious to the health of the nation were destroyed. Others which were regarded as exceedingly good for the people or were not easily available were allowed entry without duties.[100]

SŪTRĀDHYAKṢA[101]

He was the superintendent of textiles and was to supervise the

[100] *rāṣṭrapīḍākaram bhāṇḍamucchindyādaphalam ca yat* ।
mahopakāramucchulkam kuryādvījam tu durlabham ॥ – *Arth* II.21

[101] *Arth* II.23.

spinning, weaving and rolling done by the skilled weavers. Widows, disabled women, unmarried girls, recluses, female convicts, mothers of prostitutes, old female slaves and *devadāsīs* were engaged for weaving.[102] It was an important step towards fulfilling the state's responsibility to provide work to the needy and weaker sections of the society. They should be given additional allowances and recognition to take work from them on holidays.[103] If they do not spin the specified quantity, deductions should be made from their wages. According to a special provision, the *sūtrādhyakṣa* could send, through female slaves, raw material to such women as did not want to come to the manufactory, whose husbands were absent, who were widows, disabled or unmarried or who wanted to be self-reliant, to weave it at their residences.[104] If anybody gazed at the face of women workers or engaged them in irrelevant talks, he was punished.[105] If the superintendent did not pay them wages in time, he too was punished. But if a woman worker did not do work even after pocketing the wages, her thumb was chopped off. Stealing causing loss of, as also running away with the material of the manufactory could lead to physical or monetary punishment.[106]

SĪTĀDHYAKṢA[107]

He was the superintendent of agriculture and was expected to be familiar with agricultural and horticultural sciences as well as the

---

102 *ūrṇavalkalakārpāsatūlaśaṇakṣaumāṇi ca vidhavānyaṅgākanyā-pravrajitādaṇḍāpratikārinībhī rūpājīvā-mātṛkābhirvṛddharājadāsībhirvyupa ratopasthānadevadāsīdhiśca kartayet* । – *Arth*

103 *tithiṣu pratipādanamānaiśca karma kārayitavyāḥ* । – *Arth*

104 *yāścāniṣkāsinyaḥ proṣitavidhavā vyaṅgāḥ kanyakā vātmānam bibhṛyustāḥ svadāsībhiranusārya sopagraham karma kārayitavyāḥ* । – *Arth*

105 *stryāḥ mukhasamdarśanenyakāryasambhāṣāyām vā pūrvaḥ sāhasadaṇḍaḥ* । – *Arth*

106 *bhakṣitāprahṛtāvaskanditānām ca vetaneṣu ca karmakarā-ṇāmaparādhato daṇḍaḥ* । – *Arth*

107 *sītādhyakṣaḥ kṛṣitantraśulbavṛkṣāyurvedajñastajjñasakho* । *vā sarvadhānyapu ṣpaphalaśākakandamūlavāllikyakṣauma-kārpāsabījāni yathākālam gṛhṇīyāt* । – *Arth* II.24

śūlvaśāstra. With the help of experts in these sciences, he was to store seeds of different crops at the suitable time and get them sown in the cultivable land according to the seasons. The *sītādhyakṣa* could lease out unsown fields to other farmers for cultivation with the provision that they would give to the state half of their produce.[108] Such fields could also be leased out to landless labourers. In such cases one-fourth or one-fifth of the produce should be given to them.[109] Workers of the farmers, namely, *gopāla*s, slaves, servants and artisans were provided with wages and other allowances according to their work.[110] The *sītādhyakṣa* got proper platforms and godowns constructed for storage.[111] No fire was allowed to be lighted near them, but provision for water in the vicinity should be made.[112]

SURĀDHYAKṢA[113]

He was the superintendent of excise and regulated the trade, manufacture, contract, sale and purchase of wines in urban, rural and cantonment areas. Barring those who had licence to carry wine with them, all persons were ordered to drink in bars only.[114] There were separate shops for superior and inferior wines.[115] Spies posted at the drinking bars to take note of all the visitors to them and the consumption of wines as also the expenditure in them.[116] The superintendent also got prepared the *ariṣṭa*s for medicinal use under

---

108 *yathartuvaśena ā bījavāpāḥ* । – *Arth*

109 *vāpātiriktamardhasītikāḥ kuryuḥ* । *svavīryopajīvino vā caturthapañcabhāgikāḥ* । – *Arth*

110 *ṣaṇḍavāṭagopālakadāsakarmakārebhyaḥ yathāpuruṣaparivāpam bhaktam kuryāt* । *sapādapaṇikamāsam dadyāt* । *karmānurūpam kārubhyo bhaktavetanam* । – *Arth*

111 *prakarāṇām samucchrāyān balabhīrvā tathāvidhāḥ* । – *Arth*

112 *anagnikāḥ sodakāśca khale syuḥ parikarmiṇaḥ* । – *Arth*

113 *Arth* II.25.1.

114 *pānāgāreṣu vā pibeyurasañcāriṇaḥ* । – *Arth*

115 *anyatra duṣṭasurāyaḥ tāmanyatra vikrāpayet* । – *Arth*

116 *tatrasthāḥ prakṛtyautpatikau vyayau gūḍhā vidyurāgantuḥśca* । – *Arth*

the instructions of the physicians.[117] Persons selling wines on festivals without the licence were punished, however, there was a provision for granting permission to drink on festivals, in festive gatherings and on journeys for four days.[118] Excise duties were imposed after taking into consideration the daily sale of the wines, the quantities of their consumption and the amount of cash received.[119] It is important to know that the state was always in search of avenues to provide work to the weaker sections of the society. Therefore, it was eager to employ women and children for the lighter task of preparing the essential ingredients of wines and in their manufacture.[120]

SŪNĀDHYAKṢA[121]

He was the superintendent of butcheries who prohibited the capturing and killing of such animals, birds and fishes as lived within the precincts of the royal forest and hermitages. However, those hunters who killed the harmful and ownerless animals were rewarded by the superintendent. They had to pay to the state one-sixth of their profits.[122] The sale of meat was strictly regulated. Saleable meat must be fresh and correctly weighed.[123] Those who sold unhygienic meat were punished.[124]

GAṆIKĀDHYAKṢA

He was the superintendent of prostitutes. It appears there were two classes of prostitutes – some under the service of the state and others private. Sons of prostitutes could be appointed as *cāraṇa*s under

---

117 *cikitsakapramāṇāḥ pratyekaśo vikārāṇāmariṣṭāḥ* । – *Arth*

118 *utsavasamājayātrāsu caturaḥ sauriko deyaḥ* । – *Arth*

119 *anhaśca vikrayam vyājīm jñātvā mānahiraṇyayoḥ* ।
tathā vaidharaṇam kuryāducitam cānuvartayet । – *Arth*

120 *surākiṇvaviacyam striyo bālāśca kuryuḥ* । – *Arth*

121 *Arth* II.26.

122 *pravr̥tta hiṁsānāmparigr̥hītānām ṣaḍbhāgam gr̥hṇīyāt* । – *Arth*

123 *mānsam sadyohatam vikrīnīran ... tulāhīnam hīnāṣṭaguṇam* । – *Arth*

124 *pariśūnamaśiraḥ pādāsthi vigandham svayammr̥tam ca na vikrīṇīran* ।
– *Arth*

certain circumstances.[125] The old female attendants of the prostitutes could serve in the royal storehouses or kitchen.

It was the duty of the superintendent to enter into his register, the income of the prostitutes from different sources and prevent them from being extravagant.[126] Rape on an unmarried girl, with or without her consent, was punishable.[127] A person guilty of forcibly keeping a prostitute in his house or causing injury to her was heavily fined.[128] A prostitute refusing to oblige even after charging her fees was also fined. The jugglers, dancers, singers, *cāraṇa*s, brother-runners, call-girls, etc. also came under the jurisdiction of the *gaṇikādhyakṣa*.[129] Normally, a prostitute had to pay, as tax, her two days' income monthly to the state.[130]

NĀVĀDHYAKṢA[131]

He was the superintendent of boats and ships and was expected to be familiar with all important water-routes, sea-routes, river-routes, lake-routes, tank-routes, etc. Fishers, sea-borne traders touching the ports, users of state boats for transport and dealers in conches and pearls had to pay specified taxes.[132] The superintendent was to follow the rules made by the superintendent of ports.[133] He was to rescue the boat and give relief in taxes in lieu of the loss suffered

---

125 *Arth* 27.27.

126 *bhogam dāyamāyam vyavamāyatim ca gaṇikāya nibandhayet ativyayakarma ca vārayet* । – *Arth*

127 *akāmāyāḥ kumāryā vā sāhase uttamo daṇḍah sakāmāyāḥ pūrvaḥ sāhasadaṇḍaḥ* । – *Arth*

128 *gaṇikāmakāmām ruṁdhatu niṣpātayato vā vraṇavidāraṇena vā rūpamupaghnataḥ sahasradaṇḍaḥ* । – *Arth*

129 *etena natanartakagāyakavādakavāgjīvanakuśilavaplavakasa-ubhika-cāranastrīvyahāriṇām striyo gūḍhājīvāśca vyākhyātaḥ* । – *Arth*

130 *rūpājīvā bhogadvyaguṇam māsam dadyuḥ* । – *Arth*

131 *nāvadhyakṣaḥ* । – *Arth* II.28

132 *śaṅkhamuktāgrāhino* । – *Arth*

133 *pattanādhyakṣanibandham paṇyapattanacaritram nāvādhyakṣaḥ pālayet* । – *Arth*

by its occupants.[134] Boats of the pirates as also those bound for the enemy countries or transgressing the rules of oceanic trade should be destroyed.[135] The *nāvādhyakṣa* was to allow only those big boats to sail on big rivers which were manned by a crew of five experts.[136] Ports should be provided for their anchoring and vigil should be maintained to see that persons inimical to the state did not enter them. Bypassing the ports or landing houses was fined.[137] Brāhmaṇas, ascetics, children, the old, the sick, envoys and pregnant women were allowed to proceed without paying any tax after showing their papers bearing the seal of the *nāvādhyakṣa*.[138] Only those foreigners could enter into the country who had passports.[139] Persons suspected to be abductors, smugglers of valuables, secret documents, arms, poisonous drugs and firearms and going without passports were to be arrested immediately.[140] Unloading of unauthorized or overweighing articles were confiscated.[141]

GO 'DHYAKṢA[142]

He was the superintendent of cattle. He was assisted by a number of employees such as *gopālaka* (rearer of cows), *piṇḍāraka* (rearer of buffaloes), *dohaka* (milkman), *manthaka* (churner of the curd) and

---

134 *mūḍhavātāhatām tam pitevānugṛhṇīyāt* ।
udakaprāptam paṇyaśulkamardhaśulkam vā kuryāt । – *Arth*

135 *hinsrikā nirghātayet amitraviṣayātigāḥ paṇyapattana-cāritropa-ghaṭikāśca* ।
– *Arth*

136 *śāsakaniyāmakadātraraśmigrāhakotsecākādhiṣṭhitāśca mahānāvo ... mahānadīṣu prayojayet* । – *Arth* II.28

137 *baddhatīrthāścaitāḥ kāryāḥ rājadviṣṭakāriṇām taraṇabhayāt* । – *Arth* II.28

138 *brāhmaṇapravrajitabālavṛddhavyādhitaśāsanaharagarbhiṇyo-nāvādhyakṣa-mudrābhistareyuḥ* ।
– *Arth* II.28

139 *kṛtapraveśāḥ pāraviṣayikāḥ sārthapramāṇāḥ viśeyuḥ* । – *Arth* II.28

140 *parasya bhāryyām kanyām vittam vā harantam ... gūḍhasārabhāṇḍaśāsana-śastrāgniyogam viṣahastam dīrghapathi-kamamudram copagrāhayet* ।
– *Arth* II.28

141 *pratyanteṣu tarāḥ śulkamātivāhikam vartanīm ca gṛhṇīyuḥ* । – *Arth* II.28

142 *gopālakapiṇḍārakadohakamanthakalubdhakāḥ* ... ।
kṣīraghṛtabhṛtā hivatsānupahanyuritī vetanopagrāhikam ।। – *Arth* II.29

lubdhaka (hunters of wild animals). They were either paid in cash or kind, but they could not have any share in milk in the interest of calves. There were royal stables where the private cows were kept for protection from cattle-lifters on payment of tax. Royal cattle were stamped. Lifting or killing of cows was punished by death sentence. Sick and old cattle were treated with medicines. The *gopālaka*s were to inform the *go 'dhyakṣa* about natural and unnatural death of the cattle. Dealers in cattle were to give to him, as tax, one-fourth of the price of each cattle. There were fixed quantities and varieties of fodder for cattle, according to their needs.

VIVITĀDHYAKṢA[143]

He was the superintendent of pastures, which were to be protected from thieves and wild animals. He was to provide for wells, tanks, gardens and orchards in areas bereft of water.[144] Hunters were appointed to inform about the presence of the smugglers and enemies in the forests. Functions of the *vivitādhyakṣa* included the supervision of *dravya* forests, elephant forests and the collection of taxes for travels for protection against thieves, for carrying overweighing goods, for affording protection to cows and for other business transactions.[145]

MUDRĀDHYAKṢA

He was the superintendent of the department of passports. He used to issue passports to the incoming and outgoing people after charging a *māṣaka* from each of them as tax.[146] Travelling without passports was punishable with fines.[147]

---

143 *coravyālabhyānnimnāraṇyāni śodhayet* । – *Arth* II.34

144 *anudake kūpasetubandhotsān sthāpayet puṣpaphalavātānśca* ।
– *Arth* II.34

145 *dravyahastivanājīvam vartanīm corarakṣaṇam sārthātīvāhyam gorakṣam vyavahāramr ca kārayet* । – *Arth* II.34

146 *mudrādhyakṣo mudrām māṣakeṇa dadyat* । – *Arth* II.34

147 *dvādaśapaṇamamudro janapado dadyāt* । – *Arth* II.34

AŚVĀDHYAKṢA[148]

He was the superintendent of horses, who maintained a register with entries regarding how the horses were procured, their breed, age, colour, identification marks, etc. Proper stables were provided to house them. They were fed properly according to their needs. There were physicians to treat them. There were a large number of attendants to look after them.

HASTYĀDHYAKṢA[149]

He was the superintendent of elephants, who was responsible for protecting elephant-forests, constructing their stables, determining their food and its quantity, their training, equipment and medical treatment. He was also to arrange for their special training for warfare. There were a host of caretakers to cater to the needs of elephants.[150]

RATHĀDHYAKṢA[151]

He was the superintendent of chariots, who employed chariot-makers for construction and repair of chariots. War chariots were called *saṁgrāmika rathas*. He was to arrange for wages and allowances for all the employees of chariotry, such as *sārathīs* and *rathikas*. The former were the charioteers and the latter chariot-makers.[152]

PATYĀDHYAKṢA

He was the superintendent of infantry and was expected to be aware of the character of different categories of the army, namely, the *maula-bala* (hereditary army), *bhr̥tya-bala* (mercenary army), *śreṇī-bala* (army of the corporations), *mitra-bala* (allied army), *amitra-bala*

---

148 *Arth* II.30.

149 *Arth* II.31.

150 *Arth* II.32.

151 *sa rathakarmāntān kārayat* । – *Arth* II.33

152 *ākarmabhyaścabhr̥tānām* । – *Arth* II.33

(army made up of deserters of the enemy) and an *aṭavī-bala* (army of foresters). He was required to be familiar with different aspects of warfare including low land warfare, arrays of soldiers, strategies, ditch-battles, aerial, nocturnal and day warfare.[153]

It was enjoined upon all superintendents to work in close cooperation with accountants, clerks, experts in coins, caretaker of the *nīvī* and the chief superintendent.[154] Each superintedent checked accounts of his department everyday, every five days, fifteen days, a month, four months and a year. If he was found guilty of fabrication, he was fined.[155] The functions of the superintendents of Kauṭilya were those of a magistrate, a judge and a police officer, all rolled in one person. Their work was checked by the *pradeṣṭā*.[156] They were selected from the highest grade of the *amātyas*.[157]

Provincial Civil Service

RĀṢṬRĪYA

The Mauryan empire was divided into a number of provinces called *deśa*s or *rāṣṭras*.[158] According to the Jūnāgaṛh Inscription of Rudradāman I, Puṣyagupta Vaiśya and Tuṣāspa were *rāṣṭrīya*s (governors) of Saurāṣṭra Province under Candragupta Maurya and Aśoka respectively. The *Arthaśāstra* uses the term *rāṣṭrapāla* for the governor, drawing a salary of 12,000 *paṇa*s.[159]

Both Puṣyagupta Vaiśya and Tuṣāspa did not belong to the royal family, the latter was even a Greek (Yavana). Thus, the Mauryan

---

153 *nimnasthalaprakāśakūṭakhanakākāsadivārātriyuddhavyāyām ca vidyāt* ।
– *Arth*

154 *Arth* II.9.

155 *Arth* II.7.24, 30, 34.

156 *Arth* IV.9.1.

157 *amātyasampadopetāḥ sarvādhyakṣāḥ śaktiśaḥ karmasu niyojyāḥ* ।
– *Arth* IV.9.1

158 *deśe rāṣṭrapālamantapālam vā sthāpayitum* । – *Arth* V.1

159 *Arth* V.3.7.

civil service was not a caste-based, rigidly closed organization. Able people, irrespective of their castes, religion and even nationality were recruited to it. However, princes (*kumāras*) were also appointed as governors of the provinces. It was certainly so in cases of Ujjayinī and Takṣaśilā. The *Divyāvadāna* has it that Bindusāra had appointed Aśoka as the governor at Takṣaśilā. When Aśoka became the king, he appointed Kuṇāla, his grandson, as the governor of Takṣaśilā.[160] Later, Aśoka associated a *mahāmātra* with the governor with a view to give greater efficiency to the administration. It is interesting to note that the *kumāra* and the *mahāmātra* received royal instructions directly from the king independently of each other. Thus, they were both answerable to the king directly.[161] That the governors were responsible not only for protecting the life and property of the people and ensuring social justice, but also for undertaking philanthropic work, is evident from the Jūnāgaṛh Inscription which informs us how the Sudarśana lake was built by Puṣyagupta Vaiśya and enlarged by Tuṣāspa for irrigational purposes. Jaugaḍa and Dhauli Separate Rock Inscriptions suggest that the provincial governors had their own council of ministers.

The province was divided into *sthānīyas* of 800 villages each. A *sthānīya* had a number of *droṇamukhas*. Each *droṇamukha* comprised 400 villages. A *droṇamukha* consisted of *kharvaṭikas* of 200 villages each. A *kharvaṭika* was further divided into *saṁgrahaṇas* of 100 villages each.[162] The administrative head of a *sthānīya* was called

---

160 *Divyā*, p. 430.

161 KRE I: and for this purpose I shall cause a *mahāmātra* to go forth on tour every five years, who will neither be harsh nor fiery but gentle in action so that being aware of this object (avoidance of causeless imprisonment or harassment) will not according to my instructions. But from Ujjain the Kumāra will send forth this class of officers and will not overstep three years in like manner from Takṣaśilā.

MRE I: By command of the prince viceroy and the *mahāmātras* from Suvarṇagiri, the *mahāmātra* at Isila should be asked about (their) health and (then) addressed as follows.

162 *Arth* II.1.

sthānika. He was one of those officers who received land-grants from the king. But they were not authorized to sell or mortgage the donated land.[163] He was also to keep details about residents of the *durga* with regard to their castes, numbers, occupations, income and expenditure and the state revenue from the *durga*.[164] He was to function under overall supervision of the *samāhartā*, and was thus essentially a revenue officer. His revenue the records were checked by the *pradeṣṭā*, and finally by the *samāhartā*.[165] He maintained a register with entries regarding the numbers of males and females, children and the old, their character, occupation, cultivated and unclutivated land, information about the incoming and outgoing persons, income and expenditure of the inhabitants of one-fourth of the *janapada* and the town which came under his jurisdiction. In the *janapada* he worked under the *pradeṣṭā* and the *samāhartā* and in the town under the *nāgaraka*. The *samāhartā* used to keep a vigil over his work through his spies. The *sthānika* was also responsible for collecting taxes and punishing the tax-evaders.[166] A thorough census, therefore, was absolutely necessary for proper collection of taxes as also for ensuring the security of the people and their property. Thus, the *sthānika* was a revenue officer and also a police officer.

RĀJUKAS

The origin of the word admits of at least two interpretations:

1. *Rajju* means a cord. This is why a police officer in the *Arthaśāstra* is called *cörarajjuka*, as he used to tie thieves with cord. *Rajjuka* may be an abbreviated form of *corarajjuka*.
2. *Rajju* also means a unit of land measurement. So *rajjuka* may stand for a land survey officer.

---

163 *vikrayādhānavarjam* । – *Arth*

164 *evam durgacāturbhāgam sthānikaścintayet* । – *Arth* II.36

165 *Arth* II.35.7.

166 *Arth* IV.13.10.

This appears to be more tenable because the *Jātaka*s describe him as measuring land by means of a cord and fixing its boundaries. What is more important is that he has been designated as *amacca* (*amātya*).[167] This shows two things: first, the *rājuka* was a high officer, and second, he was a land survey officer. Megasthenes also refers to him when he speaks of officers who measured the land, collected taxes and superintended the occupations connected with the land.[168]

During the reign of Aśoka they attained higher status and respectability. In RE III he states:

> Everywhere in my dominion, the *yukta*s, the *rājuka*s and the *prādeśika*s shall proceed on tour, every five years as well for this purpose (propagation of *dhamma*) as for other business – meritorious is heartening to mother and father, meritorious is liberality to friends, acquaintances and relatives, to brāhmaṇas and śramaṇas, meritorious is abstention from the slaughter of animals, meritorious is small expense and small accumulation ....

We may infer from this quotation that the *rājuka*s had occupied higher position than the *yukta*s but were lower than the *prādeśika*s. In addition to their original functions of land-surveyors in the country-side, they were entrusted with the task of propagating *dhamma*.

But their further elevation is vividly described in PE IV. To quote,

> The *rājuka*s have been set by me over many hundred thousand people. Any reward or punishment by them has been placed by me under their sole control – why? – in order that the *rājuka*s may perform their duties with confidence and without fear, cause welfare and happiness to the people of the provinces and confer favours. They will make themselves acquainted with what gives

167 Aśoka, p. 59.

168 McCrindle 1877: 86.

> happiness or pain and exhort the people of the provinces as well as those devoted to *dhamma* – how? – so that they may gain happiness here and hereafter. ... Their (convicts) relatives will indeed propitiate some (or the *rājuka*s) in order to grant their life ....

The same inscription informs us that the rewards and punishments were put under their control with a view to ensuring *vyavahāra-samatā* (uniformity in legel procedure) and *daṇḍa-samatā* (uniformity of punishment).

All things put together go to prove that Aśoka had made the *rājuka*s the highest welfare, administrative and judicial officers in the countryside. Now the appeal of the convicts, even of those condemned to death would be considered, not by the *dhamma-mahāmātra*s or *prādeśika*s or *nagara-vyāvahārika*s, but by the *rajuka*s alone. For the material happiness of the people in the countryside they would undertake philanthropic activities and grant favours and concessions to the needy. Side by side they would keep on propagating the tenets of *dhamma*.

Probably, the census work, which was done by the *gopa* and the *sthānika* in the countryside, was also taken over by *rājuka*s under Aśoka.

Though working in provinces, the *rājuka*s were appointed by the king and received instructions from him through the central officers termed as *puruṣa*s.[169]

YUKTAS

The *Arthaśāstra* states that a check on the *yukta*s, inter alia, leads to the increase in the treasury.[170] Thus, he was a revenue officer; so as the *upāyukta*.[171] They were among those revenue officers who

---

[169] PE IV & VI.

[170] *yuktapratiṣedhaḥ ... koṣavṛddhiḥ* । – *Arth* II.8

[171] *tatropayuktanidhayakanibandhaka ... anekaikaśonuyuñjita* । – *Arth* II.8

could easily misappropriate the government money. Kauṭilya has counted as many as forty ways of such misappropriation.[172] Kauṭilya observes that the fish living in the water cannot be seen drinking it, so also the *yukta*s dealing with revenue are not seen defalcating it.[173] The direction of the flight of birds in the sky may be known. But the concealed intentions of the working *yukta*s cannot be known.[174] When their defalcation was detected, their whole property could be confiscated and they were demoted.[175] However, Kauṭilya concludes his observations on a pleasant note, suggesting that all employees of the revenue department were not dishonest and that many of them worked sincerely and hard to increase the treasury justly and watched the interest of the king. Kauṭilya recommends that such honest officers should always be retained on high posts.[176]

*Yukta*s find mention in the Aśokan incriptions also. RE VIII states of *yuktas*, *rājuka*s and *prādeśika*s in that order. It suggests that the *yukta*s were subordinate to *rājuka*s. Besides their revenue work, they were instructed by Aśoka to proceed on tours every five years for the propagation of *dhamma*.[177]

Village Administration

The rural administration was carried on the close cooperation of three officers – the *sthānika*, the *gopa* and the *grāmika*. The *sthānika*, as referred to earlier, was the highest of the three, who supervised the work of the *gopa*. The latter in turn supervised the work of the *grāmika* who was the lowest in the list of rural administration.

---

172 *teṣām haranopāyāścatvārimśat* । – *Arth* II.8

173 *matsyā yathāntaḥ salile caranto jñātum na śakyāḥ* । *salilan pibantaḥ yuktāstathā kāryavidhau niyukta jñātum naśakyā dhanamādadānāḥ* । – *Arth* II.9

174 *api śakyā gatirjñātum patatām khe patattrinām* ।
na tu pracchannabhāvānām yuktānām caratām gatiḥ । – *Arth* II.9

175 *āśrāvayeccopacitān viparyasyecca karmasu* । – *Arth* II.9

176 *na bhakṣayanti ye tvarthān nyāyato vardhayanti ca nityādhikārāḥ kāryāste rājñāḥ priyahita ratāḥ* । – *Arth* II.9

177 *Arth* RE III.

GOPA

He was in-charge of a group of five to ten villages.[178] He was to maintain a register to enter into it the boundaries, cultivated and uncultivated land, places of worship, bridges, cremation grounds, free kitchens, watering sheds, places of pilgrimage, pastures, motorable and *kaccā* roads, number of houses, sales deeds and remissions, taxpayers and non-taxpayers.[179] The total number of the population was to be entered in the register, caste-wise, occupation-wise, sex-wise, age-wise as also the number of cattle. Its entries should include the character and means of income and expenditure.[180] Thus, it covered the thorough work of complete census taken up by the *samāhartā* in the *janapada* of which the village was the lowest territorial unit.

Both the *sthānika* and the *gopa* were accountable to the *pradeṣṭā*. The duties of the former two were also to collect taxes and suppress powerful anti-social elements interfering with the administration. Under instructions from the *samāhartā*, spies closely watched every activity and segment of villages. Thus, the *gopa* was also a magistrate, a revenue officer and a police officer in his area.

GRĀMIKA

He was the village headman also called *grāmakūṭa* on whom also the *samāhartrā* set his spies.[181] His name does not appear in the list of salaried officers of the state. So he appears to be the representative of the villagers who ran the village administration with the help of the elders, of the village, its neighbours and attendants. In the event of

---

178 *tatpradiṣṭaḥ pañcagrāmīm daśagrāmīm vā gopaścintayet* । – *Arth* II.35

179 *sīmāvarodhena grāmāgrāḥ akr̥ṣṭākr̥ṣṭasthalakedārārāmaṣaṇḍavāṭavanavā-stucaityadevagr̥hasetubandhaśmaśānasatraprapapuṇyasthānavivītapathi-samkhyāṅenakṣetrāgrammetena sīmnām kṣetrāṇām ca maryādāraṇyapa thipramāṇasampradānavikrayānugrahaparihāranibandhān kārayet* ।
– *Arth* II.35

180 Ibid.

181 *grāmakūṭamadhyakṣam vā satri brūyāt* । – *Arth* IV.3

the sale of a house its sale price was publicly announced in front of the forty neighbouring families. Before a field, garden, bridge, tank or reservoir was sold, its price was also proclaimed in the presence of the elders of the neighbouring village. Then it was purchased by the highest bidder. Thus, the *grāmika*, the *grāma-vṛddha*s and the neighbouring (*sāmanta*) families played an important role in the life of villagers.[182] Disputes regarding the boundary of two villagers were also settled by their neighbours or leaders of groups of five or ten villagers. In case of disputes regarding fields, neighbouring elders of the village were sought for the settlement.[183] That the *grāma-vṛddha*s continued to be important in the reign of Aśoka also is seen from the fact that he used to meet and hear them on his *dhamma-yātrā*s (RE VIII). It appears in some major disputes, families of the neighbouring villagers were involved in an effort to reach a settlement.[184] Removing of boundary marks, or illegal occupation of land, etc. was punishable. Thus, the *grāmika* had to function as a policeman also. He was assisted by a number of attendants (*grāma-bhṛtaka*s) in the discharge of his duties. They constituted the salaried staff of the state, drawing 500 *paṇa*s each.[185] If neighbours and elders were unable to settle a land-dispute, then it was referred to commonly accepted pious or neutral persons. If they too could not find a solution, the disputed land was taken over by the state. The state also took over such land as had no claimant.[186]

Those undertaking the construction work in public interest were rewarded. Such persons as built new tanks or bridges were exempted

---

182 *sāmantacatvāriṁśatkulyā gṛhapratimukhe veśma śrāvayeyuḥ* ।
– *Arth* III.9

183 *sīmāvivādam grāmayorubhayoḥ sāmantā pañcagrāmī daśagrāmi vā ... kuryāt* ।
kṣetravivādam sāmantagrāmavṛddha ... kuryuḥ । – *Arth* III.9

184 *sarva eva vivādāḥ sāmantapratyayāḥ* । – *Arth* III.9

185 *grāmabhṛtaka ... pañcaśatāḥ* । – *Arth* V.3

186 *teṣām dvaidhībhāve yato bahavaḥ śucayonumatā vā tato niyajcheyuḥ madhyam vā gṛhṇīyuḥ tadubhayam paroktam vāstu rājā haret pranaṣṭa-svāmikam ca* ।
– *Arth* III.9

from taxes for five years. If they got the old ones renovated, they were freed from the payment of taxes for four years. If they were extended, the persons responsible for the extension were granted three years exemption from taxes.[187]

City Administration

NĀGARAKA

According to Kauṭilya, the city administration was done by the *nāgaraka*[188] with a number of officers working under him. The city was divided into four wards, each under a *sthānika*. In each ward there were *gopa*s looking after groups of ten, twenty or forty families.[189] The *gopa* regulated the stay of travellers in *dharmaśālā*s. Those who looked extravagant or heavy drunkards automatically became suspects in the eyes of administration.[190] The *gopa* or the *sthānika* was to be informed about a physician who treated wounds of a person secretly. The owner of the house was to report to the *gopa* about the incoming and outgoing persons of his house. All types of suspects were to be handed over to the *nāgaraka*, with a view to preventing accidents of fire, people were prevented from lighting fire during the hottest hours of midday in summer.[191] For fire-fighting the householders were asked to keep ready water-filled pitchers and pools, ladder, axe and other necessary equipment in front of their houses in summer. Smiths and artisans working at fire were made to settle in one single part of the city.[192] The administration saw to it that water-filled pitchers in hundreds and thousands were kept arranged in roles in lanes, markets, road-crosses, main entrances to the city,

---

187 *taṭākasetubandhānām navapravartane pāñcavarśikaḥ pratihāraḥ bhagnotṣṛṭānām cāturvarśikaḥ samupārūḍhānām traivarśikaḥ* । – *Arth*

188 *nāgarako nagaram cintayet* । – *Arth* II.36

189 *daśakulīm gopo viṁśatikulīm catvāriṁśatikulīm vā* । – *Arth*

190 *ativyayakartaramatyahitakarmanam ca nivedayeyuḥ* । – *Arth* II.36

191 *agnipratīkāram ca grīṣna madhyamayorahnaścaturbhāgahyoḥ* । – *Arth* II.36

192 *agnijīvina ekasthān vāsayet* । – *Arth* II.36

the storehouses, and stables.[193] Gynaecologists and physicians were given passports.[194] The Nāgaraka was to protect different routes, tunnels and lost property.[195] He was to release children, old, sick and destitutes from prisons on certain auspicious days.[196] Creating nuisance at places of pilgrimage, sources of water, temples and government establishments were punishable with varying fines. Throwing of carcasses on roads was similarly punishable. Disposal of the dead at any place other than cremation and burial grounds also invited penalty. Curfew was imposed during certain hours of the night, the beginning and end of which was announced by blowing trumpets. People were not allowed to move about during the curfew. Police guards (*rakṣiṇaḥ*) on duty to enforce these rules, were kept themselves very busy.[197]

Megasthenes does not speak of the *nāgaraka*. Instead he mentions a thirty-member Municipal Board of Pāṭaliputra, divided into six committees of five members each. Each committee was entrusted with a specific task.

The first committee looked after artisans and craftsmen. Kauṭilya speaks of a variety of articles produced by them.

The second committee looked after foreigners. That there was a separate committee to look after them, testifies that the number of foreigners living in the capital must have been considerable. Kauṭilya also refers to foreigners coming to the country with passports.

The third committee was in-charge of registering births and

---

193 *rasthyāsu kuṭavrajāḥ sahasram tiṣṭheyuḥ catuṣpathadvārarājaparigraheṣu ca* । – *Arth*

194 *sūtikā citītsakapretapradīpayānanāgarikatūrya-prekṣāgninimittam drābhiścāgrahyāḥ* । – *Arth*

195 *nityamudaksthānumārgabhūccannapathapaprapră-kārarakṣāvekṣaṇam ... rakṣaṇam* । – *Arth*

196 *bandhanāgāre ca bālavṛddhavyādhitānāthānām jātanakṣatrapaurṇamāsīṣu visargaḥ* । – *Arth*

197 *dvitīye paurajānapadānām kāryāṇi paśyet* । – *Arth* I.19.10

deaths. We have already seen how Kauṭilya recommends a complete census which included births and deaths also.

The fourth committee supervised sales and purchases as also weights and measurements. These activities were given due importance by Kauṭilya also.

The fifth committee was in-charge of goods which were sold after being duly stamped, the new being separated from the old. This is exactly what Kauṭilya also wanted to be done.

The sixth committee collected customs duties on things which were sold. Kauṭilya also refers to *śulka* and a number of other taxes.

We may infer that all big towns like Pāṭaliputra had such municipal boards which enjoyed autonomy. The *nāgaraka* of Kauṭilya must have kept a watch over their working without unduly interfering with their work.

Judiciary

The king was the highest court of justice. Kauṭilya[198] has observed that the royal edicts (*rājaśāsana*) constituted the highest source of law. It is something which the earlier law-givers had never allowed to happen. Nilakantha Sastri is of the opinion that the (*rājaśāsana*) got precedence over other three sources of law – *dharma, vyavahāra* and *carita* – for the first time under the impact of the Greeks whose Syrian empire touched the western boundary of the Mauryan empire. This is likely. But B.P. Sinha seems to be most authentic when he says that the *rājaśāsana* even in the Mauryan period was not regarded as the substantive law.[199] It should be taken to mean only the regulatory law. In other words, the king, as in the past, was not the enactor of law. He could only enforce it. What the king did was only to make rules to regulate the existing laws of the country without changing the fundamental sources of law.

---

198 *dharmasya vyavahāraśca caritram rājaśāsanam vivādārthaśca catuspādaḥ paścimaḥ pūrvabādhakaḥ* ı – *Arth* III.1

199 *CHB*, vol. I, part 1, p. 560.

That the king disposed of cases is borne out by Megasthenes' account which informs us that even when his body was being massaged, the king kept of hearing cases. Aśoka wanted his petitioners to be ushered in at all places and hours. Kauṭilya also informs us that the king entered the court every morning at a fixed hour and looked into the affairs of the subject.[200]

Besides the king, there were a number of regional courts located at (1) *janapada-sandhi* (border of the two states), (2) *saṁgrahaṇa* (3) *droṇamukha*, and (4) *sthānīya*. Each of these courts was presided over by three judges of the rank of the *amātyas*. These judges were technically known as *dharmasthas*.[201] Kauṭilya has nowhere graded these courts either as lower or upper ones. So it appears that they were independent of and equal in status, to each other. Appeals against their judgements lay directly in the king's court. The mention of three judges with regard to each court is also interesting (4.1.1). One would be tempted to conclude that they sat in ones, twos and threes, consituting the single bench, division bench or full bench. But it seems more likely that every case was heard by the three judges sitting together. These three judges were appointed in each court with a view to ensuring majority judgement in case the two judges differed from one another.

It would appear from Kauṭilya that the judges decided cases mainly on the basis of witnesses who were known as *sākṣīs*. Sometimes the services of the spies were also utilized to find out the truth.[202] The judge was to adjure the witness in front of the brāhmaṇas or a water-pitcher or fire before he was called upon to give his evidence.[203] Adjuration was practised to make the witness speak truthfully. In the event of difference of opinion among the witnesses, the judge was to accept the evidence of either the majority of witnesses or those who are known for their truthfulness or of

200 *upasthānagataḥ kāryārthinām ...*। – *Arth* I.18.1

201 *dharmasthastrayo 'mātyā*। – *Arth* III.1.1

202 *Arth* IV.4.6-11.

203 *brāhmaṇodakumbhāgnisakāśe śākṣiṇah parigṛnhīyāt*। – *Arth* III.11.34-37

those who are acceptable to both parties in dispute.

As mentioned earlier, the judges were drawn from such *amātyas* as had passed the *dharmopadhā*,[204] for they were most suited for upholding *dharma*. Even so, if a judge was found guilty of dereliction of his duty, he was punished. Not putting questions to right persons, prompting a person to reply in a certain manner, threatening a person or refusing to hear him, deciding cases arbitrarily or adjourning the case without sufficient reason, etc. constituted dereliction of duty on the part of the judge.[205] If the clerk of the court deliberately altered the proceedings, he too was punished.[206] As these judges are said to be working under the *samāhartā*,[207] they appear to have administered justice in rural areas. Kauṭilya speaks of *paura-vyāvahārikas* who were evidently city-judges.[208] He was given a salary of 12,000 *paṇas* per annum. In the Kaliṅga RE II Aśoka refers to him as *nagara-vyāvahārika*. To quote him:

> For this purpose has this document been here written: in order that the *mahāmātras* who are the city-judges may be devoted to eternal rules of conduct and that causeless imprisonment or causeless harassment of the town's people may not take place.

It is clear from this that the city-judges were of the *mahāmātra* rank and that they dispensed justice in towns and not in villages.

Along with the *samāhartā*, the *pradeṣṭāraḥ* have also been mentioned by Kauṭilya. There were two types of courts in his times – *dharmasthīya* courts and *kaṇṭaka-śodhana* courts. The former dealt with the disputes between citizens, while the latter decided disputes between the citizens and the state. *Dharmasthīya* courts

---

204 *tatra dhaimopadhāśuddhān dharmasthīyakaṇṭaka-śodhaneśu sthāpayeta* ।
– *Arth* I.43

205 *Arth* IV.9.13-16.

206 *lekhakaḥ ... na likhati ... anuktam likhati ... sāhasadaṇḍaḥ* ।
– *Arth* IV.9.17

207 *Arth* I.9.3.

208 *Arth* I.11.1.

were presided over *dharmastha* judges. The *kaṇṭaka-śodhana* courts were held by *pradeṣṭāraḥ*.[209] Being of *amātya* rank, they were given an annual salary of 8,000 *paṇas*.[210] They performed judicial as well as police duties. The latter included searching thieves outside forts.[211] They were entrusted with the task of supervising the work of the superintendents of departments[212] and kept a watch over the artisans and their employees. So they combined in them the functions of a magistrate, a judge and a police officer. They seem to be the *prādeśika*s of the Aśokan inscriptions.

*Cāraka*s (lock-ups) and the *bandhanāgāra*s (prisons) were put under the charge of the *dharmastha*s and the *pradeṣṭā*s respectively. The *cāraka*s seem to have housed under-trial people, while the *bandhanāgāra*s were meant for convicts. There were separate prisons for men and women.[213] If the jailor was found guilty of freeing prisoners illegally from prisons, he was punished.[214]

If brāhmaṇas, ascetics, women, minor, helpless and the sick could not be present in the court at the time of the hearing of their cases, judges were granted special power to look into their cases themselves so that they did not lose their cases by default.[215]

It will also appear from the above discussion that the Mauryas had no separate department of police. Functions of the police were performed by executive, revenue and judicial officers. Thus, the *samāhartā*, the *sthānika*, the *gopa*, the *grāmika*, the *nāgaraka*, the *pradeṣṭā*, the *sannidhātā*, etc. were entrusted with police functions also.

On the whole, The Mauryan civil service with devices of regular supervision and cross-checkings from top to bottom and always

---

209 *Arth* IV.9.1.

210 *Arth* II.5.40, IV.9.22.

211 *Arth* IV.20.22.

212 *Arth* III.20.22.

213 KRE II.

214 *Arth* II.9.20-24.

215 *Arth* II.1.7.

kept on its toes by a thorough system of espionage and counter-espionage suitably served the needs of the empire. Aśoka made it conscious of its functions by issuing a warning that due discharge of duties rather than an attempt to flatter the king would win them his favour.[216] The Mauryan civil service made more effective by bestowing upon it various powers and privileges. From the examples of the prime minister and the *purohita* it appears that the central civil service in many cases was provided accommodation at the capital.[217] Their good living was ensured. Low-paid officers were paid both in cash and kind.[218] In the events of deaths, births and illness, they were provided help by the state. If they died in harness, their dependents were given sustenance.[219] While they were on duty, they could not be arrested (III.1.22). An incentive to efficient officers was given in the form of advance increments. To avoid delay and inconvenience, power to disburse salaries and effect postings and transfers was delegated to superintendents (II.9.32). However, officers were appointed on probation and were confirmed on their posts only after they had proved their worth.[220] All officers were paid regular salaries in cash.[221] In times of distress, they were provided with cattle, land and forest produce also.

---

216 *Arth* V.3.28-31.

217 *Arth* II.9.31-36, IV.9.1.

218 *etāvatabharaṇe* ...। – *Arth* V.3.2

219 *karmasu bhr̥tānām putradāra bhaktavetanam babheran*।
pretavyādhitasūtikākr̥tyeṣu-caiṣāmarthamānakarma kuryāt।।
– *Arth* V.3.1

220 *Arth* III.20-22.

221 *Arth* V.3.

6

Civil Service during the Foreign Rule of the Indo-Greeks, Śakas, Pahlavas and Kuṣāṇas

THE rule of the Indo-Greeks, Śakas, Pahlavas and the Kuṣāṇas coincided with that of the Śuṅgas and the Sātavāhanas. Thus, India witnessed the flowering of two types of polity at one and the same time. Whereas the main features of the foreign polity are brought to light mainly by their coins and inscriptions, those of the indigenous one are revealed mainly by the *Manusmṛti,* and to a small degree by Patañjali and the Sātavāhana inscriptions. It is interesting to note that there are many common features between the two, suggesting some sort of interaction between them.

The Śuṅga–Sātavāhana Civil Service

The political contents of the Brāhmanical revivalism as symbolized by the arrival of the Śuṅgas and the Sātavāhanas are best illustrated by the *Manusmṛti* which, mostly, gives a traditional account of Hindu polity.

The word *amātya* continued to denote the civil service in general.[1] Sometimes civil servants were called *sahāya*s of the king.[2] The *Manusmṛti* contains several references to prove that the highest of the civil servants were drawn from the pool of *amātya*s. For instance,

---

1 *Manu* VII.141, IX.234.

2 *Manu* VII.31, 36, 55.

the finance officer is said to be of the status of an *amātya*.[3] So was the case with the head of the police department.[4] The ambassadors too were recruited from amongst the *amātyas*.[5] It is important to note that the Nāsik Cave Inscription of Gautamīputra Sātakarṇi belonging to the eighteenth year of his reign also speaks of the *amātyas*, Viṣṇupālita and Śivagupta.[6] The Nāsik Cave Inscription of the twenty-fourth year of the same ruler refers to another *amātya* named Śyāmaka posted at Govardhana.[7] Śivaskandila was another *amātya* under Vāsiṣṭhīputra Pulumāvi according to the Nāsik Cave Inscription of the same ruler belonging to the twenty-second year of his rule.[8] Another Nāsik Buddhist Cave Inscription is important insofar as it refers to Bhaṭṭapālika, a daughter of a *rājāmātya*.[9] The *rājāmātya* cannot be taken to mean as an *amātya* of the king, because all *amātyas* were appointed by and working under the king. Nor can it mean the prime minister, for he has been termed as *amātya-mukhya* by Manu.[10] Our contention is that the terms, *rājāmātya* and *kumārāmātya* were reserved for that class of the *amātyas* who were granted the royal status by virtue of their proven loyalty and talent. The Guptas preferred the term *kumārāmātya* as against *rājāmātya* used by the Sātavāhanas.

As the *amātyas* denoted the civil service, the *sacivas* stood for the councillors.[11] According to Manu, the ministers were a desideratum for a good governance of the country. To quote him,

> even an easy undertaking is difficult to accomplish single-handedly. What to say of the state which yields large

---

3 *Manu* VII.60.

4 *amātye daṇḍāyatto* । – *Manu* VII.65

5 *Manu* VII.63-64.

6 Luder's List No. 1125.

7 Ibid., No. 1126.

8 Ibid., No. 1124.

9 Ibid., No. 1141.

10 *Manu* VII.141.

11 *Manu* VII.54, 120.

revenues.[12] The king was obliged to function on the advice of the ministers.[13]

That the *amātyas* and *sacivas* were different from each other is made clear by Manu when he speaks of their appointment separately. To quote him,

1. The king should appoint seven or eight ministers whose ancestors have been royal servants, who were versed in the sciences, heroes, skilled in the use of weapons and descended from noble families who have been tried.[14]
2. The king should appoint *amātyas*, men of integrity who are wise, firm, well able to collect money and well tried.[15]

The former category was the ministerial one whose main function was to advise the king on all important matters. Though councillors, they were expected to possess military knowledge as well. Two qualities that were given the special consideration at the time of their appointment were heredity and noble birth. They were to be consulted first separately and then collectively.[16]

Though the king consulted his ministers on all important issues, there was nothing to prevent him from overriding their resolution, if he so desired. So it is not always easy to agree with Jayaswal (1934) that "the king is not given even the power of vetoing".[17] Manu himself says that the king was to consult all ministers or some of them or none.[18]

---

12 *api yatsukaram karma tadapyekena duṣkaram* ।
viśeṣato 'sahāyena kintu rājyam mahodayam ॥ – *Manu* VII.55

13 *Manu* VII.30-31.

14 *maulān śāstravidaḥ śūrān labdhalakṣyān kulodgatān* ।
sacivān sapta cāṣṭau vā prakurvīta parīkṣitān ॥ – *Manu* VII.54

15 *anyānapi prakurvvīta śucīn prajñānavasthitān* ।
samyagardhasamāhartṛnamātyān suparīkṣitān ॥ – *Manu* VII.60

16 *teṣām svam svamabhiprāyamupalabhya pṛthakpṛthak* ।
samastānām ca kāryeṣu vidadhyāddhitamātmanaḥ ॥ – *Manu* VII.57

17 *HP*, II, p. 118.

18 *sārdham taireka vā* । – *Manu* VII.151

The latter category comprised the executive officers who manned different departments of the government. In the appointment of both categories of the functionaries, the word *parīkṣitān* has been used. Ordinarily it means tried. But it may mean *upadhītān* as well. In that case, the officers had to get through four *upadhā*s (tests) – *dharmopadhā, arthopadhā, kāmopadhā* and *bhayopadhā* – prescribed by ancient Indian political thinkers.

The prime minister (*amātya-mukhya*) was invariably a brāhmaṇa[19] and was vested with powers to transact all business during the illness of the king.[20] The king depended heavily on him for the execution of all resolutions. In fact, the entire administration came under his purview.[21] The *parama mantra*s (the most secret deliberations) were to be held with him only.[22]

Besides the ministers, Manu mentions the *purohita* (royal priest) and the *ṛtvija*s (brāhmaṇas, expert in sacerdotal art). It appears that their functions were primarily sacrificial and ritualistic.[23]

Manu advised the king to keep the royal treasury and the state under direct charge.[24] Special care was taken to appoint only the brave, the skilful, the high-born and the honest for the collection of revenue.[25] The Sātavāhana Inscriptions used the word *hairaṇyaka* which may mean a treasurer-in-charge of the revenues in cash.[26] The collection and maintenance of other forms of revenue might have been the work of the *bhāṇḍāgārika*.[27]

---

19 *Manu* VII.58.

20 *sthāpayedāsane tasmin khinnaḥ kārye kṣaṇe nṛṇām* । – *Manu* VII.141

21 *Manu* VII. 58-59, XII.100.

22 *Manu* VII.58.

23 *tesya gṛhāṇi karmāṇi kuryurvaitānikānica* । – *Manu* VII.78

24 *nṛpatau koṣarāṣṭre āyante* । – *Manu* VII.65

25 *Manu* VII.62.

26 Luder's List Nos. 993, 996.

27 Ibid., No. 1141: Mentions a *bhāṇḍāgārika*, Agigataṇaka who was also a *rājāmātya*.

Both the *senāpati* and the *balādhyakṣa* figure in the *Manusmṛti*. While the former was the commander-in-chief of the army, the latter was only a commander under him.[28] The Sātavāhanas had a *mahāsenāpati* under them.[29] It may be presumed that he had several *senāpati*s under his command. The *Manusmṛti* has it that *gulma*s (military guards) were stationed at villages and groups of villages to ensure security of the people.[30] The Luder's list refers to a *gaulmika* who must have been a captain of *gulma*.[31]

Since Manu makes a distinction between *senāpatya* and *daṇḍanatṛtva*, it can be inferred that while the former suggests military functions, the latter suggests police functions. The *nāyaka* may well mean a police officer rather than a military captain.[32] Otherwise too, the separation of the military department from the police department is suggested by Manu when he speaks of *senābala* and *daṇḍa-vaināyikī kriyā* separately.[33] The police was placed under the charge of an *amātya*.[34]

In the same breath Manu speaks of *dūta* (ambassador) on whom depended the peace or its opposite – the war.[35] The Vidiśā Garuḍa Pillar Inscription has it that Antialkidos, the Greek king of Taxila, had sent Heliodoros, his *dūta* at the court of Bhāgabhadra, a Śuṅga king.[36] Manu advises the king to appoint such person as *dūta*, who is well-versed in all sciences.[37]

---

28 *Manu* VII.189.

29 Luder's List Nos. 1124, 1146: Which tells us that *mahāsenāpati*, Medhuna had prepared the draft of a village grant under Vāsiṣṭhīputra, Pulumāvi.

30 *Manu* VII.114, 190.

31 Luder's List No. 1200.

32 Ibid.

33 *Manu* VII.65.

34 *amātye daṇḍayātto daṇḍe vaināyikī kriyā nṛpatau koṣarāṣṭre ca dūte sandhiviparyayau* । – *Manu* VII.65

35 Ibid.

36 Luder's List No. 669.

37 *Manu* VII.63.

The Nāsik Cave Inscription of Gautamīputra Sātakarṇi (year 24) refers to a document of the gift of a field drafted by a *pratihāra-rakṣī* (doorkeeper).[38]

There were spies technically known as cārāḥ[39] and sañcārāntakas[40] to collect information and watch the conduct of the government servants as well as the people in general. It appears that there was a separate department for cārakarma.[41] The king was to personally visit by turns all other officials; he was to properly explore their behaviours in their districts through spies appointed to each, because the king should protect his subjects against those officials who seize the others' property.[42]

Similarly, the local government was entrusted to the care of a minister.[43] He looked after the villages and the districts.

The king used to be the highest court of justice. However, Manu avers that "if the king does not personally investigate the lawsuits, he is to appoint a learned brāhmaṇa to try them".[44] He was assisted by three accessors.[45]

Patañjali, in his *Mahābhāṣya*, speaks of a *śaulkika*[46] (customs officer). The same officer has been mentioned as *śulkādhyakṣa* in the *Milindapañha* which is not chronologically very much distant from the Indo-Greek period.

The *navakarmika*, who figures in the Sātavāhana inscriptions, was the overseer of public works.[47] Whether he was the same as

38 Luder's List No. 1126.

39 *Manu* VII.122.

40 Luder's List No. 1200.

41 *Manu* VII.81.

42 *sa tānanuparikrāmet servvāneva sadā svayam* ।
teṣām vṛttam pariṇayet samyagrāṣṭreṣu taccaraiḥ ॥ – *Manu* VII.122

43 *rājñonyaḥ sacivaḥ snigdhastāni paśyedatandritaḥ* । – *Manu* VII.120

44 *niyuñjyādvidvāṁsam brāhmaṇam kāryadarśane* । – *Manu* VIII.9

45 *Manu* VIII.4-7.

46 *Mahābhāṣya* IV.2.104.

47 Luder's List No. 987.

karmāntika[48] cannot be said with any amount of certainty. Probably, the *navakarmika* and the *karmāntika* both belonged to the Public Works Department. The former probably was entrusted with the construction of new works; the latter was in-charge of the repairs and preservation of the old ones. There might have been a separate superintendent of waterworks called *pāṇiyagharika*.[49]

Towns received special attention of the government. Each town was put under the charge of a city officer called *nagarādhikṛta*.[50]

Manu has put him among the high ranking officials.[51] His jurisdiction over the town was all embracing[52] and the intelligence men and police officers stationed in the town took their orders from him.[53] An inscription speaks of a *nagarākṣadarśa*,[54] who might have been a judicial officer at the town level and might have assisted the *nagarādhikṛta* in the disposal of the judicial cases.

Manu has given a good account of the village administration. To quote him,

> The king has to appoint a lord over each village as well as lord of ten villages, lord of twenty villages, lord of a hundred, and lord of a thousand. The lord of one village himself shall inform the lord of ten villages of the crimes committed in his village and so on.
>
> The lord of one village shall obtain those articles which the villagers ought to furnish daily to the king, such as food, drink and fuel. The ruler of ten villages shall enjoy one *kula* of land, ruler of twenty-five *kula*s, the ruler of 100 villages one village and

48 Luder's List 1186.

49 Ibid., No. 1279.

50 *Manu* VIII.122.

51 *uccaih sthānam* । – *Manu* VII.121

52 *sarvārthacintana* । – *Manu* VII.121

53 *rājñaḥ rakṣādhikṛtāḥ, cārāḥ* । – *Manu* VII.122

54 Luder's List No. 1351.

the lord of 1,000 villages a town.[55]

Thus, the headman of the village was *grāmaṇī*, that of villages *dāśī*, of twenty villages *viṁśī*, of 100 villages *sateśa* and of 1,000 villages *sahasreśa*.[56] It is a graded list of rural functionaries. The villagers of a lower unit could appeal against their headman to the headman of the higher rank. These functionaries were not salaried officers of the state and were maintained by the villagers themselves, out of their resources and cultivable land. This is indicative of the fact that the villagers enjoyed local self-government. As mentioned earlier, there was a minister[57] for local government to supervise the work of the local bodies.

A Nāsik Cave Inscription of Gautamīputra Sātakarṇi informs us that documents regarding the land grants were kept by *mahāmiyas* (record-keepers).[58] Probably each village headquarters had their office.

The *Manusmṛti* states of the *mahāmātras*, who were high officers.[59] They are referred to in the Sātavāhana inscriptions also[60] separately from *amātyas*.[61] It may be assumed that they constituted a special class of officers to keep a watch over specified functional areas.

The *yuktas* were the middle rank executive officers,[62] who might have been entrusted with jobs of different nature. *Ājñaptis*

---

55 *yāni rājapradeyāni pratyaham grāmavāsibhiḥ annapānendhanādīni grāmikastānyavāpnuyāt । daśī kulantu bhuñjīta viṁśi pañcakulāni ca । grāmam grāmaśatādhyakṣaḥ sahasrādhipathiḥ puram ।* – *Manu* VII.116-19

56 *Manu* VII.115, 120.

57 *rajño 'nyaḥ sacivaḥ snigdhastāni paśyedatandritaḥ* । – *Manu* VII.120

58 Luder's List No. 1125.

59 *Manu* IX.259.

60 Luder's List No. 1144.

61 Luder's List Nos. 994, 1105, 1124-26.

62 *Manu* VIII.34.

mentioned in some inscriptions probably belonged to the same category.[63] For drafting letters and documents there must have been the *rājalipikāras*.[64] The prefix *rāja* implies that they were central employees. *Lipikāras* must have been employed by the provincial and district administration as well. Where there were no especially trained *lipikāras*, the task of drafting documents in regard to grants was performed by such officers as *amātyas*,[65] *senāpatis*[66] and even *pratihārarakṣīs*.[67] The epigraphic evidence has it that kings used to employ their physicians called *rājavaidyas*.[68] The departmental heads were known as *adhyakṣas*.[69] The actual number of the civil servants must have varied in accordance with the requirements of the government, for Manu says that "the king has to appoint as many persons as the due performance of his business requires".[70]

The Indo-Greek Civil Service

The Yavana invasion of the second century BCE brought about the Indo-Greek rule in India. Though the Yavanas had, at one point of time, reached as far as Pāṭaliputra and had overrun the whole of northern India,[71] but due to the civil war amongst them they could not stay in northern India for long.[72] First their dominion dropped back to Mathurā, where coins of Strato I and II are found, and ultimately shrank to the territory of Punjab. This territory too was

---

63 Luder's List No. 1327.

64 Ibid., No. 271.

65 Ibid., No. 1125.

66 Ibid., No. 1124.

67 Ibid., No. 1126.

68 Ibid., Nos. 1190-93.

69 *Manu* VII.81.

70 *Manu* VII.61.

71 *tathā sāketamākramya pāñcālān mathurānstathā* ।
yavanāḥ duṣṭavikrāntāḥ prāpsyanti kusumadhvajam । – *Gārgī Saṁhitā*

72 *madhyadeśa na sthāsyanti yavanāḥ yuddhadurmadāḥ teṣāmanyon-yasambhāvāḥ bhaviṣyanti na saṁśayaḥ* । – *Gārgī Saṁhitā*

for the greater part of their rule governed by two rival houses – East Punjab by the descendants of Euthedemos and West Punjab by those of Eucratides. Though the Indo-Greek rule continued in India in some measure, for about 150 years, it has left behind it very meagre evidence of their polity. The main source of their history is their coins which throw little light on their political set-up. Therefore, it is very difficult to write much about their civil service.

The *Milindapañha,* which deals with the career and achievements of Menander, informs us that he had a council of ministers.[73]

The Greek had divided their dominions into provinces (satrapies) and districts (eparchies). The former were put under the charge of the strategoses,[74] who were essentially military governors and the latter under the Meridarkhs.[75] One of the main features of the Indo-Greek rule was the joint rule system (*dvairājya*). As coins have revealed, Lysias and Antialtidas, Agathokleia and Strato I, Strato I and Strato II and Hermaios and Calliope ruled conjointly. Under the system the junior colleague received all the training and experience under the guidance of his senior partner whom he generally succeeded after his death.

Since the Greek coins very often portray the city-deities, it can be inferred that the cities under the Indo-Greek rule enjoyed autonomy. The fact that the *grāmaṇī,* also called the *grāmika,* has been referred to in the preceding and succeeding ages makes it reasonable to suppose that he played a leading role in managing the affairs of the village during the Indo-Greek period as well.

The *Milindapañha* speaks of the *śulkādhyakṣa,* who was the customs officer during this age. That a Greek engineer Agesilaos had served under Kaniṣka is a good enough reason to suppose that such engineers called *navakarmika* must have existed under the Indo-Greek rulers also.

---

73 *Milindapañha,* pp. 4, 19-20.

74 *SI,* p. 111.

75 *SI,* p. 109: Swāt Relic Vase Inscription.

Śaka–Pahlava Civil Service

The Śaka–Pahlavas, particularly the Śakas, issued a host of inscriptions and coins which shed enormous light on their civil service. Like the Indo-Greeks, the Śakas and the Pahlavas of north-west India had also divided their kingdom into provinces and districts. The former were put under the charge of the Strategos (military governor) and the latter under Meridarkhs[76] (governors).

The system of joint-rule (*dvairājya*) was also adopted by the Śakas and the Pahlavas from the Indo-Greeks. Under it the king was called *mahākṣatrapa* and the associated sub-king, *kṣatrapa*. On the death of the former the latter assumed the title of *mahākṣatrapa* and associated someone else as *kṣatrapa* with him. To illustrate, on the coins found at Mathurā Rājuvula was ruling as *mahākṣatrapa* of Mathurā and he had associated *kṣatrapa* Soḍāsa with him. On later coins the same Soḍāsa has been called as *mahākṣatrapa*.[77] Similarly, Azes I and Azilises ruled conjointly as *mahākṣatrapa* and *kṣatrapa* at Taxila. Later, Azilises became the *mahākṣatrapa* and he associated Azes II as *kṣatrapa* under him. According to the general practice, the name of the *mahākṣatrapa* in Greek appeared on the obverse of the coins and that of the *kṣatrapa* in Kharoṣṭhī on the reverse of the coins. The Pārthian king Gondopharnes, who was a *mahākṣatrapa*, had associated Aspavarman as his *kṣatrapa*.[78] At different points of time Gondopharnes and Abdagases were ruling as *mahākṣatrapa* and *kṣatrapa* respectively. According to the Andhau inscription, *mahākṣatrapa* Caṣṭana was ruling conjointly with *kṣatrapa* Rudradāman I.[79] Later, Rudradāman I became the *mahākṣatrapa*.

The word *amātya* occurs in the Jūnāgaṛh Inscription of Rudradāman I. Therein Suviśākha has been called by this designation

---

[76] *CII*, vol. I, I.5: Taxila Copper Plate Inscription records the construction of a *stūpa* by the Meridarah.

[77] *CAIBM*, pp. 111-16.

[78] *PMC-I*, Plate XV, p. 35.

[79] *SI*, p. 167.

and has been shown as ruling over Ānarta and Surāṣṭra on behalf of his master Rudradāman I. Clearly, the term, which occurs as *amacca* as well, during the Śaka–Sātavāhana period, denotes the civil service providing high functionaries of the state.

The Jūnāgaṛh Inscription also speaks of the *mati-saciva*s and the *karma-saciva*s under the Śakas. The former were councillors, whereas the latter were executive officers. The designations of some of the important *karma-saciva*s are preserved in the Śaka inscriptions.

The Mathurā Stone Inscription, belonging to the period of *mahākṣatrapa* Soḍāsa, mentions a *gañjavara* (treasurer) who incidently was a brāhmaṇa.[80]

That many of the posts had become hereditary during the Śaka period is proved by Gunda Stone Inscriptions of the time of Rudrasiṁha I, which says that Senāpati Rudrabhūti was the son of Senāpati Bāpaka.[81] It also preserves the information that the completely Indianized Śakas had started calling their commander-in-chief as *senāpati*.

The designation *mahādaṇḍanāyaka* may mean the chief police officer.[82]

The Śaka inscriptions mention chief queens, but they did not enjoy any political power. However, they are shown as doing mostly philanthropic work and making religious gifts. For instance, the Mathurā Lion Capital Inscription records the enshrinement of the Buddha's relics and improvization of an endowment by the chief queen of Mahākṣatrapa Rājuvula.[83] The word *yuvarāja* also occurs in the same inscription which uses it for Kharaosta. However, his functions have not been spelled out in any Śaka record. But his nomination as *yuvarāja* during the reign of the ruling king must

---

80 Luder's List No. 82: As discussed earlier, the term *rājāmātya* may denote the higher position.

81 Ibid., No. 963.

82 *SI*, p. 181.

83 *CII*, vol. II, 1.48.

have laid to rest all conjectures and disputes regarding succession and also afforded him an opportunity to gain administrative and military experience.

As under the Kuṣāṇas, so also under the Śakas and the Pahlavas, there was no office of the *bhaṇḍāgārika*.

There is a reference to a *nigama-sabhā* in a Nāsik Cave Inscription of the time of Nahapāna. Most probably it meant a municipal corporation.[84] Thus, while the village autonomy was very much preserved under the leadership of the *grāmaṇī*, the *nigama-sabhā*s ensured, to a great extent, the autonomy of the town under the Śakas.

An important feature of the Śaka civil service was its cosmopolitan character. Suviśākha, the *amātya* of Rudradāman I was a Pahlava, according to the Jūnāgaṛh Inscription. The Mathurā Stone Inscription of the time of Mahākṣatrapa Soḍāsa informs us about the appointment of a brāhmaṇa as a treasurer.[85]

Kuṣāṇa Civil Service

The Kuṣāṇa polity had inherited several elements of the Greek, Śaka–Pahlava and Indian polity and introduced several others to suit its extensive empire based on autocracy and military force. Fortunately, there are a number of literary, epigraphic and numismatic sources which furnish us with valuable information regarding its civil service.

The *Saddharmapuṇḍarīka*[86] opines that the *bodhisattva*s must never serve the *rājaputra*s, the *rājamahāmātra*s and the *rājapuruṣa*s. These words actually constitute the civil service. It uses the word *rājāmātya* also.[87] However, such words as *amātya*s, *mantrī*s and *saciva*s do not occur in the Kuṣāṇa inscriptions. But it does not means that they did not exist during their rule.

---

84 *SI*, p. 158.

85 Luder's List No. 82.

86 *Saddharmapuṇḍarīka*, p. 180.

87 Ibid., p. 288.

In fact, the *Divyāvadāna*, which belongs to the second-third century CE, refers to the word *pariṣadyam*[88] which means the members of the *pariṣad*. It used to assist the king. At another place, the same source speaks of the evil ministers advising the king to oppress the people with burdensome taxes. It is not clear whether the *pariṣad* and the council of ministers were identical or two separate bodies. Probably the latter alternative seems to be more natural. The *Divyāvadāna*[89] uses the word *tulaka* for a councillor. He must have been the member of the council of ministers.

Besides the ministers, the Kuṣāṇas had a well-organized civil service. The names of some of the high functionaries of the state were Vasumitra, who presided over the Fourth Buddhist Council, Aśvaghoṣa who was the vice-president of the same council, Pārśva and Māṭhara, the great celebrities, Caraka, the royal physician and Saṅgharakṣa, the king's chaplain. Incidently the *rājavaidya* is mentioned in the inscription as well.[90]

Since the Kuṣāṇa state was military in character, its records mention the *daṇḍanāyaka* or the *mahādaṇḍnāyaka* frequently. A Mathurā inscription of the fourth year of Kaniṣka's reign refers to the *mahādaṇḍanāyaka*, Hummiyaka Caṇyakka.[91] The Maṇikiālā Inscription of the same ruler contains the name of *daṇḍanāyaka*, Lala who worked in collaboration with *kṣatrapa* Vespasi.[92] According to the Māṭ inscription, the *mahādaṇḍanāyaka* figures in the reign of Huviṣka also.[93] There is a good deal of controversy regarding the interpretation of the word *daṇḍanāyaka*. To A. Stein,[94] he was "the prefect of police" performing the functions of a Greek Strategos. But since the Greek Strategos was essentially a military governor rather than a police

88 Puri, 1965, *India under the Kuṣāṇas*, p. 85.

89 *Divyā*, p. 562.

90 Luder's List Nos. 1190-3.

91 Bajpai, *PIHC*, 1958, p. 68.

92 *SI*, p. 138.

93 *JRAS*, 1924, p. 397.

94 *Rām* (tr.), 1,VIII.975.

officer, A. Stein's interpretation brings us nowhere, for the *daṇḍanāyaka* could either be a prefect of the police or a military governor. J.F. Fleet's (1963) opinion[95] that he was "the great leader of forces" makes him look like a military leader. When James Princep[96] calls him an "administrator of punishment" or a "magistrate" he combines in him the police and judicial functions. According to U.N. Ghoshal,[97] he was the commander-in-chief of the army. B.N. Puri's (1965) suggestion[98] that the *daṇḍanāyaka*s were feudatory chiefs appointed by Kuṣāṇa kings required to render civil and military help is not beyond doubt, for they were not always feudatory chiefs. The office of the *daṇḍanāyaka* had come into existence much earlier than the Kuṣāṇas. And it existed separately from that of the *senāpati* or *balādhikṛta*. So it may appear that the *daṇḍanāyaka* was essentially a police officer who performed magisterial functions also. In that case the *mahādaṇḍanāyaka* would mean the chief police officer. As regards the *daṇḍapāla*s,[99] they appear to have been police officers of a lower rank.

The Kuṣāṇas seem to have had a Public Works Department whose help must have been sought in the construction of a host of *stūpas*, *caitya*s and *vihāra*s. Probably the Greek engineer (*navakarmika*) Agesilaos belonged to it and had got the great relic tower the built at Puruṣapura. Besides the *navakarmika*, the *vihāra-karavahena* (architect of *vihāra*s) find mention in the Maṇikiālā Stone Inscription of Kaniṣka.[100] According to the Surkh Koṭal inscriptions, a temple called Kaneshko Oanindo Bagolaggo (Kaniṣka victorious sanctuary) was repaired by one Nokonzoko, probably an engineer.

That the Kuṣāṇas had preserved the institution of the diplomatic envoys (*dūta*s) is proved by the Annals of the Later Han Dynasty which

---

95 *CII*, vol. 3, p. 16.

96 Princep's *Essays-I*, p. 23.

97 *Indian Historiography and other Essays*, pp. 177-79.

98 *India under the Kuṣānas*, p. 84.

99 *Mahāvastu Avadāna*, p. 18.

100 *SI*, pp. 138-39.

tells us how the Chinese general Pan Chao had arrested the envoy of the Yueh Chi King (Kaniṣka) who demanded the hand of a Chinese princess for his master. We are again told that Po-tiao (Vāsudeva II) had sent an embassy to China in 230 CE. Earlier ambassadors from the Kuṣāṇa court visited the Roman Emperor, Antoninus Pius (138-61 CE).

The phrase *daivaputraśāhiśāhānuśāhī* in the Allahabad Pillar Inscription represents the descendants of the great Kuṣāṇas. The same inscription speaks of their *viṣaya*s (districts) and *bhukti*s (provinces) into which the Kuṣāṇa empire must have been divided. These territorial units were ruled by the *mahākṣatrapa*s and the *kṣatrapa*s. The Sārnāth Inscription of Kaniṣka I speaks of Mahākṣatrapa Kharapallan and Kṣatrapa Vanaspara. Then, there is the famous case of Soter Megas who seems to have ruled over the Indian dominion of Kadphises II as the latter's governor. Powerful governors like him were even allowed to issue coins in their names. At least the coins of Soter Megas suggest such a possibility.

The system of joint rule was preserved by the Kuṣāṇas also. Annals of the Later Han Dynasty tell us that Tien-tchou (India) was conquered by Wima Kaḍphises. The discovery of his father's (Kujūla Kaḍphises) coins in Taxila[101] can be explained only by the theory that the Indian provinces were conquered by Wima Kaḍphises as *yuvarāja* or joint ruler during his father's times.

That Kaniṣka I ruled with Vāsiṣka as his subordinate can be assumed by the following factors:

1. Kaniṣka I's dates range from year 1 to year 23.
2. Rājan Vāsiṣka was ruling in the year 22 according to the Sāñcī inscription.

Similarly Vāsiṣka[102] and Huviṣka[103] seem to have been associated as rulers is suggested by the fact that both of them were ruling in the year 28.

---

101 John Marshall, *Taxila*, 1, p. 67.

102 Luder's List No. 161: Sāñcī Bodhisattva Inscription of the year 28.

103 *EI*, XXI, pp. 55 ff.: Mathurā Inscription of the year 28.

At any rate the Sārnāth inscription of the year 3 does not leave us in any doubt that Mahākṣatrapa Kharapallana and Kṣatrapa Vanaspara were ruling conjointly[104] over the eastern provinces with the headquarters at Sārnāth.

The local self-government seems to have continued during the reign of the Kuṣāṇas as well, for we hear of the *grāmika* in their inscriptions. The Mathurā Jain Inscription of the year 40 records the dedication of an image by the wife of Grāmika Jayanāga and the daughter-in-law of Grāmika Jayadeva.[105] The Mathurā Jain Inscription of the year 84 records the setting up of an image by the wife of a *grāmika* during the reign of *mahārāja rājādhirāja devaputra śāhī* Vāsudeva. The Post-Mauryan inscriptions keep on mentioning *grāmaṇī*,[106] *grāmabhojaka*[107] and *grāmeyakayukta*.[108] These testify that the village administration was allowed to continue under the supervision of the village headman (*grāmaṇī-grāmika*) with the assistance of the freeholders of land (*grāmabhojaka*s) and the staff of the village *sabhā* (*grāmeyakayukta*). The Kuṣāṇas kept an eye over the functioning of the *grāma-sabhā*s through the *grāma-svāmī*s who were the *kṣatrapa*s according to the Peshawar Inscription.[109] The inscription also suggests that the high functionaries of the state were allotted villages in lieu of their salaries. It is just possible that low ranking officers were paid in cash. The old Greek practice of portraying city-deities on the coins was almost discontinued with the gradual expanding the frontiers of the empire. The Kuṣāṇa set-up was

104 *EI*, VIII, p. 173: First inscription: *sahakṣatrapena vanasparena kharapallanena ca* ।

Second inscription: *mahākṣatrapena kharapallanena saha kṣatrapena vanasparena*.

105 Luder's List No. 48.

106 Ibid., No. 1333.

107 Ibid., No. 1200.

108 Ibid., No. 1327.

109 Sharma, 1968, *Aspects of Political Ideas and Institutions in Ancient India*, pp. 169-70.

totally unlike the set-up of Greek city states. So the disappearance of the city-deities on the Kuṣāṇa coins should not be interpreted as indicative of the loss of village autonomy under their rule. The continuing local self-government is further suggested by the four seals at Bhītā with the legend *nigama* or *nigamasa* in the Kuṣāṇa script. They reveal that the municipal corporations had an active life under Kuṣāṇas as well. Further, the Kaṅkālī Ṭīlā in Mathurā has yielded a number of inscriptions referring to not only the *grāmika*, but also the *śreṣṭhī*s (bankers) and the *sārthavāha*s (caravan-leaders) who, like their counterparts in the Gupta period, must have played an important role in the district administration, especially when they had acquired great wealth and prestige due to the increased foreign trade during the Kuṣāṇa period.

The fact that copperplates were inscribed at the instance of the king, as was the case after the conclusion of the Fourth Buddhist Council, proves that the Kuṣāṇa civil service had some royal scribes as well. They were called *rājalipikāra*s.[110] It had on it the royal physician (*rāja-vaidya*) also.[111]

110 Luder's List No. 271.

111 Ibid., Nos. 1190-93.

7

Gupta Civil Service

THE administrative structure has been termed as *lokatantra* by Kālidāsa.[1] Obviously it rested on the civil service, which is denoted by a number of technical words, such as *amātyas*,[2] *tīrthas*,[3] *adhikārapuruṣas*,[4] *niyuktas*[5] and *kumārāmātyas* mentioned in Gupta inscriptions.[6]

As in earlier periods so also in the Gupta period, ancient Indian thought did not admit of any form of autocracy. However, great and powerful the king might have been, he could not play the Bourbon or the Stuart. He was ordained to run the government not singly but with the aid of his ministers and other civil servants. Kāmandaka, the renowned law-giver of the Gupta period, clearly lays down that the king should engage himself in the welfare of the people with the assistance of his ministers and the civil servants.[7]

As shown earlier, the word *amātya* clearly denoted the civil service in the pre-Gupta period. The use of the word *kumārāmātya* came in vogue during the Gupta period. There has been a good deal of controversy as to what this word precisely means. It is made up of

---

1 *Śāk*, p. 154.

2 *Raghu* XIX.47.

3 *Raghu* XVII.68.

4 *Raghu* V.63.

5 *Raghu* V.29.

6 *API.*

7 *Nītisāra* 8.1.

two words *kumāra* and *amātya*. This led J.F. Fleet (1963) to believe that the *kumārāmātya* was the councillor of the crown-prince.[8] Beni Prasad (1928) has almost similar ideas when he interpreted *kumārāmātya* as the minister of the prince viceroy.[9] But the epigraphical evidence of the Gupta period clearly mitigates against this interpretation. In inscriptions, the *kumārāmātya* has very often been associated with the king and not the crown-prince. For instance, the Allahabad Pillar Inscription describes Hariṣeṇa as the *kumārāmātya* of the monarch Samudragupta himself. The Karamadaṇḍa Inscription describes Pr̥thvīṣeṇa as the *mantrī*-cum-*kumārāmātya* of Kamāragupta I. Some other scholars have come forward with yet another interpretation of the word *kumārāmātya*. A.S. Altekar (1949), for instance, thinks that the *amātya* who started his career straight as a minister was termed *kumārāmātya*.[10] But this interpretation, at the very face of it, appears to be superfluous. Ministership, which presupposed vast experience and expertise and was obtainable after numerous tests and trials, could not have been bestowed upon the youth in such a large number as to have necessitated the organization of a special class in the cadre.

Even more untenable is R.D. Banerji's thesis that the *kumārāmātya*s were divided into three categories.[11] In the first category were the *kumārāmātya*s equal to the rank of the princes. The second category of *kumārāmātya*s consisted of such of them as were at par with the crown-prince. And to the third category belonged those *kumārāmātya*s who were as powerful and respectable as the king himself. His whole thesis is based upon misconception. The word *kumārāmātya* cannot mean an *amātya* of the rank of a *kumāra* (prince). Had it been so, he would not have been placed under the subordination of a commoner governor. For the Damodarpur Copper-Plate Inscription informs us that Vetravarman, a *kumārāmātya* and also a *viṣayapati* of Koṭivarṣa, was working under

8 *CII*, vol. III, p. 160.

9 *State in Ancient India*, p. 296.

10 *State and Government in Ancient India*, p. 339.

11 *Age of the Imperial Guptas*, pp. 73-74.

the *uparika* (governor) of Puṇḍravardhana-bhukti.[12]

Again, the phrase *yuvarājapādīya-kumārāmātya* does not mean a *kumārāmātya* holding the status of a crown prince. Actually it means a *kumārāmātya* working under a crown prince. That a *kumārāmātya* was equal to the king himself is fantastic, for a civil servant, however important, cannot be put at par with his master who appointed him and allowed him to work during his pleasure. Moreover, no literary work of the Gupta period contains the slightest indication that there were three categories of the *kumārāmātya*s.

It is true that the Karamadaṇḍa Inscription uses the term *kumārāmātya* both for Śikharasvāmin, the father and Pr̥thvīṣeṇa, his son. But it is two meagre an evidence to generalize that the *kumārāmātya* was one who had hereditary right to the office of the state, as R.C. Majumdar and R.G. Basak would make us to believe.[13] The Allahabad Pillar Inscription calls Hariṣeṇa as *kumārāmātya*, but does not use this designation for his father who was also a functionary of the state.

The *kumārāmātya*s of the Gupta period are shown manning various types of offices. Hariṣeṇa of the Allahabad Pillar Inscription was a minister of war and peace as also the chief police officer. Pr̥thvīṣeṇa of the Karamadaṇḍa Inscription was a minister. The Damodarpur Copper-Plate Inscription (Nos. 1 and 2) speak of Vetravarman as the head of the district administration. These references falsify V.R.R. Dikshitar's view (1952) that the *kumārāmātya*s were basically treasury officers.[14] It is most likely that the *kumārāmātya*s and *amātya*s, both denote the ancient Indian bureaucracy. Whereas the *amātya*s stood for the common run of civil servants, the title *kumārāmātya* was conferred on such *amātya*s as were knighted for some special merit or service.

Kauṭilya has made it very clear that the high functionaries of

---

12 *EI*, XV, pp. 130 and 133.

13 *History of Bengal*, vol. I, p. 284, *State and Government in Ancient India*, p. 339.

14 *Gupta Polity*, p. 157.

the state were appointed from amongst the *amātyas* who constituted the bureaucracy of the state. Kāmandaka also describes the *amātyas* as comprising the officials of the state.[15]

The Gupta civil service had developed certain special features which sets it apart from the Mauryan civil service. With the glorification of monarchy, the general royal title *rājā* of the Mauryan period was quietly dropped for a more grandiloquent royal title *mahārājādhirāja* during the Gupta period. Like the Gupta monarchy, the Gupta civil service too adopted more high sounding designations for it. For instance, the *daṇḍanāyaka* of the earlier periods became *mahādaṇḍanāyaka*. Similarly the *aśvapati* assumed the greater title *mahāśvapati*. The *akṣapaṭalika* was now called *mahākṣapaṭalika*. Such examples can be multiplied to demonstrate the process of greater glorification and assumption of more powers with regard to the Gupta bureaucracy.

The civil service also tended to be more and more hereditary. The phrase *anvaya-prāpta-sācivya* used in the Gupta epigraphs amply brings out this tendency. According to the Karamadaṇḍa Inscription, both the father and the son were appointed as *mantrī-kumārāmātya* by Kumāragupta I. The Jūnāgaṛh Inscription informs us that Skandagupta had appointed Parṇadatta as well as his son Cakrapālita on higher posts.

Prior to the Gupta period, a functionary of the government was generally given one office. But it seems that the Gupta monarchy started a new system of putting more than one office under the charge of an officer. For instance, according to the Allahabad Pillar Inscription, Hariṣeṇa was a *kumārāmātya*, a *sāndhivigrahika* and a *daṇḍanāyaka* all in one. Even his father Dhruvabhūti was a *khādyatpākika* and also a *mahādaṇḍanāyaka* according to the same inscription. The Udayagiri Cave Inscription No. 1 has it that the Gupta dynasty was served by three generations of the *sanatānāka* family as feudals – Mahārāja Chagalaga, his son Mahārāja Viṣṇudāsa

---

15 *KāmN* 4.25-27.

and the latter's son Mahārāja Soḍhala.[16] This practice probably came in vogue to give recognition and reward to a functionary of outstanding merit. This bestowal of additional responsibilities was marked in the cases of *kumārāmātyas* and not mere *amātyas*. The former belonged to the knighted class of the bureaucracy. It is unnatural to assume that a vast country like India, with a long history of trained and multifunctional bureaucracy, suddenly ran short of efficient officers so as to force the Gupta emperors to resort to the device of combining several offices under one person.

The *Arthaśāstra* of Kauṭilya leaves us in no doubt that the Mauryan civil servants were paid in cash. But there seems to have been some change in the mode of payment to the Gupta civil servants. If Fa-hien is to be believed, the bodyguards, functionaries and attendants of the king received emoluments and pension.[17] The word emolument may well mean donations of land. However, the discovery of a huge numeber of gold coins of the Guptas may indicate that the major part of salaries to the civil servants continued to be paid in cash even now.

Whereas all high officials of the state were appointed by the Mauryan monarch, at least some of them could be appointed by the provincial governors as well during the Gupta period. The Vaigram Copper-Plate Inscription tells us that Kulavr̥ddha, the *viṣayapati*, was appointed by the monarch. This explains why he has been called *bhaṭṭāraka pādānuddhyāta* in that record. On the other hand, the Dāmodarpur Copper-Plate Inscription has it that the *uparika* of Puṇḍravardhana-bhukti had himself appointed his *viṣayapati*.[18]

There seems to have been concentration of high Mauryan functionaries at the capital. But with the decentralization of powers at the centre, and the growing importance of the regional officers, the latter had their own headquarters in important towns of their

---

16 *CII*, vol. III, p. 21.

17 Ho Chong-Chum, *Fa-hien's Pilgrimage to Buddhist Countries*, Chinese Literature, 1965, No. 39, p. 154.

18 *AI*, XV p. 130.

respective regions. Some of these headquarters were located at Vaiśālī, Magadha, Nāgara and Tīra, etc.[19]

There was a preponderance of brāhmaṇas in the Gupta bureaucracy. The Udayagiri Cave Inscription speaks of a brāhmaṇa official under Candragupta II.[20] Karamadaṇḍa Inscriptions clearly speak of the brāhmaṇa Śikharsvāmin and Pṛthvīṣeṇa respectively.[21] This was mainly because brāhmaṇas were traditionally the most educated and well-versed in the sources of law. Kātyāyana, the law-giver of the Gupta period, also ordains that the *amātya*s should be brāhmaṇas. But since the Guptas themselves were not brāhmaṇas and had freely appointed their officers on merit irrespective of their religion, so much so that Āmrakārddava, the commander of Candragupta II's forces was a Buddhist according to the Sāñcī Inscription. It can safely be inferred that there was no bar on the appointment of the non-brāhmaṇas on government posts. At least the feudal chiefs of the Guptas had some non-brāhmaṇas as their officials. For instance, Sarvadatta, an *uparika*, under the *parivrājaka*s seems to have been a vaiśya.[22]

Besides the *amātya*s and the *kumārāmātya*s, the Guptas had *saciva*s and *mantrī*s under them. It is difficult to agree with P.L. Gupta (1970) that the *saciva*s and the *amātya*s under the Guptas were synonyms, mainly because the qualifications laid down by Kāmandaka are similar.[23] Since all the officials of the state were the drawn from the pool of the *amātya*s, their basic qualifications were bound to be similar. But in the majority of the literary sources, the *saciva* stands for the *mantrī*. The following literary evidences of the Gupta period leave us in no doubt that the *mantrī*s and the *saciva*s were synonyms:

---

19 *ASI, AR, 1913-14*, p. 104, seal 300, *Nalanda and Its Epigraphic Materials*, pp. 51-53, *ASI, AR, 1903-04*, p. 109, seal 22.

20 *CII*, vol. III, p. 36.

21 *EI*, X, p. 71.

22 *CII*, vol. III, p. 36.

23 *Gupta Sāmrājya*, p. 386.

1. *Raghu* XVII.50: *mantraḥ pratidinam tasya babhūva saha mantribhiḥ* (he held daily consultations with his *mantrīs*).
2. *Raghu* IV.87: *sacivasakhaḥ* (the *saciva*s were the companions of the king).
3. *Raghu* I.34: *tena dhṛjagato gurvī saciveṣu nicikṣipe* (during his absence, he entrusted the adminstration to *saciva*s).
4. *Raghu* 1.34: *saciveṣu*
5. *Raghu* VIII.17: *mantribhiḥ*

The importance of the ministers is brought out by the fact that Kāmandaka regarded *mantra-śakti* to be superior to the *prabhāva-śakti* and *utsāha-śakti*.[24] Only that person was recommended for the ministerial post whose devotion to the country was unquestionable.[25] If the council of ministers is destroyed, the king and the people are also destroyed.[26]

Even the evidence of the Jūnāgaṛh Inscription of Rudradāman I, cited by Gupta, does not make *amātya*s and *saciva*s synonyms. The *mati-saciva* and the *karma-saciva* mentioned therein were *mantrī*s and executive officers, both drawn from the cadre of *amātya*s.

Since Kāmandaka uses the words *amātya* and *mantrī* together and advises the king to consult both,[27] they were the civil servants and the ministers respectively. In the Mandasor Inscription the term *saciva* stands for a minister.

Certain terms used for the ministers in literary evidences bring out some other salient features of the Gupta bureaucracy:

---

[24] *prabhāvotsāhaśaktibhyām mantra-śaktiḥ praśasyate* । – *KāmN* XIII.7

[25] *mantrayeteḥ kāryāṇi sahāptena vipaścitā* ।
āptam mūrkhamanāptam ca mantriṇam parivarjayet ॥ – *KāmN* XII.4

[26] *KāmN* XII.13.

[27] *KāmN* 8.1.

1. They have been termed as *maula* in the *Raghuvaṁśa*, XII.12, suggesting the hereditary nature of their offices.
2. *mantribhiḥ nītiviśāradaiḥ* in the *Raghuvaṁśa*, VIII.77, would make it amply clear that the *mantrī*s were expected to be expert in *nīti* (polity).
3. *mantrī-vr̥ddhān* in the *Raghuvaṁśa* XVIII.71 and *vr̥ddhaiḥ amātyaiḥ* in the *Raghuvaṁśa*, XIII.66, points towards the fact that age and experience were regarded to be additional qualifications of bureaucrats.
4. The use of the words *bhavān*[28] and *ārya*[29] for ministers aver the high esteem in which they were held.

The *Mālavikāgnimitra* speaks of the *mantrī-pariṣad* as well.[30] Kāmandaka calls it *mantrī-maṇḍala*.[31] The Bilsāḍ Inscription of Kumāragupta I reign informs us that one Dhruvaśarman was honoured by the *pariṣad*.[32] Just as in the Aśokan inscription, so also in the Bilsāḍ inscription, the *pariṣad* stands for the *mantrī-pariṣad* which is the same as the *mantrī-maṇḍala* of Kāmandaka. On this ground, it is unnecessary to identify it with an Academic Assembly and not a council of ministers. Conferment of honour by the council of ministers does not come into conflict with the council's deliberative functions. It is in keeping with the Vedic traditions of the *sabhā* and the *samiti* which had multidimensional functions. The *mantrī-pariṣad* seems to have been presided over by the prime minister called *mantrī-mukhya* in the *Mudrārākṣasa*.[33]

Like earlier periods, the Gupta period too seems to have had two

---

28 *Mālavikā*, p. 11.

29 *Śāk*, p. 198.

30 *kañcukī-deva evamamātyapariṣade vijñāpāyāmi … mantri-pariṣadopeyevameva darśanam* । – *Mālavikā*, Act V

31 *dvādaśeti manuḥ prāha ṣoḍaśeti br̥haspatiḥ*। *uśanā viṁśatiriti mantriṇām mantrimaṇḍalam*। – *KāmN* 12.48

32 *CII*, vol. III: *pārṣadā mānitena*।

33 *Mudrā*, Act II.

institutions – the ministers and the council of ministers. According to Udayagiri Cave Inscription No. II, Vīrasena was a minister under Candragupta II. The Karamadaṇḍa Inscription of the Gupta era 117 speaks of Śikharasvāmin as a *mantrī* of Candragupta II. He was also called the *kumārāmātya* suggesting thereby a civil service. The Karamadaṇḍa Inscription suggests the existence of the ministers. According to Kauṭilya, the number of the king's ministers, who were always at his disposal for consultation, was three or four. Kāmandaka, who regarded Kauṭilya as his model, might not have ordained much differently. However, Kāmandaka does not shed any light on the number and composition of the *mantrī-pariṣad*. The number of its members might have varied in accordance with the requirements of the state. But Kāmandaka described elaborately the functions of the *mantrī-pariṣad*. It was basically a deliberative body entrusted with the task of examining all important issues with their pros and cons and taking decisions and guarding the secrecy of its deliberations.[34] Kālidāsa also refers to the ministers several times in his works.[35] Kāmandaka advises the king to hold meeting with his ministers at such places as were inaccessible even to birds.[36] At the time of their appointment, utmost care was taken to see that only such persons were chosen for ministerial posts as could guard the secrets of the state.[37] Their other requisite qualifications included, inter alia, high birth, erudition, valour, morality, diplomatic expertise, prudence, enterprise, healthy physique and forbearance. They should also be natives of the country.[38]

The *Mālavikāgnimitra* also gives some important information regarding the working of the *mantrī-pariṣad*. According to it, the agenda of its meeting was prepared by the king. It was not necessary for him to be present in the meetings. Normally, its decisions were

---

34 *KāmN* XII.30.

35 *Raghu* VIII.17, XII. XIII, 71; *Vik*, p. 87.

36 *KāmN* XII.42-47.

37 *KāmN* XII.42-47.

38 *KāmN* IV.24-30.

conveyed to him by the *kañcukī*. However, the most important of them were conveyed to the king by an *amātya*.

Though the council of ministers was a deliberative body, yet, since it was manned by the *purohita* and the ministers of proven intellect and loyalty, it was greatly respected by the king who, in most cases, must have accepted its decisions. However, the king was free to accept or reject them according to his own discretion.[39]

The ministers performed a variety of functions. Their main function was to advise the king on all important issues.[40] They looked after the administration in the absence or on death of the king.[41] They made all necessary arrangements for the consecration of the new king.[42] It was the minister, probably the prime minister, who conveyed the decision of the council of ministers to the king.[43] The king's reaction to the resolution of the council of ministers was again conveyed back to it by the same minister.[44]

The ministers were expected to study every issue carefully, take a decision of a known issue, remove doubts from a doubtful issue and thoroughly understand the issue which is not fully known.[45] The king had no hesitation in accepting the decision of the ministers arrived at unanimously and firmly. The decision of the ministers became all the more imperative for the king if it was irreproachable

---

39 *Mālavikā*, Act I

40 *mantraḥ pratidinam tasya babhūva saha mantribhiḥ* ı – *Raghu* XVII.50

41 *Raghu* XIV.4.52-54.

42 *Vik*, p. 136.

43 *amātyo vijñāpayati-vidarbhagatamanuṣṭheya-mavadhāritamasmābhiḥ* ı
devasya tāvadabhipretam śrotumicchāmiti ı – *Mālavikā*, V, p. 103

44 *deva amāyto ... vijñāpayati-kalyāṇīdevasya buddhi* ı *mantripari-ṣadopeyetadeva darśanam* ı – *Mālavikā*, V, p. 103

45 *avijñātasya vijñānam vijñātasya viniścayaḥ* ı *arthadvaidhasya sandehacchedanam śeṣadarśanam* ı

yatra mantrimanassāmyam yatra ceto na śaṅkate
yatra santo na nindanti tatra parīyācenikirṣitam ı – *KāmN*, XII.31

by noble persons.[46] But in case of doubt, the king had the authority to return the proposal to the ministers for reconsideration.[47] The king was advised to subjugate his personal opinion to the collective opinion of his ministers.[48]

A large number of the designations of the Gupta officials have come down to us through epigraphs and literary sources. Some of the most important from amongst them belonging to the central civil service were as follows:

YUVARĀJA

He was the crown-prince and normally succeeded his father. But it was not necessary for him to be the eldest son. Candragupta I, according to the Allahabad Pillar Inscription, had nominated Samudragupta, probably in preference to his elder brother (Kāca?) to succeed him. Candragupta II was *tatparigṛhīta* of Samudragupta (chosen by Samudragupta) as his successor, though Rāmagupta was elder to him. Sometimes, the *yuvarāja* has been called *yuvarāja-bhaṭṭāraka* in the Gupta inscriptions. He had his own *kumārāmātya*s under him. Crown-princes assisted their fathers in administrative and military matters. When the Mehrauli Pillar Inscription mentions that the breeze coming from southern oceans was laden with the fragrance of Candra's valour, it seems to suggest that Candragupta II had taken part in his father's (Samudragupta's) southern expedition.

Candragupta II had appointed Govindagupta as the governor of Tīrabhukti. He was the governor of western Mālavā under Kumāragupta I. Ghaṭotkacagupta was appointed governor of eastern Mālavā by his father Kumāragupta I. Skandagupta had successfully repulsed the invasion of Puṣyamitra as the crown-prince under his father Kumāragupta I, according to the Bhītarī Pillar Inscription. The Nālandā seal of Samudragupta has it that the Kumāra Candragupta

---

46 *KāmN* XII.39.

47 *KāmN* XII.40.

48 *dhṛtepi mantre mantrajñāiḥsvayam bhūyo vicārayet* I *tathā vartteta mantrajño yathā svārtham na pīḍayet* I – *KāmN* XII.40

II had worked as *dūtaka* in a land transaction in Kramila *viṣaya* during the reign of his father.[49]

The literary evidence of the period sheds much light on the office of the *yuvarāja*. The princes were called *kumāras*. But after he was consecrated (*yuvarājyābhiṣeka*[50]), he came to be known as *yuvarāja*.[51] The consecration has been referred to by Kāmandaka in the following manner:

> *vinayopagrahān bhūṭyai kurvīta nṛpatiḥ sutān* । *avinītakumāram hi kulamāśu viśīryate* ॥
>
> *vinītamaurasam putram yauvarājyebhiṣecayet* ।

Since he was to assist his father in civil and military matters and was allowed to use his seal and have his own council of ministers, it was poetically put as if sovereignty was partly transferred to him.[52]

PUROHITA

He was the royal priest and by virtue of his sacerdotal, legal and academic profundity, he was probably the most reliable councillor of the king. If Kāmandaka is to be believed, he was also a member of the council of ministers.[53] In accordance with the Vedic tradition, he could wield weapons and took part in military expeditions as well.[54] If the *Mālavikāgnimitra* is to be believed, he used to receive a monthly salary.[55] He has been referred to as *purodhā* as well[56] and has been shown as sitting with the king and advising him.[57] According

---

49 *EI*, vol. XXV, p. 50.

50 *Vik*, pp. 136, 18.

51 *Raghu* III.35.

52 *Raghu* III.28, 35-36, 38.

53 *KāmN* IV.31.

54 Dikshitar, 1929, *Hindu Adminstrative Institution*, p. 115.

55 *dakṣiṇām māsikam purohitasya* । – *Mālavikā*, p. 87

56 *Raghu* XIX.54.

57 *Śāk* V.

to Kāmandaka,[58] he was well-versed in the three Vedas, *Daṇḍanīti* and *Atharvaveda* and performed daily rituals for the welfare of the kingdom.

QUEEN

During the Vedic period, the queens used to be *ratnin*s wielding great political influence. But by the time of the Guptas, they came to be divested of that influence. Except in the case of Kumāradevī, who shared power with her husband Candragupta I, under special circumstances, there is no other Gupta queen with political functions. Of course, they were called *mahādevī*s and were mentioned as mothers of the ruling monarchs in the latters' inscriptions, but they did not share regal power. They sometimes had their seals as well. One such seal belonging to Dhruvasvāminī, has come to light bearing the following inscription:

> *mahārājādhirāja śrī candragupta-patni mahārāja śrī govindagupta-mātā mahādevī śrī dhruvasvāminī* ।

However, Kālidāsa avers that in the absence of the male heir, pregnant queen could wield power and her orders were faithfully carried out. To quote,

> *maulaih sārdhaṁ sthavirasacivairhemasiṁhāsanastha* ।
> *rājñi rājyam vidhivadasiṣadbhartukhahatajña* ॥
> – *Raghu* XIX.57

AKṢAPAṬALIKA[59]

Ever since the Mauryan period, the *akṣapaṭalika* had continued to be an important officer. *Akṣapaṭala* would technically mean the records office. Hence, *akṣapaṭala* was in-charge of that office. He used to maintain the deeds and documents pertaining to the sale, purchase and income of the land. It appears that during the Mauryan period,

---

58 *trayyām ca daṇḍanītyām ca kuśalaḥ syāt purohitaḥ* । *atharvavihitam nityam kuryācchāntikapauṣṭikam* । – *KāmN* IV.31

59 *Mauryan Polity*, p. 157.

he was a central officer, whereas during the Gupta period, he worked at the village level.

SABHYA

The Allahabad Pillar Inscription speaks of *sabhya*s who would mean members of the *sabhā*. The *sabhā* was apparently a central assembly which was presided over by the king himself. One of its main functions was to nominate the successor to the throne. The above inscription tells us how it had selected Samudragupta as Candragupta I's successor, setting aside the claims of other *tulya-kulaja*s. However, Bṛhaspati refers to the *sabhya*s as performing judicial functions with the *prāḍvivāka*. It is difficult to agree with Dikshitar (1952) that the *sabhā* "must have been similar to the *paura-jānapada* organization",[60] for the *paura-jānapada* theory of Jayaswal is highly dubious.

PRĀḌVIVĀKA

He was the chief justice, next only to the king in judicial hierarchy. He could use the king's seal. He presided over the *mudrita* courts.[61] He was assisted by seven, five or three *sabhya*s in the discharge of his judicial functions.[62] According to law-givers, the *prāḍvivāka* had to be preferably a brāhmaṇa.[63]

SENĀPATI

The Sāñcī Inscription of GE 93 refers to Āmrakārddava, who was the commander of Candragupta II and had fought and won many battles for his master. The commander-in-chief of the army was known as *senāpati*,[64] though the army was also led by the king[65] as

---

60 *Gupta Polity*, p. 151.

61 *Bṛhaspatismṛti* I.63, *Kātyāyanasmṛti* LV.71-81.

62 *Gupta Polity*, p. 184.

63 *Viṣṇusmṛti* III.72-3.

64 *Mālavikā*, p. 11.

65 *Raghu* IV.

also the heir-apparent[66] personally.

The Mandasor Inscription of Govindagupta refers to Dattabhaṭṭa as a *senāpati* under Prabhākara, the governor. He was the son of Vāyurakṣita who himself was the *senāpati* of Govindagupta.[67] The *senāpati* was probably known as *mahābalādhikṛta* also.

The Karamadaṇḍa Inscription mentions a *mahābalādhikṛta* named Pṛthvīṣeṇa under Kumāragupta I. Earlier, he was a *mantrī*, but was later promoted to the post of the *mahābalādhikṛta*. In that capacity, he seems to have been the executive chief of both civil and military administration. The *mahābalādhikṛta* had a number of *aśvapati*s (commanders of the cavalry), *bhaṭāśvapati*s (commanders of the infantry and cavalry) and *mahāpīlupatis*[68] (commanders of the elephant force). The *Mudrārākṣasa* calls the commander of the elephant force as *gajādhyakṣa*. It also refers to the commanders of the cavalry and elephants as *hastyaśvādhyakṣa*s.[69] The ordinary troops were known as *cāṭa*s and *bhaṭa*s, who were sometimes given to entering villages and exacting money from them (Khoh Copper Plate Inscription of Mahārāja Hastin).

It is significant to note that the Maitraka rulers who were the governors of Saurāṣṭra under the Guptas used the title *senāpati* for themselves. For instance, Bhaṭārka was one such ruler.

According to Kāmandaka, the *senāpati* should be one who could know the mind of the army, who was of noble family, a native of the country and who would act in conformity with the science of *daṇḍanīti*, one possessed of the qualities of energy, heroism, forgiveness, patience, amiableness and richness, one endowed with power and manliness, who was depended upon by his followers for their support, who was expert in the knowledge of animals like

---

66 *Raghu* XVII.31-32.

67 *EI*, XXVII, p. 12.

68 *CII*, vol. III, p. 260; *ASI, AR, 1911-12*, pp. 52-53, *1903-04*, pp. 101-02; *SI*, p. 343.

69 *Mudrā*, Act III.

horses and elephants, a clever administrator, who was conversant with all countries and their languages, who could undertake nocturnal attacks, who could bridge rivers and cross mountains and who was never afraid of the enemy.[70]

There is another term *mahābalādhyakṣa* according to the Gupta inscriptions. It is not certain whether he was the same as *mahābalādhikṛta*. But the probability is that he was second in command to *mahābalādhikṛta*. The *gajādhyakṣa* and the *aśvādhyakṣa* referred to in the *Mudrārākṣasa* and the other *adhyakṣa*s of the divisions which worked under him. However, the overall in-charge of the war office was the *mahābalādhikṛta*.[71] Pṛthvīṣeṇa was one such under Kumāragupta I.

Kāmandaka Nītisāra XIX.45-53 mentions *nāyaka*s who were troop commanders. They formed the *vyūha* and led their *pravīra puruṣa*s (skilled soldiers) in military campaigns, sharing their trials and tribulations.

SĀNDHIVIGRAHIKA

In the Allahabad Pillar Inscription, Hariṣeṇa has been described, inter alia, as the *sāndhivigrahika* (minister of peace and war) of Samudragupta.[72]

The Udayagiri Cave Inscription speaks of Śāba Vīrasena as the *sāndhivigrahika* of Candragupta II. It is this inscription which clearly alludes to the hereditary character of the Gupta civil service, for it describes Vīrasena of having secured ministership by heredity (*anvaya-prāpta-sācivya*). But since it describes Vīrasena's other qualities as well, we may well presume that merit was basically the

70 *KāmN* XIX.27-43.

71 *Mālavikā*, p. 198.

72 V.R.R. Dikshitar observes that he "could not have therefore been a regular military officer, but he enjoyed the status of a high military official". But this observation is untenable, because there is no evidence to show that honorary titles were given to the Gupta bureaucracy. Moreover, military details given in the Allahabad Pillar Inscription suggest that Hariṣeṇa had accompanied his master on his expeditions.

criterion for high appointments. Vīrasena is again said to be the resident of Pāṭaliputra, the capital of the Guptas which might have maintained the Gupta secretariat.

It is unnatural to presume, as done by P.L. Gupta (1970),[73] that such illustrious officers as Hariṣeṇa were kept out of the council of ministers. It is also likely that he kept a watch on the *sāmanta*s and allies and formulated policies towards them.

In the *Mālavikāgnimitra*[74] the minister informs the king, through the chamberlain, that the king of Vidarbha had sent two girls as present to him. This minister may be identified with the *sāndhivigrahika*.

KOŚĀDHYAKṢA

Like some other law-givers, Kālidāsa has also advised the king to keep the *kośa* under his direct control.[75] But the counting of money (*gaṇanā*) associated with a bureaucrat in the *Abhijñānaśākuntalam* permits of several officers like *samāhartā* in the department of revenue.[76] The officers of the treasury were generally covered by the term *kośagṛhe niyuktāḥ*.[77]

MAHĀPRATIHĀRA

He was the chief of a horde of palace officials, the chief chamberlain. His name also occurs on Vaiśālī seal discovered by J. Bloch. He can be identified with the *antarvaṁśika* of the *Arthaśāstra* of Kauṭilya and the *kañcukī* of Sanskrit literature.[78] He carried a *hemavetra* (golden staff) as a symbol of his authority.[79]

---

[73] *Gupta Sāmrājya*.

[74] *Mālavikā*, Act V.

[75] *Raghu* V.1.29, XVII.60.81.

[76] *arthajātasya gaṇanābahulatayaivameva paura-kāryamavekṣitam* ।
– *Śāk*, p. 209

[77] *Raghu* V.29

[78] *Vikram*, p. III, *Sāk*, p. 154.

[79] *Kumāra* III.41.

We come across another important functionary of the palace called *dauvārika*.[80] He seems to have regulated the entrance into and exit from the palace. He must have worked under the overall supervision of the *kañcukī*.

The harem in the expansive palace was looked after by the *pratihārī*, the *dauvārika*, the *yavanī*s (Greek-females) and *avarodha-rakṣaka*s in general.[81]

The *kañcukī* of the Gupta palace performed, inter alia, the functions of the Aśokan *stryadhyakṣa-mahāmātra*.[82]

All these officers must have been assisted by a number of other doorkeepers, generally covered by the term *dvārasthaḥ*.[83] The guards of the harem were called *avarodha-rakṣaka*s.[84]

The overall security of the palace was entrusted to a special team of vigilance men called *pratyavekṣaka*s.[85] The bards who sang in praise of the king to awaken the king or during his marches and auspicious occasions were known as *bandinaḥ*, *bandiputrāḥ* and *sūtātmajāḥ*.[86] They have been spoken of as *vandakajana* in Bhītarī Pillar Inscriptions of Skandagupta.

The king had a heavy schedule of work. Those who heralded hours of his works during day and night were called *vaitālikāḥ*.[87]

POLICE OFFICERS

Among the police officers one has been mentioned as *daṇḍapāśika* whose office is alluded to as *daṇḍapāśādhikaraṇa* on one of the Vaiśālī seals, discovered by J. Bloch. The main function of the officer seems

80 *Śāk*, p. 62.

81 *Raghu* VI.20, 26, 59.

82 RE XII.

83 *Kumāra* VI.48.

84 *Raghu* VII.19.

85 *Śāk*, p. 198.

86 *Raghu* IV.6, V.65.

87 *Mālavikā*, p. 32, *Śāk*, p. 157.

to have been to apprehend criminals and tie them with *pāśa* (rope). The other police officers mentioned in the Gupta records were *dāṇḍika* and *cauroddharaṇika* (*ASI, AR* 1911-12, pp. 54-55; 1903-04, p. 108).

The police guards who carried the criminals to the courts under their custody (*Vik*, p. 124) and also apprehended the thieves (*pāṭaccaras*) and burglars (*gaṇḍabhedakas*) were called by the general term *rakṣiṇaḥ*. They could put them in fetters (*nigaḍabandhanena kṛtvā* – *Māl*, pp. 64, 79) or in prisons (*Raghu* VI.40). In towns the police force was put under the command of the *nāgarika* who was earlier known as *nāgaraka* in the *Arthaśāstra* of Kauṭilya (*Śāk*, pp. 182-86).

The overall in-charge of the police force seems to have been *daṇḍanāyaka* or *mahādaṇḍanāyaka* though he has been taken to mean chief justice by some scholars (*Gupta Empire*, p. 49). Both, Hariṣeṇa and his father Dhruvabhūti, were *mahādaṇḍanāyakas* according to the Allahabad Pillar Inscription. This officer has also been mentioned in the Vaiśālī seal belonging to the period of Govindagupta. The *mahādaṇḍanāyaka* seems to have been performing civil functions as well, since we find him and the *cāṭas* and the *bhaṭas* (policemen and soldiers) present at the time of land transactions.[88]

VINAYA-STHITI-SAṀSTHĀPAKA

This officer has been mentioned in a Vaiśālī seal.[89] His work seems to have been the interpretation and enforcement of sacred laws and ensuring the moral and ethical values in the society.

DŪTA

He was an envoy who was sent to other kingdoms to make important negotiation. The *Mālavikāgnimitra* describes such an envoy being sent by the king of Vidarbha to Agnimitra.

---

88 *EI*, vol. XV; *Gupta Inscriptions*, p. 169.

89 *ASI, AR, 1903-04*, p. 109.

Kāmandaka has mentioned three categories of the *dūtas*.[90] The *śāsanaharas* were one of them. The *śāsanahārins* of Kālidāsa may be identified with them. Chapter XIII of the *Nītisāra* of Kāmandaka deals with the qualifications and functions of the *dūtas*. Unmindful of their personal discomforts and discomfitures, they should keep on pursuing their objectives. For this, they were to be conversant with the topography and language of the enemy state and sow seeds of dissensions in it.

ADHIKARAṆIKA

The *Mṛcchakaṭika* informs us about this judicial officer who presided over the city-court called *adhikaraṇa-maṇḍapa*.[91] According to the Dāmodarpur Copper Plate Inscriptions, the district headquarters were called *adhiṣṭhānas* in which were located these *adhikaraṇas* (district offices and courts).

ANTAPĀLA

He was entrusted with the task of guarding the frontiers and looking after the forts. The *Mālavikāgnimitra* speaks of Vīrasena, the brother-in-law of Agnimitra, as such an *antapāla*.[92]

DHARMĀDHIKĀRI[93]

He has been mentioned in the *Abhijñānśākuntalam* (p. 40) and seems to have been the head of the Department of Religion. Among other things, he took care of ascetics living in forests. His functions were different from the *purohita* who had much more far-reaching areas of supervision under him.

---

[90] *nisṛṣṭārtho mitārthaśca tathā śāsanahārakaḥ* । *sāmarthyāt pādato hīno dūtastu trividhaḥ smṛtaḥ* ॥ – *KāmN* XIII.3

[91] *Raghu* III.68, *Mṛccha*, Act IX.

[92] *asti devyāḥ varṇāparo bhrātā vīraseno nāma sa bhartrā* । *narmadātīre antapāladurge sthāpitaḥ* ॥ – *Mālavikā*, p. X

[93] *yaḥ pauraveṇa rājñā dharmādhikāre niyuktaḥ* । – *Śāk*, p. 40

KHĀDYUTPAKIKA

This designation has been used for Hariṣeṇa in the Allahabad Pillar Inscription. It has been taken to mean the officer controlling superintendents of the royal kitchen.

SPIES

The Sanskrit[94] words generally used for them were *cāra, praṇidhi* and *apasarpa*. They were the king's eyes through which he saw everything in his kingdom.[95] They also operated secretly in enemy countries. According to Kāmandaka, a spy should be skilled in the interpretation of internal sentiments by conjecture and by external gestures, of accurate memory, polite and soft of speech, agile in movements, capable of bearing with all sorts of privations and difficulties, quick-witted and expert in everything.[96] Their main function was to frequent important places and collect information beneficial to his state.[97]

Provincial Government

GOPTĀ

Technically the word means *protector*, but had come to be used for the governor of a province (*deśa*). The Mandasor Inscription has it that Bandhuvarman was the governor of Mālavā under Kumāragupta I. He has been called *bandhuriva prajānām* in the inscription. According to the Jūnāgaṛh Inscription,[98] Parṇadatta was the *goptā* of Saurāṣṭra under Skandagupta.

Great care was taken to ensure that only a highly talented person was appointed as a governor, specially in important provinces. The Jūnāgaṛh Inscription tells us how Skandagupta kept on brooding

---

94 *Raghu* XIV.13, 32, XVIII.48, *Kumāra* II.6, 7.

95 *Raghu* XVIII.48, *Kām* XIII.28.

96 *Kām* XIII.26.

97 *Kām* XIII.49.

98 Jūnāgaṛh Inscription.

many days and nights as to who should be offered the governorship of Saurāṣṭra. Ultimately his choice fell on Parṇadatta, who in his opinion, was the only man (*ekaḥ*) to shoulder such an important responsibility by virtue of his being modest (*vinīta*), truthful (*satya*), straightforward (*ārjava*) and of unimpeachable integrity (*viśuddha*).

His main responsibility seems to have been the protection of the province, vulnerable to the Hūṇa invasion. But he was also expected to look after the general welfare of the people. This explains why Parṇadatta had got repaired the Sudarśana Lake which had been an important irrigational project of the region ever since the days of Candragupta Maurya.

UPARIKA

Besides the *deśa*, we hear of another territorial division *bhukti* during the Gupta period. It is important to know that whereas the western rocords of the Guptas mention *deśa*, the eastern inscriptions use the word *bhukti* in them. We are not sure whether *deśa* and *bhukti*, both meant a province or only the former meant a province, whereas the latter stood for a commissionery of modern days. Some of the *bhukti*s of the empire were Puṇḍravardhanabhukti, Tīrabhukti and Magadhabhukti under *uparika*s.

There is a good deal of controversy regarding the actual meaning of the word *uparika*. According to some scholars, it is associated with *uparikara* – an extra tax on the land produce.[99] But the formation of the word *uparika* from *uparikara* cannot be explained under any grammatical rule. P.L. Gupta (1970) seems to be nearer the truth when he says that *upari* means higher and that the *uparika* would be a higher officer, e.g. a commissioner. The Dāmodarpur Copper Plate Inscription Nos. 1 and 2 speak of Vetravarman as a *viṣayapati* under the *uparika* of Puṇḍravardhana-bhukti. Very frequently the princes were appointed as *uparika*s. For instance, the Tumain Inscription tells us that Kumāragupta I had appointed prince Ghaṭotkacagupta

[99] Saletore, 1943, *Life in Gupta Age*, p. 258.

as the governor of Erikiṇa (Eraṇ).[100] The Dāmodarpur Copper Plate Inscription No. III informs us that Brahmadatta, the *uparika* of Puṇḍravardhana-bhukti under Budhagupta, was called *mahārāja.* Sometimes, the governor was called *uparika-mahārāja,* as in the Dāmodarpur Copper Plate Inscription No. 4. In the Gunaighar Inscription, the governor of Vainyagupta, *mahārāja* Rudradatta, has been called *pādadāsa* (Vassal).

Vaiśālī has yielded several seals containing the names of *balādhikaraṇa, raṇabhāṇḍāgārika, daṇḍapāśādhikaraṇa, mahādaṇḍanāyaka* and *mahāpratihāra,* suggesting thereby that the *uparika* had a large number of high functionaries to run the provincial administration. The titles of the *uparika* included *mahārāja, mahā-sāmanta* and *senāpati.*

In the Khoh Inscription of Mahārāja Hastin, an officer named *bhogika* has been mentioned. He was probably the same as the *uparika.*

Interestingly enough, Bṛhaspati brings out the requisite qualifications of an *uparika.* According to him, he should be possessed of sound and steady physique, should be valiant, handsome, presentable, liberal, energetic and expert. He should be capable of administering justice in legal disputes in order to maintain impartiality and morality.[101]

BHOGIKA

Gupta Inscriptions speak of this officer.[102] If Dikshitar (1952) is

---

[100] *EI,* vol. II, p. 210: In the fifth Dāmodarpur Copper-Plate Inscription the *uparika* of Puṇḍravardhana-bhukti, Devabhaṭṭāraka has been designated as Rājaputra (*EI,* vol. XV, p. 142).

[101] Viśvarūpa on *Yājñavalkyasmṛti* I.307 – *avikāryo 'vikalendriyaḥ pratāpavān subhagaḥ sumukho 'kṛpaṇāpramādī dakṣo dākṣiṇya-cāritrarakṣanārthamadhikaraṇasandigdhavivekākṛduparikaḥ syāt* । Also see *D.R. Bhandarkar Commemoration Volume,* pp. 231-33.

[102] *CII,* vol. III, p. 100.

correct, his position was higher than that of a *viṣayapati* and lower than that of a *sāmanta* who was the minister-in-charge of the province.[103]

RĀJASTHĀNĪYA

This term occurs in the Gupta inscriptions.[104] J.F. Fleet (1963) would make us believe that he was "one who belongs to a *rāja-sthāna* (king's abode)" or "one who occupies the position of a *rājan*". In either case, he was a prince who was generally appointed as a governor.

The provincial administrative set-up closely resembled the central one. The Provincial Civil Service was also denoted by the term *kumārāmātya*. If a *kumārāmātya* belonged to the Central Civil Service, he would sometimes specifically be designated as *paramabhaṭṭāraka-pādīya kumārāmātya* as against *yuvarāja-pādīya kumārāmātya* who belonged to the Provincial Civil Service. The designation of many of the officers in the provincial cadre were not very different from those in the centre cadre. Their officials find mention in Gupta records:

DAṆḌANĀYAKA

Probably, he combined in him the duties of a military commander and a magistrate. Several of them were put under the charge of a *mahādaṇḍanāyaka*.

DAṆḌAPĀŚIKA

He was an ordinary police officer who worked under the head of the police department called *daṇḍapāśādhikaraṇika*.[105]

BALĀDHIKARAṆIKA

He was evidently the officer-in-charge of the military department.[106]

---

103 *Gupta Polity*, p. 244.

104 *CII*, vol. III, p. 157.

105 *ASI, AR, 1903-04*, p. 108.

106 Ibid.

RAṆABHĀṆḌĀGĀRIKA

He was the officer-in-charge of the war finances.

VINAYASTHITISTHĀPAKA

As mentioned earlier, he was the officer-in-charge of the Department of Religion. Some would like to take him as an officer-in-charge of the Department of Justice.[107]

PĀṬYUPARIKA

He was the officer-in-charge of the Department of Accounts.

AUDRAṄGIKA

This term has been derived from the word *udraṅga* (a tax on permanent tenants). As such, *audraṅgika* was the tax-collector.

CAURODDHARAṆIKA

He was evidently a police officer whose main function was to apprehend thieves.

SĀDHANIKA

He appears to have been a judicial officer whose main function was the disposal of the cases arising out of the debts and fines.[108]

AGRAHĀRIKA

He was the officer-in-charge of the *agrahāra*s, land grants generally made to the brāhmaṇas.

AURṆASTHĀNIKA

This word has been derived from *urṇa* (wool). So *aurṇasthānika* would most probably be an officer-in-charge of the wool manufactories.

---

107 *ASI, AR, 1903-04*, p. 109.

108 Gunaighar Inscription II.15-16.

BHOGAPAṬIKA

The *bhoga* is a technical word, meaning tax collected in kind such as vegetables, pulses, curd, *ghī*, fruits, etc. *Bhogapaṭika* would be an officer-in-charge of such collections for the benefit of the government functionaries touring the countryside.

TADĀYUKTAKA

He was perhaps the treasury officer.

HIRAṆYASAMUDĀYIKA

He was likely to be the mint-master supervising the minting of coins.

ĀVASATHIKA

He was the officer looking after the construction and maintenance of the *āvasatha*s or *dharmaśālā*s.

DEVADRONĪ SAMVADDA

He was an officer looking after temple properties.

According to Dikshitar, provincial governors were usually attended and assisted by a body of what may be called personal secretaries who served as the channel of communication between him and the administrative officers under him and convey to them his orders. These officers were called *dūta*s, *dūtaka*s and *ājñādāyaka*s. They did perform, inter alia, the functions referred to by Dikshitar. But they do not appear to have been the counterparts of modern personal secretaries. As discussed earlier, they were either envoys or messengers or representatives of the government supervising important land-transactions. His titles in the Gunaighar Inscription of Vainyagupta, namely *pañcādhikaraṇoparika*, *pāṭyuparika*, *purapāloparika* and *mahāsāmanta* would project him as much more than a personal secretary of a governor.

District Administration

VIṢAYAPATI

The Gupta inscriptions shed some light on district civil service also. The most important of them was the *viṣayapati* in-charge of the district administration, having his headquarters called *adhiṣṭhāna*. As early as Samudragupta, we find two of his districts – Kramila and Gayā – mentioned in the Nālandā and Gayā Copper-Plates.[109] Several names of the *viṣayapatis* of the Gupta period have also come down to us. According to the Dāmodarpur Copper Plate Inscription No. 5, Koṭivarṣa *viṣaya* was ruled by Svayambhudeva. The inscription probably belongs to the reign of Viṣṇugupta.[110] His district office was called *adhiṣṭhānādhikaraṇika*. From the Gunaighar Inscription we learn that the *viṣayapati* sometimes held the designation of *kumārāmātya*.

As mentioned earlier, Kulavṛddha, for instance, was a *viṣayapati* according to the Vaigrām Copper Plate Inscription.[111] The district administration was carried on by a district board called *viṣaya-pariṣad* consisting of the following functionaries:

1. *nagara-śreṣṭhī*: He was the representative of the mercantile community and was the president of the *nagara-sabhā*.
2. *sārthavāha*: He was the representative of the traders' guilds.
3. *prathama-kulika*: He represented the artisans.
4. *prathama-kāyastha*: Sometimes he was called as *śreṣṭha-kāyastha*,[112] both terms meaning the foremost among the *kāyasthas* or scribes. There is hardly anything to warrant P.L. Gupta's (1970) suggestion that he represented the intelligentsia.[113] It seems that the *kāyasthas* had developed into a numerous class of

---

109 Nālandā and Gayā seals of Samudragupta.

110 Dāmodarpur Copper-Plate Inscription No. 5.

111 Vaigrām Copper-Plate Inscription.

112 Farīdpur Inscription of Dharmapāla.

113 *Gupta Sāmrājya*, p. 392.

scribes and the best among them were included in the *viṣaya-pariṣad* to prepare and preserve documents. To some extent Dikshitar's (1952)suggestion that he acted as chief secretary appears to be plausible.[114]

The local bodies of the *viṣaya*s were so powerful during the Gupta period that even the *viṣayapati* could not purchase land without following the set rules. The Nandapur Copper-Plate Inscription has it that Catramaha, the *viṣayapati*, wanted to purchase a piece of land to donate it to a brāhmaṇa. He could do it only after the *samvyavahārī*s and *kuṭumbī*s were satisfied with the validity of the proposed transaction. The Vaigrām Copper-Plate Inscription makes it clear that the *samvyavahārī*s were the *mahattara*s of the local body.

DŪTAKA

In fact, he was a civil servant placed at the disposal of the district administration. But since he had to deal with land-transactions at villages, he was concerned with both the district and the village administration. The Gunaighar Copper-Plate Inscription contains some important information in this regard. According to it, Mahārājaśrī Vainyagupta, at the instance of his functionary Mahārāja Rudradatta, had issued this order granting land in Kantedadaka-*grāma*, to a Buddhist *vihāra* for improvization of insense, flowers, lamps, etc. for worship, lodging, boarding and clothing and medicines to the ill and materials for the repair of the *vihāra*.

The above inscription tells us that Mahāsāmanta Mahārāja Śrī Vijayasena had acted as the king's *dūtaka*. As was the practice in the Gupta period, Vijayasena held several other offices as well. He was also the *mahāpratihāra*, *mahāpīlupati* (commander of the elephant army), *pañcādhikaraṇa* (president of the five officers) and *pura-pāla-uparika* (president of the board of city-mayors).

The *dūtaka* communicated the information regarding the royal donation to the three *kumārāmātya*s suggesting thereby that he held a

---

114 *Gupta Polity*, pp. 157-58.

higher position than the *kumārāmātyas*. He has also been mentioned in the Khoh Inscription of Mahārāja Hastin.

The Gupta Inscriptions refer to a number of functionaries carrying out the functions assigned to them by the *viṣaya-pariṣad*:

1. *dhruvādhikaraṇika*: He was the officer-in-charge of the agricultural produce.[115]
2. *agrahārika*: *Agrahāra* was a piece of land donated to the brāhmaṇas or temples. The officer who looked after these *agrahāras* was called *agrahārika*.[116] He is mentioned in the Bihar Stone Pillar Inscription.
3. *śaulkika*: *Śulka* was the term used for the customs duties collected by the government. The customs officer was thus called *śaulkika*.[117]
4. *gaulmika*: He was the officer-in-charge of the forest produce.[118] Both *śaulkika* and *gaulmika* are referred to in the Bihar Stone Pillar Inscription.
5. *utkheṭayita*: He was an officer working in the Department of Taxation.[119]
6. *bhaṇḍāgārādhikṛta*: He was the treasury officer.[120]
7. *talavāṭaka*: He was the police officer.[121]
8. *akṣapaṭalika*: He was officer-in-charge of the archives or records office.[122] Since his office – the *akṣapaṭala* – was to prepare and preserve the deeds and documents pertaining to sale, purchase

115 *CII*, vol. 3, p. 170.

116 Ibid., p. 52.

117 Ibid.

118 Ibid.

119 *EI*, vol. XII, p. 75.

120 Ibid.

121 *CII*, vol. 3, p. 217.

122 Ibid., p. 190.

and revenue at the district level, he must have been a very important officer.

It is significant to know that the name of the *akṣapaṭalika* occurs in the list of central civil service during the Mauryan period. But in the Gupta period, he was essentially a district officer.

9. *kartṛ*: The *akṣapaṭalika* was assisted by a number of *kartṛ*s in drafting documents. They were also called *śāsayatṛ*s.[123]

10. *divira*: This is the term used for a number of clerks and scribes who assisted their officers in various ways.

    The district administrative headquarters was called the *adhikaraṇa* which must have housed a lagre number of district officers.

11. *āyoktaka*: He was the administrative officer of another territorial unit called *vīthī*. Many districts in the Gupta empire had a number of *vīthī*s in them. The Pahāṛpur Copper-Plate Inscription speaks of a *vīthī* named Dakṣiṇānśaka.[124] The Kulaikuri Copper-Plate Inscription refers to the Śṛṅgavera *vīthī*.[125]

The Dāmodarpur Copper-Plate Inscription throws light on the district administration. It was carried on by a district council manned by the following:

1. Kumārāmātya Vetravarman was the *viṣayapati* of Koṭivarṣa.
2. Dhṛtipāla, the *nagaraśreṣṭhī* (president of the chamber of commerce).
3. Bandhumitra, the *sārthavāha* (representative of the guilds of merchants).
4. Dhṛtimitra, the *prathamakulika* (president of the guilds of artisans).

---

123 *EI*, vol. 12, p. 79.

124 Ibid., XX, p. 61.

125 *IHQ*, vol. XIX, p. 24.

5. Sāmbapāla, the *prathama kāyastha* (chief secretary).

Village Administration

Like the district administration, the village administration too finds mention in the Gupta inscriptions.

GRĀMIKA[126]

Also called *grāmeyaka* and *grāmādhyakṣa*, he was the head of the village administration. In the *Arthaśāstra* of Kauṭilya, his name does not occur in the list of salaried officers of the state. He seems to have represented villages in the Mauryan period. However, we are not sure whether he was an official of the state or the people under the Guptas. In the task of running the village administration, he was assisted by a number of functionaries.

The proposal for land donations was very often mooted through him. According to the Dāmodarpur Copper-Plate Inscription, Nābhaka, the *grāmika* had forwarded a proposal for the purchase of land for residential purposes for certain brāhmaṇas.

AKṢAPAṬALIKA

As in the district, so also in the village, he looked after revenue records.

AṢṬAKULĀDHIKARAṆA

R.D. Banerji was of the opinion that he was an officer put in-charge of each group of eight villages.[127] Basak, depending upon the literal translation of the term, thought that he was an officer-in-charge of each group of eight families in the village.[128] Depending upon Buddhaghoṣa's commentary on the *Mahāparinirvāṇa-Suttanta*, which makes *aṣṭakula* to mean a judicial body, K.K. Dasgupta held that the

---

126 *CII*, vol. III, pp. 112, 256; *IA*, vol. V, p. 155.

127 *JASB*, vol. V, NS, p. 460.

128 *EI*, vol. XV, p. 137.

aṣṭakulādhikaraṇa was a village court presided over by eight judges.[129] His view appears to be most tenable. P.L. Gupta's (1970) objection[130] to this view on the basis that the *aṣṭakulādhikaraṇa* has been mentioned along with the *grāmika* and *mahattaras* in the Dhanaidah and Dāmodarpur copper plates and that they had informed the people about the application for the purchase of a piece of land does not cut much ice. It only suggests that the *aṣṭakulādhikaraṇa* was a village court of the nature of a *loka adālata* which involved the local people not only in deciding disputes but also in disposing of such matters as might lead to disputes.

PUSTAPĀLA

He was an officer at the village and *vīthī* levels functioning as a recordkeeper. In all land transactions, he was, first of all, consulted regarding the nature and ownership of land which was sold, bought or gifted.[131] It was on the basis of his report that the *āyuktaka* accepted the proposal for land transaction.[132]

VALATKAUŚANA

D.C. Sircar (1942) thinks that he was the representative of the state at the village level.[133] The Gayā and Nālandā seals of Samudragupta, which mention him, would suggest that he was basically a tax-collector.

Vīthī Administration[134]

To quote Dikshitar,

> It is possible that only the big villages, difficult of being

---

129 *IC*, vol. V, pp. 110-11.

130 *Gupta Sāmrājya*, p. 396.

131 Dāmodarpur Copper-Plate Inscription No. 1.

132 Ibid.

133 *SI*, p. 271.

134 *IHQ*, vol. XIX, pp. 21ff.

administered efficiently by *viṣayapati*s single-handed, were divided in that manner.

Its chief administrator was the *āyuktaka*. He administered the *vīthī* with the help of the following:[135]

1. *mahattara*s (elders),
2. *kuṭumbī*s (householders),
3. *pustapāla*s (recordkeepers),
4. *kāyastha*s (clerks),
5. *kulika*s (representatives of artisans).

The combined testimony of the inscriptions referring to the *viṣaya*s, *grāma*s and *vīthī*s point towards multidimensional functions of their local bodies:

According to the Nālanda seal, a land grant was made to a brāhmaṇa named Jayabhaṭṭasvāmī. The Gayā seal speaks of another land grant to brāhmaṇa named Gopadevasvāmī. The Dhanaidah Copper-Plate Inscription informs us of the sale of land for making a donation to a brāhmaṇa called Varāhasvāmī. Of all the Copper-Plate Inscriptions, probably, the Kulaikuri Copper Plate Inscription gives greatest details referring to the sale of land and the procedure and functionaries involved in such sales. It has mention to territorial units of the *grāma* and the *vīthī* as also to functionaries such as *viṣayapati*s, *āyuktaka*s, *kuṭumbī*s, *adhikaraṇika*s, *samvyavahārī*s, *kulika*s and *pustapāla*. The Dāmodarpur Copper-Plate Inscription No. 1 refers to an application of a brāhmaṇa named Karppaṭika for the purchase of a piece of land and for making a permanent arrangement for the performance of a regular Agnihotra with its income. The Dāmodarpur Copper-Plate Inscription No. 2 refers to the official donation of a piece of land to a person for the regular performance of the *pañca-mahāyajña*s.

According to the Dāmodarpur Copper-Plate Inscription No. 5, a person from Ayodhyā had made an application to the *viṣayapati* for

---

135 *ASI*, AR, *1903-04*, p. 109; *SI*, p. 333, Fleet No. 14.

a grant of land to make provision for the repairs of a temple which had developed breaches (*khaṇḍa*) and cracks (*phuṭṭa*) and also for making *bali, caru, satra, gavya, dhūpa, puṣpa, madhuparka* and *dīpa* available for the worship.

This land did not belong to one single village, but was spread over four or five villages. As was the case with all land-transactions, the application thus made was referred to the *pustapāla*s. Their *prathama* (chief) would examine all transactions. After it was found in order (*yukta*), the deed was ordered to be made on a copper plate.

Dāmodarpur Copper-Plate Inscriptions tell us that the sale, purchase or transfer of the land could not be effected without the sanction of the government. However, the government allowed land transactions on the basis of *nīvī-dharma* which stipulated that the purpose, generally religious or charitable, for which the land grant was made, should permanently be fulfilled and financed out of the income from the sanctioned land. This is why great care was taken to examine all aspects of such a land transaction. The application for the sale or purchase of land was made to the *pustapāla*s. They placed it before the *pariṣad* consisting of the *mahattaras*, *aṣṭakulādhikaraṇa*s, *grāmika*s and *kuṭumbī*s. The *pariṣad* notified the proposal for the knowledge of all the villages. Thereafter, the *pariṣad* inspected the land and asked for the report from the *pustapāla*s. If the proposal was found in order, the *pustapāla*s recommended the sale of the land on the basis of *nīvī-dharma*.

The government sanctioned the sale of its land to private persons only if such a sale did not put the government exchequer to any loss, on the other hand, generally such land as was fallow (*khila*), bereft of vegetation (*astamba*) and incapable of yielding any revenue to the government (*samudaya-bāhya*). It was ensured that the sale would not involve any payment of compensation to its owner (*apratikara*).

It was at the instance of the governor, Rudradatta that the King Vainyagupta had made a gift of an *agrahāra* to a Mahāyānist *saṅgha*. Rudradatta had also made an earlier gift to the same *saṅgha* to provide *cīvara, piṇḍapaṭa, śayana, aśana* and medicines as also to maintain and repair its *vihāra*. Thus, it is clear from the Gunaighar Inscription that functions of the governor included financial assistance to religious establishments without prejudice to their sectarian nature. It should be noticed that the monarch of this governor was Vainyagupta who was a Śaiva.

City Administration[136]

PURAPĀLA

He looked after the city administration. The Jūnāgaṛh Inscription of Skandagupta informs us that Parṇadatta, the Governor of Saurāṣṭra, had appointed his son Cakrapālita as the administrator of Girinagara. The *purapāla* was authorized to use his own seal. Vaiśālī has yielded such a seal with the inscription:

vaiśālyadhiṣṭhadhikaraṇasya.

The *purapāla* was also called *nagarādhyakṣa*[137] (mayor of the city). Cakrapālita was thoroughly examined (*parīkṣya*) by his father Parṇadatta before he was given this post. The Jūnāgaṛh Inscription refers to a number of qualities which a *nagarādhyakṣa* should possess. He should be free from debts (*anṛṇya*), must be eloquent (*vākya*), well-mannered (*dākṣiṇya*), smiling and amiable (*pūrvasmitabhāṣa*), possessed of liberalities (*dāna*) and honour-giving (*māna*).

The *purapāla* who was the president of the *nagara pariṣad* was also called *puroga*, and *nagara rakṣaka*. The use of the word *upadhā* in plural in relation to Cakrapālita in the Jūnāgaṛh Inscription indicates that high officials of the state had to go through four tests – *dharmopadhā, arthopadhā, kāmopadhā* and *bhayopadhā* – before

---

136 Jūnāgaṛh Inscription.

kṣamā prabhutvam vinayo nayaśca ।
śauryam vinā śauryamahārccanan ca ॥

dākṣyam damo dānamadīnatāca । *dākṣiṇyamānṛṇyamaśūnyatā ca* ... ।

ityevametānadhikānato 'nyān guṇān parīkṣya svayameva pitrā ।
yaḥ sanniyukto nagarasya rakṣām viśiṣya pūrvānpracakāra samyak ॥

137 *Raghu* IV.26.

they were appointed on a particular post in accordance with their aptitude and qualifications.

It appears that the Guptas had a secretariat at their capital (*mūla*), it housed the officers of several high functionaries of the state. At least the royal court of justice presided over by the king was held daily at the capital.[138] The secretariat seems to have worked under the overall supervision of *sarvādhyakṣa*. It might also have stored and preserved documents and letters of various kinds written and read by a host of scribes.[139]

> In this way employing the fourfold administration of the government necessary to a king in its due order as far as eighteen *tīrtha*s, he (the king) obtained its fruits.[140]

---

138 *Raghu* VIII.18; *Śāk*, p. 198.

139 *Śāk*, p. 218: *patrahasta; śāk* p. 219: *patrarūḍha; Mālavikā*, p. 101: *lekha*, Ibid., p. 88: *lekhakaiḥ*.

140 *Raghu* XVII.60. Commenting on *Raghu* XVII.68, Caritravardhana speaks of the *tīrtha*s thus:

mantripurohitasenāpatyādyaṣṭādaśakam ।

Unlike the *Mahābhārata* and the *Arthaśāstra* of Kauṭilya, he mentions the designations of only three *tīrtha*s among the eighteen, namely, *mantrī*, *purohita* and *senāpati*.

8

Vardhana Civil Service

THE Vardhana period had several significant achievements to its credit. But it suffered from a multitude of deficiencies which make it look somewhat insipid in comparison to the more purposeful and rewarding periods of the Mauryas and the Guptas. The political disintegration of the country in the wake of the downfall of the Guptas, the frequent Hūṇa incursions, the later Gupta–Maukharī feud and the growing feudalization of the administrative machinery, all combined together to sap the efficiency of the civil service, and rendered the law-enforcing agencies corrupt and incompetent. In contrast to the numerous gold coins of the Guptas, which have been discovered in different parts of the country, only one gold coin of the Vardhana period, that of Harṣa, has come to light so far, suggesting, on the one hand, the paucity of gold in the country and, on the other hand, the shrinking of media of exchange in high business circles. It is to be noted that the overwhelming number of civil servants were no more paid in cash. They were allotted land for their services. Gone were the days when foreign travellers like Fa-hien could move freely through the length and breadth of the country without fear or hindrance. The insecurity that had gripped the country during the rule of the Vardhanas is attested by single fact that the Chinese traveller Yuan Chwang was waylaid by robbers more than once during the reign of Harṣa. Also gone were the days when the farmers could work on their fields without any damage to their person or cultivation even when the armies were on the march.

But the contemporary testimony of the Vardhana period brings out, in high relief, the plight of the farmers. The adversely affected cultivators have been described by Bāṇa as protesting vehemently in the following manner: "Where is the king? Whose king? What sort of king is he?" Bāṇa has gone on record that the marching armies did not spare even the *agrahāra*s of the brāhmaṇas.[1]

As literature, so also the court life and the civil service, had become pompous, heavy, artificial and extravagant during the Vardhana period. The feudal system had taken deeper roots and had brought under its ominous shadow the political and economic institutions of the country. The principle of hereditary bureaucracy was sometimes extended to unreasonable limits so much so that the aged Siṁhanāda continued to head the military organization of Harṣa even when he merited retirement from active service.

The Guptas had never allowed the harem to accompany them on their military expeditions. But if the *Harṣacarita* (*HC*) is to be believed, the ladies of the harem were taken by the king along with the army.[2] Such a practice must have made lax the discipline of the army.[3]

All these factors tended to affect adversely the civil service of the Vardhanas. Its deplorable nature and functioning are brought out by Bāṇa in a vivid manner. He has compared civil servants with sycophants, whores and spineless creatures and has observed that the poor civil servants were hardly human beings and that it did not behove a self-respecting person to enter into the service of even the lord of the three worlds because of its accompanying subservience.[4] The servant, he continues, has no independent identity, no self-

---

1 *kva rājā? kuto rājā? kīdṛśo vā rājā?* – *HC*, p. 212

2 *puraḥ saradīpikālokaviralāyamānalokotpīḍa-prasthitāntaḥ pura-karaṇīkadambike*। – *HC*, p. 206

3 During his expedition against Śaśāṅka, Harṣa's war elephants trampled over the houses and heavily damaged colonies. – *HC*, p. 206

4 *varākaḥ sevakopi martyamadhya, rājilopi vā bhogī, pulākopi vā kalamaḥ*। *varam kṣaṇamapi kṛtā manavata mānavatā, na matonamatastrailokyādhirājyotabhogo 'pi manasvinaḥ*। – *HC*, p. 225

respect and no peace. His subordination, according to him, carries him to the lowest depth of degradation.[5] He sees much evil in a man's desire to enter into the royal court.[6] While in service, he has to suffer all sorts of ignominies.

This long and bitter description of the agonies and degradation given by Bāṇa does not make only, the conditions of the menial servants of the palace look miserable, but also those of the highest officials of the state, for it follows Bhāskaravarman's message to Harṣa expressing his keenness to enter into a friendly alliance with him.[7]

Notwithstanding the poetic exaggeration in Bāṇa's account, two inferences can safely be drawn from it. First, *rājāyatta* government, supported by a coterie of newly-risen landed aristocracy, has got the better of the *sacivāyatta* government, sustained by the top bureaucracy. The landed aristocracy was most effectively represented by the *sāmanta*s who are frequently referred to in Varadhana records. While the word *sāmanta* has been used by Kauṭilya in the sense of a neighbouring king, it came to be used for a subordinated king, assured of his rule over his territory under certain obligations, such as *sarvakaradānājñākaraṇa-praṇāmagamana* as spelled out in Samudragupta's Allahabad Pillar Inscription. But the *sāmanta*s of the Vardhana period came to wield unprecedented influence and power with the king. If Bāṇa is to be believed, the emperor could not ignore the advice of his great *sāmantas*.[8] When Rājyavardhana gave expression to his desire to renounce the world after the death of

---

5 *apuṇyānām karmaṇāmācaraṇād bhṛtakasya kim prāyaścittam, kāpratti kriyā, kva gatasya śāntiḥ, kīdṛśam jīvitam, kaḥ puruṣābhimānaḥ kim nāmāno vilāsāḥ, kīdṛśī bhogaśraddhā prabalapaṅka iva sarvamādhastannayati dāruṇo dāsaśabdaḥ* ।
– *HC*, p. 224

6 *HC*, p. 223.

7 *śuna iva nijadāraparānmukhasya jaghanya-karmalagnamātmānam tāḍayataḥ … śmaśāna pādapasyeva piśācasya dagdhabhūtyā, paruṣīkṛtān rājavallabhānatasarpataḥ …* ।
– *HC*, pp. 222-24

8 *anatikramaṇavacanaiḥ pradhānasāmantaiḥ vijñāpyamaṇaḥ* ।
– *HC*, p. 178

Prabhākaravardhana, it was *sāmanta*s who were most shocked.[9] It is, therefore, reasonable to presume that the most important decisions of the state were taken more on the advice of the *sāmanta*s rather than the *mantrī*s and the bureaucrats.

The Vardhana civil service was denoted by a number of words, i.e. *rāja-puruṣas*,[10] *amātya*,[11] *kumārāmātya*,[12] *rājavallabhas*,[13] and *liao-shu* and *funchen chih shih* in Chinese.[14] Bāṇa informs us that the royal court had among others "anointed *rājā*s who were *amātyas*". There is hardly any reason to accept D. Devahuti's (1970) view that "in this case at least, *amātya* was a title of honour and not an administrative designation". The word *rājā* during this period denotes the subordinate status of a courtier. There is nothing unnatural to suppose that he, in many cases, was entrusted with administrative responsibilites and this became an integral part of the civil service, which, through the ages, had come to be denoted by the generic term *amātya*.

In the Bānskheṛā and Madhuban Inscriptions of Harṣa, the word *kumārāmātya* occurs along with a number of state functionaries. As Harṣa's adminstrative set-up was almost a true copy of that of the Guptas, it is reasonable to conclude that the official nomenclatures remained the same. Thus, a *kumārāmātya* would mean an *amātya* raised to the status of a prince, as it did in the Gupta period. We may call him a knighted *amātya*. This explains why he gets precedence over the ordinary *uparika* and the *viṣayapati* in aforesaid inscriptions.

---

9 *niḥśvatsu sāmanteṣu* । – *HC*, p. 182

10 *avanipālapuruṣagṛhītasamagrāgramīṇānīyamānopakaraṇa-sambhāram* । – *HC*, p. 142

11 *HC*, p. 181.

12 *HPS*, p. 175 fn. 7, Bāṅskheṛā and Madhuban grants of Harṣa.

13 *paruṣīkṛtān rājaballabhānatasarpataḥ* । – *HC*, p. 222

14 Hsi Yu Chi, V, 3a.

YUVARĀJA

The Vardhanas had a traditional form of monarchical government under which the eldest son normally was the *yuvarāja* who succeeded his father. But it is just possible that at times succession was decided not merely on the basis of age, but also on those of merit and aptitude. According to some scholars, Prabhākaravardhana was inclined towards his younger son Harṣa to succeed him, probably because his elder son Rājyavardhana, being a *saugata*, was not interested in the mundane responsibilities of the government and also because Harṣa was regarded as more promising and competent. Rather than supporting the above contention, the following words of Harṣa dispel all doubts that Rājyavardhana was not the heir-apparent and that Harṣa was planning to supersede him:

> Pray heaven, my brother, when he learns of our father's death … may not … assume two robes of bark or seek a hermitage as a royal sage. … Never may indifference due to transitoriness of things lead him to slight the advances of sovereign glory. … Once arrived here, may he not, when pressed by kings, display a contrary mind.[15]

The last sentence is most significant, because it shows that kings (*sāmanta*s), and certainly not without the approval of Prabhākaravardhana, had already decided in favour of Rājyavardhana's succession. Prabhākaravardhana's last words uttered to Harṣa from his death-bed were meant for Rājyavardhana as well.[16] Harṣa was supposed to assist him in his administration as his heir-apparent. And if at all these words were meant for Harṣa alone, it may alternately be reasonable to presume that Prabhākaravardhana knew of Rājyavardhana's aversion to shoulder the responsibilities of administration as his successor. Whatever be the case, the combined testimony of Yuan Chwang, the *Āryamañjuśrīmūlakalpa* and Harṣa's own records leave us in no doubt that Rājyavardhana did succeed

15 *HC*, pp. 173-74.

16 *HC*, pp. 168-69: "Succeed to this world", is a command too mean for an intending conqueror of both worlds … "support the burden of royalty … Protect the people."

his father without the least hindrance from any quarter. According to the normal practice, it was in the fitness of things that his elder son would succeed Prahbākaravardhana.

The princes were given thorough education, both academic, and military. They were associated with their father's administration. The ailing Prabhākaravardhana had deputed his sons Rājyavardhana and Harṣa to repulse the Hūṇa attack. The very fact that Harṣa later became the famous author of the three well-known Sanskrit dramas, *Nāgānanda*, *Ratnāvalī* and *Priyadarśikā* testifies that he was given education of very high order during his earlier days. The florid signature of Harṣa in the Bāṅskheṛā Inscription proves that he had mastered calligraphy. This is indirectly supported by Bāṇa who refers to florid signatures of the inscription.[17]

PRINCESSES

It is true that the princesses could not succeed their fathers and husbands in the event of their death. The most significant example is that of Rājyaśrī who could not succeed Grahavarmā, her husband, even though he had died issueless. But the Fang-chih records do say that Harṣa was "administering the government in conjunction with his widowed sister".[18]

Rājyaśrī is said to have grown up "daily increasing familiarity with friends, expert in song, dance, etc. and with all accomplishments".[19]

According to the *Life*, Rājyaśrī,

> of great intelligence ... was sitting behind the king ... as she heard the Master of the law extolling the doctrine of the Great Vehicle ...

---

17 *vibhramakṛtahastasthiti* – *HC*, p. 66. It appears that moral values were inculcated in the prince from his childhood. Bāṇa observes that the prince, in the real sense, is one who is not *durvinīta* (indisciplined). – *HC*, p. 181

18 Watters, 1904-05, I, p. 345.

19 *HC*, p. 140.

she was filled with joy and could not cease her praises.[20]

All this speaks of her intellectual taste and training.

RĀJAMAHIṢĪ

The Vedic practice of associating the queens with administrative deliberations as attested by their inclusion in the list of the *ratnin*s was abandoned long ago. However, they continued to enjoy great respectability. Yaśomatī had her own establishment with a retinue of attendants to look after her.

Among them the following deserve special mention:

1. *pratihārī*: She was the doorkeeper supervising the entry of visitors to the harem of her mistress. Bāṇa has given her name as Velā.
2. *mukhya-sakhī*: The queen had her chief female companion of her confidence; she was also known as *priya-sakhī*. Through her the queen could convey her feelings and ideas to those whom she did not directly speak to. It is to be noted that in the case of Rājyaśrī, this office was held by Patralatā.
3. *kañcukī*: He was generally an old man of great trust and kept watch over the entry point of the harem. Several of them manned vital points at the entrances.[21]
4. *dhātreyī*:[22] She was also very close to the queen and was in-charge of her personal beauty parlour, being adept in the art of hair-dressing, make-up, floral decoration, etc.
5. *kātyāyanika*:[23] She was generally an old woman of wide experience and was a personal councillor of the queen in all delicate matters.

---

20 *Life*, p. 176.

21 *kañcukībhirativṛddha iranuvatām* । – *HC*, p. 165

22 *dhātryā ca nijayā prasādhitām* । – *HC*, p. 165

23 *jaratya samstutayā dhāryamāṇām* । – *HC*, pp. 164-65

According to the convention, the chief queen's name also appeared in many of the royal records. For instance, Yaśomatīdevī's name appears along with that of Mahārājādhirāja Prabhākaravardhana in the Madhuban Copper-Plate Inscription. The same inscription contains the names of Mahāsenaguptādevī, Apsarodevī and Vajriṇīdevī as consorts of kings Ādityavardhana, Rājyavardhana I and Naravardhana, respectively. It might have been at the instance of Yaśomatī that her brother had sent his son Bhāṇḍī, aged eight, for his upbringing along with her two sons, Rājyavardhana and Harṣavardhana in the court. Prabhākaravardhana has been shown by Bāṇa as consulting Yaśomatī before he accepted Grahavarmā's proposal for the hand of Rājyaśrī. Beyond these parameters, queens had no role to play in the realm of polity. At any rate, they were not generally associated with administration in any way.

RĀJAPUTRAS

Bāṇa mentions a number of *rājaputra*s living in the court.[24] They were the princes belonging to various friendly independent or subordinate families who were kept by Prabhākaravardhana at his court like his sons. Bāṇa describes their immeasurable grief on the occasion of his patron's illness. One of them was so overwhelmed with grief that he immolated himself. Harṣa brings out in high relief the personal and affectionate relations between his family and *rājaputra*s when, shocked by the incidence of self-immolation, he observed:

> Was my father not his? Was my mother not his mother? Were we not his brothers?[25]

Bāṇa refers to a number of hereditary *kulaputra*s whose fathers and grandfathers were also patronized as *kulaputra*s in the royal court.[26]

*Kulaputra*s, in general, enjoyed a number of privileges.[27] They

---

24 *HC*, pp. 130, 155, 161, 165, 169.

25 *HC*, p. 161.

26 *pitṛpitāmahaparigrahāgatāścirantanāḥ kulaputrāḥ* । – *HC*, p. 238

27 *kliṣṭakārpaṭikakulapupralokamocitaiḥ prasādadānaiḥ* । – *HC*, p. 238

constituted the royal aristrocracy and, though the *Harṣacarita* does not shed detailed light on their utility and functions, it can safely be presumed that they must have been assigned jobs according to their aptitudes and administrative requirements.

The position of Kumāragupta and Mādhavagupta, the Mālava princes, kept at the court by Prabhākaravardhana, seems to have been a bit different from the hereditary *rājaputra*s, being treated by the king and his queen as their virtual sons. The Mālava princes, on the other hand, were described by Prabhākaravardhana as his sons attending companions and not brothers.[28]

SĀMANTAS

The institution of the *sāmanta*s had unprecedented development during the Vardhana period. It is, inter alia, corroborated by Bāṇa's categorization of the *sāmanta*s as *pradhāna-sāmanta*s, *mahā-sāmanta*s, *āpta-sāmanta*s, *sāmanta*s and even *śatru-mahāsāmanta*s and *prati-sāmanta*s.

Puṣpabhūti is said to have forced the *mahā-sāmanta*s to be his taxpayers.[29] The *āpta-sāmanta*s are seen a wailing over the serious illness of Prabhākaravardhana.[30] *Sāmanta*s were shocked to learn about Rājyavardhana's intentions of renouncing the world.[31] Their wives anointed Yaśomatī as the chief queen.[32] Bāṇa has vividly described the plight of the *śatru-mahāsāmanta*s after their defeat, capture or surrender.

They were made to wait for long hours to seek interview with the victorious king.[33] Their sons were held as hostages in the

---

28 *HC*, pp. 138-39.

29 *karādikṛtamahāsāmanta* ı – *HC*, p. 100

30 *santaptāptasāmanta* ı – *HC*, p. 100

31 *niḥśvatsusāmanteṣu* ı – *HC*, p. 182

32 *sevāsambhrāntānantasāmantasīmantinīsamāvarjitajāmbūnada-ghaṭābhiṣekaḥ* ı – *HC*, p. 167

33 *bhujanirjitaiḥśatrumahāsāmantaiḥ samantādāsevya- mānam* ı – *HC*, p. 60

royal court of the victor.[34] The Bāṅskheṛā Copper-Plate Inscription terms Śrīskandagupta as *mahā-sāmanta*. Prabhākaravardhana had despatched Rājyavardhana to fight with the Hūṇas in the company of ministers and *mahā-sāmanta*s.[35] The Aihoḷe Inscription informs us that Harṣa's feet were covered with the rays of the jewels of diadems of a multitude of *sāmanta*s, suggesting thereby that they constituted a powerful part of Harṣa's army.[36] Harṣa's Madhuban Copper-Plate Inscription uses the titles of *sāmanta* and *dūtaka* for one and the same person.[37] Another term for the *sāmanta*s of the enemy was *prati-sāmanta*.[38] The *Kādambarī* (*Kād*) speaks of the anointed *sāmantas*.[39] Some of the powerful *sāmanta*s exercised great influence on the king and they were heard by him with attention.[40] Others were not so fortunate and had to wait for the king's audience with *cowrie*s in hand and sword-blades hanging from their necks.[41] In Rājyaśrī's marriage preparations, "even kings girt up their loins and busied themselves in carrying their decorative work", set as task by their sovereign.[42]

From these accounts regarding the *sāmanta*s, certain inferences can be drawn:

1. It is not necessary, as suggested by D. Devahuti (1970),[43] that the *kulaputra*s were sons of friendly *mahā-sāmanta*s. Howsoever friendly *sāmanta*s might have been, they or their sons were not treated like sons of the king and the queen. On the other

---

34 *pratyagranīrjitasyāstamupagatavato vasantasāmantasaya bālāpatyeṣu* ।
– *HC*, p. 45

35 *HC*, p. 150.

36 *EI*, VI.1.

37 *EI*, VII.22.

38 *HC*, p. 200.

39 *mūrdhābhiṣiktena sāmantalokena* । – *Kād*, pp. 193-94

40 *anatikramaṇīyavacanaiḥ pradhānasāmantaiḥ vijñāpyamānaḥ* ।
– *HC*, p. 178

41 *HC*, p. 60.

42 *HC*, p. 124.

43 *HPS*, p. 165.

hand, Bāṇa has explicitly observed that the *kulaputras* were like the sons of Prabhākara-vardhana and Yaśomatī and like the brothers of Harṣa. The class of *sāmantas* had developed into a cadre like high functionaries of the state. This is how a *sāmanta* was a *mahā-pramātāra*[44] and another a *dūtaka*.[45]

2. *Sāmantas* had their own gradations in accordance with their importance, e.g. *pradhāna sāmanta, mahā-sāmanta, āpta-sāmanta* and *sāmanta*. The difference between a *śatru-sāmanta* and a *prati-sāmanta* is not clear. It is just possible that a *śatru-sāmanta* had no personal enemity with the victorious king and was taken to be hostile, because he was in the service of the enemy king. The *prati-sāmanta*, on the other hand, might have personally and actively against the victorious king.
3. The greatest of the *sāmantas* enjoyed great power and respectability. Some of them were even called *mūrdhābhiṣikta* like the kings.[46] Other's counsel was hardly ignored.[47]
4. The lesser ones had to perform not so respectable functions, such as holding *cowries* and acting as doorkeepers.
5. The obligations of *sāmantas* towards the king were similar to those mentioned in the Allahabad Pillar Inscription of Samudragupta, e.g. *sarvakaradāna, ājñākaraṇa, praṇāma* and *āgamana*. Very often they had to keep their sons and wives also in the royal palace. They also rendered military assistance to the king and sometimes held important offices in the civil service.
6. Yuan Chwang informs us that ministers and officials each were

---

44 Bāṅskheṛā Copper-Plate Inscription.

45 Madhuban Copper-Plate Inscription.

46 *Kād*, pp. 193-94.

47 *anatikramaṇavacanaḥ* । – *HC*, p. 180

allotted appropriate share of land for their maintenance.[48] It is reasonable to assume that the subordinated *sāmanta*s were also granted land in lieu of their services.

*Council of sāmanta*s: When the *Harṣacarita* avers that the advice of some of the *sāmanta*s could not be ignored,[49] it suggests that they had deliberative functions. In other words, there was a council of ministers which advised the king. As rightly suggested by Devahuti (1970), such a council existed at Kannauj, the Maukharī capital.

To quote Watters (1904-05), "The statesmen of Kannauj, on the advice of their leading man Bani, invited Harṣavardhana ... to become their sovereign" after the death of their king Grahavarmā. Devahuti (1970) seems to be right to sugggest that the Chinese word *liao-shu*, which has been taken to mean "statesmen" may as well mean *sāmanta*s of the council. At other places also, the *mahā-sāmanta*s have been put in the company of ministers. For instance, Prabhākaravardhana had ordered experienced ministers and the *mahā-sāmanta*s to accompany Rājyavardhana in his expedition against the Hūṇas.[50] Here the *mahā-sāmanta*s seem to have been the members of the council of *sāmanta*s. The external *āsthāna-maṇḍapa* was meant for the king, the ministers and *sāmanta*s for counselling the king.[51] This too indicates deliberative functions of some of the *sāmanta*s.

MINISTERS

The Vardhanas had ministers to advise them on all important matters. The *Harṣacarita*[52] uses the words *mantrī*, *saciva* and *amātya* for a minister. But as discussed earlier, the words *mantrī* and *saciva* are synonyms. They are sometimes called *amātya*s, because they were drawn from the pool of civil service, technically denoted by the

---

48 Watters, 1904-05, I, p. 177, Beal I, p. 88.

49 *HC*, p. 178.

50 *HC*, p. 150.

51 *HC*, p. 194.

52 *HC*, p. 199.

term *amātya*. In the *āsthāna-maṇḍapa* of Śūdraka, as indicated by the *Kādambarī*, were present the *amātya*s also. They must have included the *mantrī*s and the civil service. Separately also, *Harṣacarita* mentions the *saciva*s.[53] Yet at another place experienced *mantrī*s are shown sitting tight-lipped in the Candra-Śālikā. If the Chinese term *liao-shu* means *sāmanta*s, the other term *fu-chen-chih shih* may mean ministers.[54] Since the preceding Gupta kings had their council of ministers, it must have served as a model for the Vardhana kings. But its nature, scope, number and functions are not exactly known to us from any source.

PUROHITA

It is not certain whether the *purohita* was the member of the council of ministers. Most probably he was not. But he continued to be the king's guide on important religious matters. Bāṇa describes him as performing rituals of the birth of the princes. Fear and anxiety were writ large on his face on the occasion of serious illness of Prabhākaravardhana. Before marching against Śaśāṅka, Harṣa worshipped the priest who blessed by sprinkling water over his head. It appears by the time of the Vardhanas, the royal priest had ceased to be a political advisor or a military leader.

Different from the priest were the *gaṇaka*s, also called *daivacintaka*s in the royal service. Bāṇa makes special mention of Tāraka, the *gaṇaka*, who was well-versed in astrological science. They used to make forecasts by studying the positions of planets and recommended propitiatory rituals.

ROYAL PHYSICIAN

He commanded great respect in the palace. Bāṇa refers to Suṣeṇa, who was the royal physician of Prabhākaravardhana. The doorkeepers bowed before him in respect as he made his entry into the inner apartment of the king. Rasāyana, another royal physician

---

53 *HC*, p. 130.

54 Hsi Yu Chi, V, 3a, Beal I, p. 211, has translated these two terms as "ministers and chief ministers and magistrates".

by heredity, has been described as the master of *aṣṭāṅga* Āyurveda.[55]

PRATIHĀRA

*Pratihāra*s were the chamberlains and were well-versed in the etiquette of the court-life. The very fact that the royal palace housed the residential quarters of the *pratihāra* shows the latter's importance. We are told by Bāṇa that when Bhāṇḍī came to seek interview with Harṣa, he was housed in the *pratihāra-bhavana*.[56]

*Pratihāra*s manned the entrances to the inner and outer parts of the palace. Haṁsavega, the envoy of Bhāskaravarmā, had to contact the *pratihāra* at the gate to inform Harṣa of his arrival.[57] They prevented people from making noise which might disturb the occupants of the palace, specially the ailing ones.[58] *Pratihāra*s also carried errands. Harṣa ordered his *pratihāra* to convey his desire to *gajasādhanādhikṛta* Skandagupta that he wanted to see him. It was the *pratihāra*s who made villagers stand on the road at intervals to guide the marching soldiers to the right directions. The doorway of the *dhavalagṛha* of the palace was guarded by several cane-holding *pratihāra*s.[59] They could recognize kings and *sāmanta*s by their different crowns and ribbons. The *rājakula* was guarded by a special class of *pratihāra*s, called the *antara-pratihāra*s.[60]

*Pratihāra*s had their own hierarchy. The head of the *pratihāra*s was called *mahā-pratihāra*. Over *mahā-pratihāra*s was placed the *dauvārika* who held the golden cane as the symbol of his authority.[61] It was the *dauvārika* who looked after gifts and tributes by the king.[62] The female counterpart of the *pratihāra* was *pratihārī*.

55 *HC*, p. 160.

56 *HC*, p. 226.

57 *HC*, p. 214.

58 *pratihāranivāvananibhṛtaniḥśabdaparijane* । – *HC*, p. 225

59 *HC*, p. 155.

60 *HC*, p. 60.

61 *mahāpratihārāṇāmanantaraḥ* । – *HC*, p. 62

62 *rājadauvārikotanīyamānānekanṛpopāyanam* । – *HC*, p. 142

Besides the *pratihārī*,[63] the other person posted in the female department was the *kañcukī*, always an old man.

MAHĀSĀNDHIVIGRAHIKA

He was the minister of peace and war and as such was one of the top officers of the bureaucracy. This post was held by Avantī during the reign of Harṣa. He has been termed by Bāṇa as *mahā-sāndhivigrahādhikṛta*. On orders from Harṣa, he has demanded of independent kings to surrender to his master. It can be presumed that he had a number of *sāndhivigrahādhikṛtas* under him. All of them must have been well-versed with the principles of *maṇḍala* theory as also with the *ṣaḍāṅga* theory involving all matters of *sandhi, vigraha, āsana, yāna, saṁśraya* and *dvaidhī-bhāva.*

SENĀPATI

The king used to lead the army in person in important wars. But he had a *senāpati* (commander-in-chief) to look after the minutest details of the army including its recruitments, training, upkeep, weaponry and discipline. Bāṇa informs us that Siṁhanāda was Harṣa's *senāpati*. He is said to have been Prabhākaravardhana's friend. He was old. Bāṇa has waxed eloquent in describing his qualities. His chest bore the scars created by weapons. He had to his credit numerous victories. He had collected enormous wealth for the royal treasury and had shouldered the burden of his master. Many wicked kings were brought under control by him. He was the family priest of the brave.[64]

BALĀDHIKṚTA

Bāṇa refers to Bhāṇḍī as the son of Yaśomatī's brother. He was

---

63 *HC*, p. 130.

64 *niśitaśastraṭaṅkakoṭikuṭṭitabahubṛhadvarnākṣarapanktinirantaratayā sasakalasamaravijayaparvagaṇanāmiva kurvan parvata iva pādacārī abhramanenānādaraśrīsamākarṣaṇavidhrameṇa mandaramiva mandayan ... vāhinīnāyakamaryādānuvartanen-īśvarabhārodvahanaghṛstapṛṣṭhatavyā harabṛṣabhamiva hasanniva* । – *HC*, pp. 189-90

sent to the royal court at the age of eight and had grown up there in the company of Rājyavardhana and Harṣavardhana.[65] He had accompanied Rājyavardhana with 10,000 cavalry, on his expedition against Mālavarāja.[66] After the treacherous murder of Rājyavardhana at the hands of Śaśāṅka, it was Bhāṇḍī who had brought Rājyavardhana's army as also the captured army of the enemy and the booty of war back to the capital. Covered with injuries on his chest, he looked haggard at the loss of his master.[67] It was again Bhāṇḍī who had informed Harṣa of the capture of Kānyakubja by Gupta and Rājyaśrī's flight towards the Vindhyas. On all accounts he seems to have been a military commander, probably a *balādhikr̥ta*, though this designation has not been used for him by Bāṇa. Taking into consideration the old age of the Senāpati Siṁhanāda and numerous wars one after the other in different directions, both Rājyavardhana and Harṣavardhana must have depended upon his military services immensely. Yuan Chwang mentions him as "the great minister Po-ni", whose power and reputation were high and of much weight and he guided the "ministers and officials" of Kannauj in favour of Harṣa's succession.[68]

Bāṇa mentions a number of other military functionaries. Kuntala was the head of the cavalry.[69] Skandagupta was the head of war elephants.[70] The Bāṅskheṛā Copper-Plate Inscription of Harṣa mentions him as *dūtaka, mahāpramātāra, mahā-sāmanta* Śrī Skandagupta. It simply shows that he held more than one office. That the Bāṅskheṛā Inscription refers to the *hastyāśva- vijayaskandhāvāra* also testifies that the royal army had separate columns of war elephants and horses. Horses were put under the direct supervision

---

65 *HC*, p. 136.

66 *HC*, p. 184.

67 *HC*, p. 266.

68 Hsi Yu Chi, V, 3b.

69 *kuntalam nāma br̥hadaśvavāram rājyavardhanasya prasādabhūmim* । – *HC*, p. 186

70 *gajasādhanādhikr̥ta* । – *HC*, p. 186

of the *aśvapālas*.[71] Similarly, the camels were put under the charge of the *uṣṭrapālas*.[72] Elephants were trained by officers called *mahāmātras*[73] and *adhoraṇa*.[74] Elephants meant for carrying supplies were looked after by *nīlivākas*.[75] There were *ibhabhiṣagvaras* who treated elephants for their ailments.[76] *Pāṭipatis*[77] referred to by Bāṇa seem to have been superintendents of military barracks. Military camps were looked after by the *cāṭaka*.[78] Ordinary soldiers were known as *cāṭas* and *bhaṭas*.[79] The Madhuban and Bāṅskheṛā Copper-Plate Inscriptions speak of boats as well besides horses and elephants.[80] It stands to reason that Harṣa had a separate *nāvādhyakṣa* for his navy.

About the army Yuan Chwang has the following descriptions to make:

> the men of valour are selected to be warriors. The profession is hereditary so that they have been able to exhaust the art of war. When they are garrisoned, they guard palaces. When there is war, they act as a brave vanguard.[81]

But while Yuan Chwang refers to chariots in Harṣa's army, Bāṇa does not mention them at all. The truth is that chariots had ceased to be a regular part of the army since long.

POLICE

As in the Gupta period so also in the Vardhana period, the *mahābalādhikṛta* must have been the head of the police force. The

---

71 *HC*, p. 152.

72 *HC*, p. 160.

73 *HC*, p. 196.

74 *HC*, p. 196.

75 *bhāṇḍāgāravahanabāhyamānabahunīlīvāhike* । – *HC*, p. 204

76 *HC*, p. 172.

77 *HC*, p. 204.

78 *HC*, p. 204.

79 *HC*, p. 204.

80 *EI*, I, 72, IV, 210.

81 S. Beal I, p. 82, Watters 1904-05, I, p. 171.

*sthānapāla*s who manned *caukī*s were probably policemen.[82] So were *araṇyapāla*s (forest guards) and *nāgavanavidhipāla*s (guards of the elephant forests).[83] *Cāṭa* meant a policeman as also a soldier.[84] The *daṇḍī*s wielding rods and controlling crowds were obviously a special class of the police force.[85] The *dauḥssadha-sādhanika* may be taken to mean the superintendent of villages, as suggested by R.G. Basak,[86] but since he needed force to perform his duties, he is likely to have been drawn from the police force. Bāṇa refers to *śarīra-paricārakas* or *aṅga-rakṣaka*s (king's bodyguards) as *maula*,[87] which coupled with the above-quoted observations of Yuan Chwang attests to the hereditary character of the greater part of the police and the military force. The palace bodyguards were also known by the general term *rakṣīpuruṣa*s. They were especially employed to ensure the safety of Harṣa during his childhood. Kankati, the personal body-guard of Prabhākaravardhana too must have been a very alert police officer. He is said to have been well-equipped.[88]

DŪTA

*Dūta*s played an important role in the Vardhana administration. They were either envoys or messengers performing multifarious duties. Those who were entrusted with the task of carrying messages were called *lekhahāraka*s and *dīrghadhvaga*s. Mekhalaka was such a messenger sent to fetch Bāṇa to the royal court. As per practice, he had fastened the letter containing the message on his head. Bāṇa also refers to the *dūta*s coming from different countries.[89] They belong to the category of the envoys. It was through a *dūta* that Grahavarmā, the Maukharī king of Kannauj, had sought from

---

82 *HC*, p. 205.

83 *HC*, p. 196.

84 *HC*, p. 205.

85 *HC*, p. 208.

86 *EI*, XII, 43, 141.

87 *rakṣipuruṣaśāstrapañjaramadhyabate*। – *HC*, p. 134

88 *HC*, p. 155.

89 *sarvadeśāntarāgataiḥ dūtamaṇḍalaiḥ upāsyamāḥ*। – *HC*, p. 60

Prabhākaravardhana the hand of Rājyaśrī in marriage.[90] Kuraṅgaka was the *dīrghadhvaga* who came to Harṣa to deliver to him the disturbing news of Prabhākaravardhana's serious illness. The blue ribbon round his head had a letter under it.[91] Even the guards of forests had *dūta*s under them to send messages in time of need or help.[92]

Haṁsavega, on the other hand, was an envoy sent by Bhāskaravarmā with a message of proposed friendly alliance with Harṣa.[93] Bāṇa has used two other words – *sañcāraka* and *sarvagata*.[94] They might have combined in them the functions of a messenger and a spy.

The Bāṅskheṛā Inscription of Harṣa has described Skandagupta as *dūtaka*, *mahāpramātāra* and *mahā-sāmanta*, all in one. *Dūtaka* did not belong to the ordinary category of the *dūta*s. He was the central officer who conveyed to local officers the king's order regarding some land grant. There was no separate post of a *dūtaka*. His task could be performed by any state officer chosen by the king.

Territorial Divisions

The Bāṅskheṛā Inscription of Harṣa mentions following divisions:

(1) *grāma*, (2) *paṭhaka*, (3) *viṣaya*, and (4) *bhukti*.

The Madhuban Inscription of Harṣa mentions only:

(1) *grāma*, (2) *viṣaya*, and (3) *bhukti*.

The *grāma* (village) was traditionally the lowest unit of administration. Bāṇa speaks of the *mahattaras*[95] who were the elders of the village running the *grāma-pariṣad*, as was the case in the Gupta

---

90 *HC*, p. 141.

91 *lekhagarbhayānīlīrāgamacakarucā cīracīrikayā racitamuṇḍamālakam* ।
– *HC*, p. 151

92 *nāgavanavīthīpālādūtavṛndaiḥ* । – *HC*, p. 196

93 *HC*, p. 214.

94 *HC*, p. 35.

95 *HC*, p. 212.

period. He also refers to the *grāmākṣapaṭalika* who was the counterpart of the modern village *paṭavārī* and kept all records of the village administration.[96] He was the same as mentioned in the Gayā Seal of Samudragupta as *grāmākṣapaṭalādhikṛta*. As in the Gupta period, so also in the Vardhana period, there must have been a *grāmika* or *grāmeyaka* or *grāmādhyakṣa* heading the *grāma-pariṣad*. The *pariṣad* had a number of clerks called *karaṇī*s who normally prepared the revenue records.[97] However, the villagers did not feel as safe as they used to do during the Gupta or Mauryan period. Their cultivation was generally damaged by the marching armies.[98] They were forced by the *pratihāra*s to keep standing by the roadside to guide official marchers.[99]

The *viṣaya* was a district. It is reasonable to suppose that in imitation of the Gupta district administration, the Vardhana districts too had a *viṣaya-pariṣad* under a *viṣayapati*. The Bāṅskheṛā Inscription of Harṣa[100] informs us that this record was prepared under orders of the *mahākṣapaṭalādhikaraṇadhikṛta* Bhāna. It is thus obvious that the district had an office of the *mahākṣapaṭalika* who kept all records of the sale and purchase of the village land.

ADHIKARAṆA

It was the technical term for his office. It can be presumed that the *mahākṣapaṭalika*, the same as *mahākṣapaṭalādhikṛta*, had a number of *akṣapaṭalika*s under him at district and village levels. The *pustapāla*s must have continued their traditional job of keeping official registers. This is corroborated by Yuan Chwang's account that

> official documents (*nīla-piṭa*), containing good and bad, public calamity and good fortune, were maintained by officials.[101]

---

96 *HC*, p. 203.

97 *HC*, p. 203.

98 *HC*, p. 212.

99 *puraḥ pravṛtta pratihāragṛhyamāṇagrāmīṇaparamparaprakapitapraguṇa-vartmā* ।
– *HC*, p. 152

100 *EI*, IV, 211.

101 *Life*, p. 188.

The *Life* records that Harṣa had ordered *mahattaras* to accompany Yuan Chwang on his return journey to China. He had given to them recommendatory letters for the rulers of different countries to ensure the comfort and safety of the pilgrim.

The *mahattaras* were the elders of the district as also of the village. They were members of the *viṣaya pariṣad*. Other members of the *pariṣad* might have been the *nagara-śreṣṭhi*, the *sārthavāha*, the *prathama-kulika* and the *prathama-kāyastha*, as was the case with the Gupta District Boards.

The territorial unit of *paṭhaka* seems to have been sometimes created between the village and the district for administrative reasons. A number of villagers must have been kept under it. However, we do not know its exact administrative set up.

The Vardhana empire was divided into several *bhuktis*. The combined testimony of the Bāṅskheṛā and Madhuban Inscriptions place *rājasthānīya*, *kumārāmātya* and *uparika* before *viṣayapati*. This may indicate that the first three officers were superior to the *viṣayapati*. The Mandasor Inscription of Yaśodhavarman (533-34 CE) has to add that the *rājasthānīya* had many *deśas* under his control.[102] Under the Guptas *deśa* indicated a province of great importance like Saurāṣṭra.[103] Our conclusion is that the more important provinces (*bhukti-deśa*) were entrusted to the care of the special class of governors called *rājasthānīyas*.

Kṣemendra's *Loka-Prakāśa*[104] defines a *rājasthānīya* as "one who carries out the object of protecting subjects and sheltering them". This definition will bring *rājasthānīya* very close to a *goptā*, a term used for a governor according to Gupta records.

It may be presumed that the term *uparika* was assumed by the common run of governors. The word *bhogapati* was also used by them.

---

102 *CII*, III, p. 152.

103 *sarveṣu deśeṣu vidhāya goptṛn … sañcintayāmāsa bahuprakāram* ।
– Jūnāgaṛh Inscription of Skandagupta

104 *sitakusumavilipanavasanasatkṛtaiḥ sūtradhāraiḥ* । – *HC*, p. 142

The term *kumārāmātya* is generic in character and denotes those officials of bureaucracy who had won the status of a *kumāra* by virtue of their proven merit and loyalty. Thus, a *kumārāmātya* could be assigned to any high office including that of a governor. But he was not necessarily always a governor.

Bāṇa has given an account of the forest-dwellers who had their own settlements. The Vindhya region had such a settlement of the Śabaras.[105] The settlement and its neighbouring areas had rich forests. So the government had employed *vanapālas* (forest-guards) to prevent unauthorized wood-cutting.[106]

The Vardhana administration was carried on by several departments. A departmental head was known as *adhyakṣa*.[107] In the absence of any clear evidence, it is difficult to agree with Devahuti (1970) that Harṣa had a private secretary, generally known as *rahasi-niyukta*.[108] More likely, the king's oral orders were conveyed by *mahā-pratihāras* and *mahā-sāmantas* around him. Harṣa seems to have dispensed with the old office of *rahasi-niyukta* on account of a host of other reliable functionaries around him.

Among lesser employees Bāṇa mentions *āroha* (mahout),[109] *leśikas* (feeders for elephants),[110] *sūtradharas* (artisans),[111] *ālepakas* (masons expert in plastering),[112] *tayākarmaṇikas* (empoyees-in-charge of drinking water),[113] *cāmara-grāhīs* (cowrie-holders),[114] *paurogava* (chief cook),[115] *vastra-karmantika* (officer-in-charge of

105 *HC*, pp. 227-30.

106 *HC*, p. 227.

107 *Loka-Prakāśa*, ch. IV.

108 *yathādhikāramādikhadadhyakṣam* । – *HC*, p. 227

109 *HPS*, p. 176.

110 *HC*, p. 67.

111 *HC*, p. 65.

112 *HC*, p. 181.

113 *Kātyāyana*, p. 680.

114 *Amar* 2.8.5.

115 Kātyāyana, quoted by Aparārka, p. 599.

textile manufacturing),[116] *kaṭaka-kadambaka* (foot-soldier),[117] *karpatī* (attendants on elephants),[118] *niṣādins* (employees who took elephants for a walk),[119] *vārikas* (officers looking after personal goods of the king),[120] *kārmāḥ* (employees in general),[121] *vanapāla* (same as *araṇyapāla*)[122] and *sevaka* (servant).[123]

Not much light is thrown on the judicial system of the Vardhana period. If Kātyāyana is taken to be nearer to Harṣa chronologically, he mentions *prāḍvivāka*[124] as a judge. The *Amarakośa* defines him as a legal officer.[125] That the king who was the Supreme Court of the country could not transgress the traditional sources of law is attested by Kātyāyana in the following words:

> If a king decided (a case) by his own fiat where there is a text ... it causes ruin to the people ... but in the absence of Smṛti texts, he should carry out (judicial administration) according to the usage.[126]

Great care was taken to see that only a right type of person was appointed as a judge. Kātyāyana has it that he should be high born, just, restrained, steady, religious and industrious.[127]

R.S. Tripathi would make us believe that the term *mahāpramātāra* occurring in the Madhuban Inscription of Harṣa was probably

---

116 Kātyāyana, *HDS*, III, p. 271.

117 *HK*, p. 140.

118 *HC*, p. 78.

119 *HSI*, Yu Chi, II, 10a.

120 *Kād*, pp. 61-62.

121 Same as *karmakāra* (51, I.165).

122 *HC*, p. 227.

123 Bāṅskheṛā and Madhuban Inscriptions.

124 *HPS*, p. 181.

125 *Amar*, 2.8.5.

126 Kātyāyana quoted by Aparārka, p. 599.

127 *History of Dharmaśāstra*, III, p. 271.

entrusted with justice.[128] Bāṇa[129] uses the term *vākya-vidam-adhikaraṇa-vicāraḥ*. Here the *adhikaraṇa* is definitely a court of justice. Since there is hardly any clear evidence that the profession of lawyers had come into vogue, it is untenable to assume that the *vākya-vidam* stood for lawyers. However, the term can safely be taken to mean judicial officers, thoroughly knowing the judicial procedure.

For the expenditure of the state Yuan Chwang says:

> royal land was divided into four categories: one for the expenses of the state and ceremonial worship, one for the endowment of ministers, one for rewarding the clever, the learned and the talented, and one for requiring merit through sustenance of heretics.

This observation of the Chinese pilgrim, coupled with the fact that Harṣa had made many land-grants, suggests that payment was generally made in the form of land.

But certain job-doers were probably paid in cash as would appear from the following statement:

> Official building does not rely on Corvee, but people are rewarded according to the work they accomplish. For the purpose of manning defences and military expeditions as well as standing guard on the royal tents, appropriate numbers are invited to join the army and there is reward to be collected by those who join.[130]

Bāṇa's *Kādambarī* cautions the king and his civil servants against the temptations that they may fall into. To quote it,

> Only weak and foolish monarchs are taken in by the flattery of roguish courtiers. By looking upon himself as having alighted on

---

128 *HK*, p. 140.

129 *HC*, p. 78.

130 Hsi yu Chi, II.10a (see *HPS*, p. 205).

earth as a divine being with a super-human destiny, though in reality subject to all mortal conditions, the stupid king only wins the contempt of his people.[131]

[131] *Kād*, pp. 81-82.

9

Conclusion

THE existence of the civil service in Ancient India is indicated by a number of technical words, occurring in literature and inscriptions such as *amātya, ratnin, tīrtha, mahāmātra, adhikr̥tāḥ, narāḥ, bhr̥tya, rāja-bhāra-niyuktāḥ, sahāya, rājapuruṣa, rājayukta, rājopasevī, rājopajīvī, nr̥pasevī, kumārāmātya*, etc. Functionally, they can be classified under two heads – *dhī-saciva*s (councillors) and *karma-saciva*s (executive officers). All undertakings of the state originated from the civil service – *amātyamūlāḥ samārambhāḥ*. As early as the Vedic period, it was commonly realized that if the civil service was vigorous and energetic, the state was also vigorous and energetic. This explains why great care was taken to select the best talent of the country to man the civil service. Candidates were put to various tests, namely, *dharmopadhā, arthopadhā, kamopadhā*, and *bhayopadhā* before they were recruited to different departments of the state. With the passage of time, the civil service became very numerous as is indicated by Kauṭilya's long list of functionaries. Of the seven castes mentioned by Megasthenes, as many as three comprised the civil service. It is significant that the ancient Indian polity was dominated by the civil element rather than the military element. This is the reason why the *purohita* was given precedence over the *senāpati* and the king was advised to follow the former as a student would follow his teacher and a servant his master.

It is also not always true that appointments were made on caste considerations. The *ratnin*s were representatives of different segments of society. According to the *Mahābhārata*, Vidura, a śūdra, was highly respected by the royal family and his counsels were listened to with great attention. The same work informs us that among the thirty-seven *amātya*s, three were śūdras. Historically speaking, Mauryas did not hesitate to appoint a vaiśya (Puṣyagupta) and even a Greek (Tuṣāspa) as their governors.

Like monarchy, ancient Indian Civil Service tended to be hereditary. The *Mahābhārata* uses the word *maulaḥ* for the *amātya*s, suggesting that many of them held hereditary posts. The phrases *pitr̥paitāmaḥ* and *anvaya-prāpta-sācivya* also indicate the growing tendency of the Indian Civil Service being hereditary. This tendency grew more and more predominant with the gradual feudalization of the government machinery. Though the Mauryan period does not indicate hereditary character of the civil service, it is much in evidence during the Gupta and Vardhana periods.

Ancient history was characterized by frequent warfares. Thus, necessitated by the requirements of the time, civil servants were trained in martial art. The *Atharvaveda* describes the priest Aṅgiras as destroying the rival army. The *Rāmāyaṇa* speaks of the ministers as *śāstrajñas*.

The principle of "one man, one post" did not commend itself to the ancient Indian rulers. There was also no separation of executive functions from the judicial functions. Such high officers of the Mauryan period as the *samāhartā*, the *rājuka*, the *nāgaraka* and even the *sthānika*, *gopa* and *grāmika* were magistrates, police officers and revenue officers, all in one.

At times, one and the same officer held more than one post simultaneously. The hereditary character of the civil service and the holding of more than one office by a civil servant are most noticeable in the Gupta period. Dhruvabhūti and his son Hariṣeṇa as also Parṇadatta and his son Cakrapālita were the employees of the Guptas. Hariṣeṇa was a *kumārāmātya*, *sāndhivigrahika* and *khādyatpākika* at one and the same time. The multiplicity of offices concentrated in a single person might have occurred during the Gupta period for a variety of reasons:

1. Paucity of able civil servants,
2. Government's effort to effect economy in administration, and
3. Proven reliability of certain civil servants.

The civil service up to the Mauryan period was, by and large, paid in cash. However, certain categories of civil servants came to be paid both in cash and land grants during the Gupta period. The Vardhana period saw the unprecedented practice of paying civil servants in the form of land grants.

The ancient Indian Civil Service, at least the most important of them like the prime minister and the *senāpati* were provided residential quarters at the capital. They enjoyed a variety of perks and privileges. They were given advance increments and promotions for meritorious work. In times of their special need, such as marriages, funerals and festive occasions, the government gave them special financial assistance. During famines and droughts also, they received help from the government. Though they were kept on probation in the beginning, once their merit and loyalty were proved, they were made permanent. They could not be arrested while on duty for non-payment of debts. If they died in harness, their dependents were well looked after and some of them were even absorbed in the government services. The high ones were authorized to disburse salaries of their subordinates and effect their promotions, demotions and transfers on the spot to avoid red-tapism.

Kauṭilya had noticed the existence of certain corrupt practices in the civil service, especially in its departments of revenue. He could count as many as forty ways of misappropriation of government money by revenue officers. To detect and punish such corrupt practices, a system of periodical checking and cross-checking was devised. Deterrent punishments were also prescribed. However, Kauṭilya speaks of officers known for their honesty, integrity and loyalty and recommends rewards for their outstanding work.

Bāṇa was also critical of sycophants in central services surrounding the king and had advised him to beware of them.

In the *rājāyatta* state, the vulnerable position of the civil servants was vividly described by Bāṇa. That they had to be at the mercy of their master and were put up with uncomplimentary situations is certain. But in the *ubhayāyatta* and *sacivāyatta* states, the civil service was highly respected. In fact, nothing important in the state could take place without the initiation, concurrence and cooperation of the civil service. While enjoying great power, civil servants had to observe a code of conduct and decorum towards, and in the presence of, the king.

Many designations of the ancient Indian Civil Servants are preserved which have their near counterparts even today. To mention only a few:

1.	*Mukhyāmātya*	Prime Minister
2.	A group of three four *mantrīs*	Cabinet
3.	*Mantrī-pariṣad*	Council of Ministers
4.	*Sāndhivigrahika*	Minister of External Affairs
5.	*Mahābhāṇḍāgārika*	Minister of the Department of Supplies
6.	*Raṇabhāṇḍāgārika*	Officer-in-charge of Military Stores
7.	*Mahādaṇḍanāyaka*	Director General of Police
8.	*Mahākṣapaṭalika*	Accountant General
9.	*Mahāsenāpati*	Commander-in-chief of the Army
10.	*Samāhartā*	Collector General
11.	*Kośādhyakṣa*	Chief Treasury Officer
12.	*Sannidhātā*	Chief Revenue Officer
13.	*Rājuka*	Chief Land Surveyor

14.	*Uparika*	Commissioner
15.	*Goptā, rāṣṭrīya rājasthānīya*	Rājyapāla
16.	*Viṣayapati*	District Magistrate
17.	*Nagara-vyāvahārika, paura-vyāvaharika*	City Judge
18.	*Nagarādhyakṣa*	Nagara-praśāsaka
19.	*Grāmika, grāmaṇī, grāmeyaka, grāmādhyakṣa*	Sarpañca
20.	*Prāḍvivāka*	Chief Justice
21.	*Nyāyika, dharmāsanādhikṛta*	Judge
22.	*Vyavahāranirṇetā*	Civil Judge
23.	*Amātya, kumārāmātya, rājapuruṣa*	Civil Service
24.	*Dūta*	Diplomat
25.	*Spaṣa, cara, gūḍhapuruṣa*	Spy
26.	*Bandhanāgārādhikārī*	Jailor
27.	*Adhyakṣa*s	Heads of Departments
28.	*Sarvādhyakṣa*	Chief Secretary

While dealing with the Vedic bureaucracy, scholars have mentioned only a few civil servants. But a close scrutiny of hymns reveals a fairly developed civil service. If Sāyaṇa's commentary on the *Ṛgveda* is relied upon, we may be tempted to believe that even the *pradhānāmātya* (prime minister) had come into existence. At any rate, the *Yajurveda* clearly speaks of a minister (*mantrī*). While the words *rājanya* and *kṣatra* generally meant the kṣatriya class, sometimes they denoted the civil service. The major part of it was drawn from the kṣatriya class. At the lowest level of the village, *vrājapati* seems to have meant the leader of the village militia. The existence of the police is suggested by the words *jīvagṛbha* and *gopa*.

There are indications in the *Atharvaveda* that night-watchmen were also employed. Terms *gaṇa, varūtha* and *anīka* may mean the units of the army. Great importance was attached to the office of the *sthapati* who seems to have been the head of the department of creative arts. The *Aitareya Brāhmaṇa* speaks of the *ratnin*s as well as *saciva*s. It is likely that the *ratnin*s were the forerunners of the council of ministers, while the *saciva*s were ministers whom the king consulted daily.

During the Vedic period, suffixes *pati* and *pa* added to certain words came to denote a number of civil servants such as *gaṇapati, vrājapati, sabhāpati, sthapati, vanapa, hastipa, aśvapa*, etc.

The difference between the *rājāyatta* state and the *sacivāyatta* state is well brought out by the *Rāmāyaṇa*. While Rāvaṇa gave scant respect to the advice of his ministers, Daśaratha abided by their advice on all important issues. So great was the authority of Daśaratha's ministers that Sumantra, one of them, could afford even queen Kaikeyī to be rebuked for her misdeeds.

That the sons of the ministers were also groomed for future responsibilities is attested by the *Rāmāyaṇa* when it says that as many as seven sons of the ministers of Rāvaṇa were killed by Hanumān. The Epic gives an additional information that the ministers were trained in martial art (*śastrajña*). In the *Rāmāyaṇa* the prime minister is called *mantrī-śreṣṭha* and *mantrī-pati*. For the first time the eighteen *tīrtha*s comprising the civil service has been referred to by the *Rāmāyaṇa*. When the Epic speaks of the *purohita* and the *amātya* in the same breath, it simply suggests that technically the *purohita* was not an *amātya*, though he was consulted on all important matters by virtue of his erudition. The army was divided into units. It is suggested by the word *bhāgaśaḥ*. Diplomatic envoys enjoyed certain immunities. However, bitter their message might be, they could not be slain. However, in the opinion of Vibhīṣaṇa, his limbs could be mutilated, head shaven or body stamped with hot iron in certain cases. Though the *Rāmāyaṇa* speaks of *sandhi-vigraha*, the post of the *sāndhivigrahika* had not come into vogue. Matters of peace and war appear to have been looked after by the *senāpati*. It is probable that the construction of the *narendra-mārga* from Ayodhyā to the Gaṅgā might suggest the existence of the Public Works Department, having *vartma-karmāṇi-kovidāḥ* in it. Nala seems to have acted as the leader of the advance party of the marching army. A class of officers known as *yukta*s find mention in the *Rāmāyaṇa* for the first time.

The *Mahābhārata* also refers to the ministers as trained soldiers. The *mantrī-pariṣad* of the *Mahābhārata* included the representatives of all the *varṇa*s, including the śūdras. Vidura, though a śūdra, was highly respected for his wise counsel. *Balamukhya*s would mean commanders of units. *Adhi-senāpati* denoted the commander-in-chief, if the word *senāpati* was used for an ordinary commander. Significantly, the *Mahābhārata* uses the word *mantrī-mukhyān* in the plural. In that case they might mean the senior ministers. However, words *rājāmātya* and *pratyanantara* might stand for the prime minister. It is to be noted that the *Mahābhārata* uses *pratihāra* in singular and *dvārapāla*s in plural. This shows that the latter worked under the former. The employees of the *Mahābhārata* period were paid *vetana* as well *bhakta*. Interestingly enough, the *Mahābhārata*, for the first time, lays down a code of conduct for the civil servants.

The Mauryan civil service was unprecedented in its organization. For the first time, civil servants were graded as top ones, middle ones and average ones. For the first time again, the principle of specialization was introduced in service. The *tīrtha*s constituted the top brass of civil servants. The *mantrī*, heading the list of *tīrtha*s, might mean the prime minister assisted by his own team of council of ministers. Kauṭilya has put greatest premium on merit and proper qualifications in matters of appointments. He totally rejected Bharadvāja's extreme opinion that the king should not consult any minister for fear of the disclosure of secrets. It is he who has made a clear distinction between the ministers and the council of ministers. While the ministers formulated policies, the council of ministers, working as the secretariat, implemented them. It is to be noted that the *purohita* continued to be consulted on all important matters even after the prime minister had come into existence. In spite of the great discipline obtained in the army as attested by Megasthenes, Kauṭilya had advised the king to keep it under his direct control to eliminate the possibility of the military *coup*. K.A. Nilakantha Sastri has ignored the fact that *dauvārika* was a *tīrtha* and therefore cannot stand for a number of doorkeepers. It is difficult to agree with R.P. Kangle (1960-65) that the *praśāstṛ* of the *tīrtha* list is distinguished from *praśāstṛ* of Book X of the *Arthaśāstra*, for it would be unusual to presume that there were two totally different kinds of functionaries with one and the same designation in the service of the same king.

The *samāhartā* of the *Arthaśāstra* can easily be identified with the *dravyasañcaya-kṛta* of the *Mahābhārata*. One of the most novel functions of the Mauryan state was the census of villagers, population-wise, caste-wise, sex-wise, age-wise, occupation-wise and land-wise. Another novel function of the state was periodical checking of the revenue records done by the *gopa*, the *sthānika*, the *pradeṣṭā* and finally the *samāhartā*.

There is a good deal of difficulty in ascertaining the position of the *nāyaka*. From all accounts it appears that both *nāyaka* and *senāpati* were military leaders and that the *senāpati* was placed higher than the *nāyaka* in terms of salary, upper ranking and his mention in the company of *yuvarāja* and *kumāra*. It appears that when Kauṭilya speaks of the *senāpati* in singular number, he is the commandar-in-chief of the army. But when he refers to more than one *senāpati* – as done by the *Mahābhārata* also – he is a commandant of an unit of the army. Thus there were many *senāpati*s of different units. And in that case the *nāyaka* was the commandant of ten such *senāpati*s, all working under the command of the chief of the army, also known as *senāpati*. It should be noted that the *Mahābhārata*, in a similar situation, has used the word *adhi-senāpati* to make things clearer.

R. Shamasastry (1919) has committed the mistake of splitting *paura-vyāvahārika* into two words – *paura* for the city-officer and *vyāvahārika* for the superintendent of transaction. But it is more tenable to take it as one word and identify him with the *nagara-*

vyāvahārīka of Aśoka. In a similar fashion R. Shamasastry has taken *mantrī-pariṣadādhyakṣa* to mean two *tīrthas* – one *mantrī-pariṣad* and the other *adhyakṣa* (superintendent). But the *mantrī-pariṣad* – an assembly – can hardly be treated as an officer.

Antapāla of Kauṭilya is identifiable with *antamahāmātra* of Aśoka. But the identification of *stryadhyakṣamahāmātra* with *antarvaṁśika* is untenable, because the former looked after the interest of the whole womenfolk, whereas the latter was concerned with the ladies of the harem.

Mahāmātras of Aśoka were of the *amātya* rank and were kept reserved for specific purposes of vital importance. *Prādeśikas* and *pradeṣṭās* were one and the same. The *praśāstā* of Kauṭilya seems to have been a military officer commanding engineering and supply department of the army. The *rāṣṭrīya* and the *rāṣṭrapāla* of Aśoka and Kauṭilya respectively were provincial governors. *Rājukas* under Aśoka were the highest welfare, administrative and judicial officers in the countryside.

The Mauryan village enjoyed autonomy. Its administration was run by the *grāmika* with the help of the *grāma-vṛddhas*, *sāmanta* families and *grāma-bhṛtyas*. Likewise, the *nāgaraka* ran the city administration. His sanitary schemes and preventive measures against the outbreak of fire and anti-social activities were really comprehensive. The Mauryas had no separate department of police. Its functions were performed by the executive, revenue and judicial officers and even by the city and village administrators like the *nāgaraka* and the *grāmika*.

The civil services during the reigns of the Śuṅgas, the Sātavāhanas, the Indo-Greeks, the Śakas, the Pahlavas and the Kuṣāṇas reveal some important points of agreement and disagreement. According to Manu, the *sacivas* were ministers, whereas the *amātyas* were executive officers. Manu's word *parīkṣitān* should be taken to mean *upadhītān*. Manu has distinguished *senāpatyam* from *daṇḍanetṛtva*. So the former stands for the military functions and the latter for the police functions. Patañjali's *śaulkika* is the same as *Milindapañha*'s *śulkādhyakṣa*. The *navakarmika* of the Sātavāhana inscriptions was the overseer of the public works. The *karmāntika* also belonged to the Public Works Department. Instead of undertaking *navakarma*, he looked after repairs and preservation of old buildings. Both in the *Manusmṛti* and the Sātavāhana records, the *mahāmātra*s appear to be a special class of *amātya*s.

Interestingly, the *Milindapañha* also refers to the council of ministers.

The central point of the Śaka–Pahlava polity was the joint rule. However, the Śakas preserved the *amātya*s, the *mati-saciva*s and the *karma-saciva*s in their bureaucracy. Since the foreign rule was based on force, the *mahādaṇḍanāyaka* was given great importance under it.

The *Saddharmapuṇḍarīka* uses the words *rājaputra*s, *rāja-mahāmātra*s and *rājapuruṣa*s for civil servants. The *Divyāvadāna* speaks of the members of the *pariṣad* (*pariṣadyam*). It also uses the word *tulaka* for a councillor. Surprisingly, the Śakas, the Pahlavas and the Kuṣāṇas had no office of the *bhāṇḍāgārika*. The reference to the *nagara-sabhā* and the *grāmaṇī* testify that towns and villages continued to enjoy autonomy during the Śaka–Sātavāhana period.

The Kuṣāṇas retained the territorial divisions of *viṣaya* and *bhukti*, but put them under *kṣatrapa*s and *mahākṣatrapa*s. They continued with the joint rule also. The Sārnāth Inscription informs of the joint rule of Vanaspara and Kharapallana over eastern provinces of India. They also preserved local self-government in villages, as attested by numerous allusions to the *grāmika*, *grāmabhojaka*s and *grāmeyaka-yukta* in their inscriptions. However, the work of the *grāma-sabhā*s was supervised by the Kuṣāṇa officers named *grāma-svāmī*s. Thus, the disappearance of city-deities on their coins should not be interpreted as an evidence of the loss of village autonomy under the Kuṣāṇas. The Kuṣāṇa empire was not like the city states of the Greeks. This accounts for the discountinuance of portrayal of city-deities on their coins.

The Gupta records use the word *kumārāmātya* for civil servants besides the *amātya*. Our conclusion is that this new title was conferred on those *amātya*s who had proved their outstanding merit and had come to be treated as good as *kumāra*s. In other words, they were knighted *amātya*s. V.R.R. Dikshitar's view that *kumārāmātya*s were treasury officers goes against all available evidence, for the *kumārāmātya*s are shown as holding a variety of positions.

Holding of several posts by one and the same officer may not be taken to indicate that there was a dearth of talent in the Gupta period. It is inconceivable that a large country like India with a long tradition of trained and multifunctional civil service, suddenly ran out of efficient officers during the Gupta period which witnessed unprecedented growth in all intellectual and creative fields. Our conclusion is that several offices were entrusted to certain officers in recognition of their proven merit.

In a few cases the lower order of civil servants might have been paid in the form of land grants as well. But the discovery of a very large number of gold coins proves that civil servants, by and large were paid in cash.

The Guptas were mostly Vaiṣṇavas, but they appointed persons irrespective of their religious beliefs. For instance, Āmrakārddava was a Buddhist and yet he was made the commander of the Gupta forces by Candragupta II.

It is not likely that the *saciva*s and the *amātya*s were synonyms, as held by P.L. Gupta (1970) *saciva*s seem to have been ministers as is proved beyond doubt by the literary evidence of the Gupta period.

It is true that one Dhruvaśarmā was honoured by the *pariṣad* during the reign of Kumāragupta I. But this is hardly a strong evidence to suppose that the *pariṣad* had become only an academic body under the Guptas. Traditions of the *sabhā* and the *samiti* may point towards the multidimensional activities of the *pariṣad*.

The office of the *sāndhivigrahika* had firmly come into existence. Such illuminaries as Hariṣeṇa were appointed on this post. It is unnatural to suppose, as has been done by P.L. Gupta (1970), that such outstanding civil servants as Hariṣeṇa were kept out of the council of ministers. Again, the *mahādaṇḍanāyaka* does not appear to have been the chief justice. He was rather the Director General of Police.

The *uparika* under the Guptas enjoyed great prestige. Sometimes, he also held the titles of *mahārāja*, *mahāsāmanta* and *senāpati* and had a large number of functionaries – *balādhikaraṇa*, *raṇabhāṇḍāgārika*, *daṇḍapāśādhikaraṇa*, *mahādaṇḍanāyaka* and *mahāpratihāra* – under him.

The *rājasthānīya* seems to have been a prince who was appointed as a governor. Sometimes, a distinction was made between a central civil servant and a provincial civil servant. The former was termed as *paramabhaṭṭāraka-pādīya kumārāmātya* and the latter *yuvarāja-pādīya kumārāmātya*.

A large number of copper-plate inscriptions shed profuse light on the composition and functions of the autonomous *viṣaya-pariṣad* and *grāma-pariṣad* as also the mode of the sale, purchase and donations of land.

The Gupta records make frequent references to *dūtaka*. He seems to have been a central civil servant placed at the disposal of the district and village administration for regulating land transaction.

The Guptas appeared to have had a secretariat at the capital (*mūla*) which housed a number of high functionaries in it. It worked under the overall supervision of an officer called *sarvādhyakṣa*.

The Vardhana civil service was organized on the lines of the Gupta civil service with some departures. But it was not as efficient as the Gupta civil service was. The principle of heredity was carried to such ridiculous extent that an aged officer Siṁhanāda was retained on his post of the commander-in-chief when he merited retirement. Bāṇa has vividly criticized civil servants and courtiers in his *Harṣacarita*.

Bibliography

Original Sources

BRĀHMANICAL

Agni Purāṇa, ed. Baladeva Upadhyaya, Varanasi: Chowkhamba Sanskrit Series Office, 1966.

Aitareya Brāhmaṇa, Trivandrum, 1942.

Āpastamba Gṛhyasūtra, Varanasi: Chowkhamba Sanskrit Series Office, 1928.

Arthaśāstra of Kauṭilya, English. tr. R.P. Kangle, Bombay, 1963.

Arthaśāstra of Kauṭilya, Hindi tr. Vachaspati Gairola, Varanasi: Chowkhamba Sanskrit Series Office, 1984.

Aṣṭādhyāyī, Amritsar, Sonepat: Ramlal Kapoor Trust, 1964-68.

Atharvaveda Saṁhitā, tr. R.T. Griffith, 2 vols, Benares: E.J. Lazarus and Co., 1916-17.

Baudhāyana Dharmasūtra, Chowkhamba Sanskrit Series Office, Varanasi, 1934.

Bṛhaspatismṛti, Eng. tr. George Jolly, SBE vol. 33, Varanasi, 1935.

Dharmaśāstra of Kātyāyana, ed. N.C. Bandyopadhyaya, Calcutta, 1927.

Gāthā Śaptaśatī, Nirnaya Sagar Press, Bombay, 1911.

Harṣacarita of Bāṇa, tr. Edward B. Cowell and F.W. Thomas, London: Royal Asiatic Society, 1897.

Kādambarī of Bāṇa, tr. C.M. Ridding, London: Royal Asiatic Society, 1896.

Kauṭilya's Arthaśāstra, Eng. tr. R. Shamasastry, 6th edn, 1960.

Mahābhārata, 4 vols., Bhandarkar Oriental Research Institute, Poona, 1923 74.

Manusmṛti with Hindi tr., Chowkhamba Sanskrit Pratishthan, Delhi, 1987.

Mṛcchakaṭikam of Śūdraka, ed. R.D. Karmarkar, Poona, 1950.

Mudrā Rākṣasa of Viśākhadatta, tr. M.R. Kale, Bombay, 1900.

Nāgānanda of Harṣa, ed. and tr. M.R. Kale, Bombay, 1953.

Nāradasmṛti, Eng. tr. Jolly, SBE vol. 33, Varanasi, 1935.

Niruktam of Yāska, Gurumandala Series, Calcutta, 1953.

Nītisāra of Kāmandaka, tr. M.N. Dutt, Calcutta, 1896.

Patañjali-Vyākaraṇa Mahābhāṣya, Motilal Banarsidass, Delhi, 1967.

Priyadarśikā of Harṣa, tr. G.D. Nariman et al., New York, 1923.

Raghuvaṁśam of Kālidāsa, ed. and tr. M.R. Kale, 1922, Bombay: Goyal Narayen & Co. (5th edn, Delhi: Motilal Banarsidass, 1957).

Rāmāyaṇa Hindi tr. Ram Narayan Lal, Allahabad, 1958.

Ratnāvalī of Harṣa, ed. and tr. C.R. Devadhar and N.G. Suru, Poona, 1954.

Ṛgveda Saṁhitā, ed. Tilak Maharashtra Vidyapitha Vaidika Sansthana Mandala, Poona, 4 vols, 1933, 1936, 1941, 1946.

Śakuntalā and Other Works of Kālidāsa, tr. A.W. Ryder, London, 1912.

Śatapatha Brāhmaṇa, Eng. tr. Eggeling, SBE.

The Hymns of Ṛgveda, tr. Ralph H. Griffith, 2 vols, Varanasi: Chowkhamba Sanskrit Series Office, 1963.

The Principal Upaniṣads, Eng. tr. S.R. Radhakrishnan, George Allen and Unwin Ltd., London, 1953.

Yājñavalkyasmṛti, Nirnaya Sagar Press, Bombay, 1949.

BUDDHIST

Aṅguttara Nikāya, Eng. tr. Woodward and Hare, PTS, London, 1932-36.

Aśvaghoṣa, The Awakening of Faith, tr. Timothy Richard, Charless Skilton Ltd., London, 1960.

Dīgha Nikāya, Eng. tr. T.W. Rhys Davids, 3 vols, 1890, 1910, 1921.

Divyāvadāna, Mithila Vidyapith Prakashan, Darbhanga, 1958.

I-tsing, 1896, *A Record of Buddhist Practices Sent Home from the Southern Sea*, tr. Takakusu, J., Oxford.

Jātakas, tr. E.B. Cowell, Cambridge, 1895-1913.

Kathāvatthu, tr. Mrs. C.A.F. Rhyas Davids, Reprint, London: Pali Text Society, 1960.

Lalitavistara, ed. P.L. Vaidya, Darbhanga: The Mithila Institute of Post-Graduate Studies, 1958.

Mahāvastu Avadāna, 3 vols, Sanskrit College, Calcutta, 1963.

Majjima Nikāya, Eng. tr. Chalmers, 2 vols, London, 1926-27.

Milindaprasna, ed. R.D. Vadekar, University of Bombay, 1940.

Saddharmapuṇḍarīka, tr. N. Dutt, Asiatic Society, Calcutta, 1953.

Saṁyukta Nikāya, Eng. tr. Mrs. Davids and F.L. Woodward, London, 1917-30.

Vinaya Piṭaka, tr. Rahul Sankrityayana (in Hindi), Mahabodhi Society, Sarnath, 1935.

Watters, T. (ed.), 1904-05, *On Yuan Chwang's Travels in India*, 2 vols, London.

JAIN

Ācāraṅgasūtra, Hindi tr. S.S. Saran, Beawar, 1980.

Bhagavatisūtra, 2 vols, Surat, 1937, Jamnagar, 1940.

Kalpasūtra, SBE, London, 1892.

Pariśiṣṭaparvan, ed. H. Jacobi, Calcutta, 1932.

Uttarādhyayanasūtra, tr. H. Jacobi, SBE, Oxford, 1895.

OTHER SOURCES

Fa-hien's Account of his Travels in India, tr. J.A. Legge, *Record of Buddhistic Kingdoms*, etc., Oxford, 1886.

Giles, H.A., 1923, *The Travels of Fa-hien*, Cambridge.

Hui-Li, 1911, *The Life of Hiuen-Tsiang*, tr. S. Beal, London.

McCrindle, J.W., 1877, *Ancient India as Described by Megasthenes and Arrian*, Calcutta.

Yuan Chwang, 1906, *Buddhist Records of the Western World*, tr. S. Beal, 2 vols, London.

INSCRIPTIONS

Fleet, J.F., 1963, *Corpus Inscriptionum Indicarum*, Indological Book House, Varanasi.

Hultzsch, E., 1925, *Inscription of Aśoka*, *CII*, vol. I, London.

Konow, Sten, 1969, *Kharoṣṭhī Inscriptions*, vol. II, Indological Book House, Varanasi.

Luder's *List*, Appendix to *EI*, vol. X, Calcutta, 1912.

Sircar, D.C., 1942, *Select Inscriptions Bearing on Indian History and Civilisation*, vol. I, Calcutta.

Secondary Sources

Agnihotri, Prabhu Dayal, 1963, *Patañjali-kālīn Bhārat*, Patna.

Agrawal, V.S., 1953, *India as Known to Pāṇini*, Lucknow.

———, 1953a, *Harṣa-Carita: Ek Sāṁskṛtika Adhyayana*, Patna: Bihar Rashtrabhasha Parishad.

———, 1958, *Kādambarī: Ek Sāṁskṛtika Adhyayana*, Varanasi: Chowkhamba Vidya Bhavan.

Aiyanger, K.V. Ramaswamy, 1936, *Some Aspects of Ancient Indian Polity*, Madras.

———, Ramaswamy, 1949, *Aspects of Social and Political System of Manusmṛti*, Lucknow.

Aiyar, C.P. Ramaswamy, 1937, *Indian Political Theories*, Madras.

Aiyar, Narayan, R.A., 1925, *The History of the Hindu Law in Vedic Age and in the Post-Vedic Times down to the Institute of Manu*, Madras.

Altekar, A.S., 1949, *State and Government in Ancient India*, Benares.

Anjaria, J.J., 1935, *The Nature and Grounds of Political Obligations in the Hindu State*, Bombay.

Bandyopadhyaya, N.C., 1927, *Development of Hindu Polity and Political Ideas*, Calcutta.

———, 1927a, *Kauṭilya*, Calcutta.

Banerji, P.N., 1916, *Public Administration in Ancient India*, London.

Barua, B.M., 1946, *Aśoka and His Inscriptions*, Calcutta.

Basak, R.G., 1967, *Some Aspects of Kauṭilyan Political Thinking*, University of Burdwan.

Bhandarkar, D.R., 1929, *Some Aspects of Ancient Hindu Polity*, Benares

———, 1955, *Aśoka*, Calcutta.

Bhargava, Purushottam Lal, 1935, *Chandragupta Maurya*, Lucknow: The Upper India Publishing House (2nd revised edn: D.K. Printworld, New Delhi, 1996).

Bhattacharya, Sukhmaya, 1966, *Mahābhārata-Kālina Sāmaj*, Allahabad: Lok Bharati.

Breloer, Bernhard, 1927-34, *Kauṭilya Studies*, Bonn.

Chatterji, G.S., 1950, *Harṣacarita*, Allahabad.

Chattopadhyaya, Sudhankar, 1955, *The Śakas in India*, Santiniketan: Visva Bharati.

Chaturvedi, Sitaram, 1944, *Kālidāsa-Granthāvalī*, Kashi: Jnana-Mandala.

Chowdhury, R.K., 1953, *Ancient Indian Law and Justice*, Benares.

———, 1971, *Kauṭilya's Political Ideas and Institutions*, Varanasi.

Dandekar, R.N., *Theory of Political Ideas* (D.P.).

———, 1941, *A History of the Guptas*, Poona.

Das Gupta, R.P., 1930, *Crime and Punishment in Ancient India*, Calcutta.

Das, Ram Mohan, 1982, *Crime and Punishment in Ancient India with a Particular Reference to the Manusmṛti*, Bodh Gaya.

Devahuti, 1970, *Harṣa: A Political Study*, Oxford.

Dharma, P.C., 1941, *The Rāmāyaṇa Polity*, Madras.

Dikshitar, V.R.R., 1929, *Hindu Administrative Institutions*, Madras.

———, 1952, *Gupta Polity*, Madras.

———, 1953, *Mauryan Polity*, Madras.

Dipankar, Acharya, 1968, *Kauṭilya-Kālīna Bhāratha*, Lucknow: Hindi Samiti.

Drekmeier, C., 1962, *Kingship and Community in Early India*, California.

Ghosal, U.N., 1923, *A History of Hindu Political Theories from Ancient Times*, London.

Ghosal, U.N., 1929, *Contribution to the History of Hindu Revenue System*, Calcutta.

———, 1963, *Studies in Indian History and Culture*, Calcutta.

———, 1963-66, *A History of Indian Public Life*, vols I & II, Bombay: Oxford University Press.

Gonda, J., 1966, *Ancient Indian Kingship from the Religious Point of View*, Leiden.

Gopal, L., 1965, *The Economic Life of Northern India*, Varanasi: Motilal Banarsidass.

Gopal, M.H., 1935, *Mauryan Public Finance*, London.

Gupta, P.L., 1970, *Gupta Sāmrājya*, Varanasi.

Gyani, S.D., 1964, *Agni Purāṇa: A Study*, Varanasi.

Jayaswal, K.P., 1930, *Manu and Yājñavalkya*, Calcutta.

———, 1934, *Hindu Polity*, Calcutta.

Jha, D.N., 1967, *Revenue System in Post-Mauryan and Gupta Times*, Calcutta.

Jnani, Shiv Datt, 1967, *Vedakālīna Sāmāja*, Varanasi: Chowkhamba Vidya Bhavan.

Kane, P.V., 1930-62, *History of Dharmaśāstra*, vols I-II, Poona: Bhandarkar Oriental Research Institute.

Kangle, R.P., 1960-65, *The Arthaśāstra of Kauṭilya*, vols I-III, Bombay.

Kumar, B., 1973, *The Early Kuṣāṇas*, New Delhi: Sterling Publishers.

Lal, Angane, 1968, *Sanskrit Bauddha Sāhitya Men Bhāratiya Jīvan*, Lucknow: Kailash Prakashan.

Law, N.N., 1960, *Aspects of Ancient Indian Polity*, Orient Longman.

Majumdar, B.K., 1955, *The Military System in Ancient India*, Calcutta.

Majumdar, R.C., 1918, *Corporate Life in Ancient India*, Calcutta.

Majumdar, R.C. and A.D. Pusalkar (eds), 1951-55, *History and Culture of the Indian People*, vols I-IV., Bombay: Bharatiya Vidya Bhavan.

Mishra, B.B., 1965, *Polity in Agni Purāṇa*, Calcutta.

Mitra, Veda, 1965, *India of Dharmaśāstras*, New Delhi: Arya Book Depot.

Mookerji, R.K., 1926, *Harṣa*, London.

———, 1920, *Local Government in Ancient India*, Oxford.

———, 1943, *Candragupta Maurya and His Times*, Madras.

Narain, A.K., 1957, *The Indo-Greeks*, Oxford.

Nath, Birendra, 1979, *Judicial Administration in Ancient India*, Patna.

Pandey, Shyam Lal, 1956, *Janatantravāda: Rāmāyaṇa aur Mahābhārata-Kālīna*, Lucknow.

Panikkar, K.M., 1922, *Śrī Harṣa of Kannauj*, Bombay.

———, 1928, *The Origin and Evolution of Kingship in India*, Baroda.

Pant, R.C., 1929, *Amātya: Royal Edicts on the Principles of State Policy*, Madras.

Panthari, B.P., 1953, *Yavana Itihāsakāroṅ Kā Bhārata-Varṇana*, Varanasi: Kashi Vidyapith.

Prasad, A.D., 1968, *Corruption and Administration*, Patna.

Prasad, Beni, 1927, *The Theory of Government in Ancient India*, Allahabad.

———, 1928, *The State in Ancient India*, Allahabad.

Puri, B.N., 1957, *India in the Time of Patañjali*, Bombay.

———, 1965, *India under the Kuṣāṇas*, Bombay: Bharatiya Vidya Bhavan.

Ragozin, Z.A., 1961, *Vedic India*, Delhi.

Rai, K.K., 1965, *Aparādha aur Daṇḍa*, Varanasi.

Ram Gopal, 1959, *India of Vedic Kalpasūtras*, Delhi: National Publishing House.

Ramaswami, P.N., 1962, *Essentials of Indian State-Craft*, Bombay.

Rao, M.V. Krishna, 1953, *Studies in Kauṭilya*, Mysore.

Saletore, R.N., 1943, *Life in the Gupta Age*, Bombay.

Sarkar, B.K., 1939, *Political Institutions and Theories of the Hindus*, Calcutta.

Sastri, K.A. Nilkantha, 1957, *Comprehensive History of India*, vol. III, Bombay/ Madras: Bharatiya Itihas Parishad.

——— (ed.), 1967, *Age of the Nandas and the Mauryas*, Delhi.

Sen, S.N., 1956, *India Through Chinese Eyes*, Madras.

Shamasastry, R., 1919, *The Kauṭilya's Arthaśāstra*, Mysore.

Sharma, Ram Sharan, 1965, *Indian Feudalism*, Calcutta.

———, 1968, *Aspects of Political Ideas and Institutions in Ancient India*, Delhi: Motilal Banarsidass.

Shastri, A.M., 1969, *India as Seen in Bṛhatsamhitā*, Delhi.

Shastri, J.L., 1944, *Political Thought in the Purāṇas*, Lahore.

Shastri, T. Ganapati, 1924-25, *The Arthaśāstra of Kauṭilya*, Trivandrum.

Shastri, Udayavir, 1925, *The Kauṭilya Arthaśāstra*, Lahore.

Sikdar, J.C., 1964, *Studies in the Bhagavti Sūtra*, Muzaffarpur.

Singh, Shivaji, 1972, *Evolution of Smṛti Law*, Benares.

Sinha, B.P., 1974, *The Comprehensive History of Bihar*, vol. I & II, Patna.

Sinha, H.N., 1938, *Sovereignty in Ancient Indian Polity*, London.

Sircar, D.C., 1966, *Land System and Feudalism in Ancient India*, Calcutta.

Spellman, J.W., 1964, *Political Theory of Ancient India*, London.

Stein, Otto, 1921, *Megasthenes and Kauṭilya*, Wien.

Thakur, Upendra, 1979, *Corruption in Ancient India*, Delhi.

Thapar, R., 1961, *Aśoka and the Decline of the Mauryas*, London.

Topa, I., 1941, *The Minister as a Kingmaker*, Allahabad.

Tripathi, H.N., 1965, *Prācīna Bhārata Meṅ Rājya aur Nyāya-pālikā*, Delhi.

Upadhyaya, B.S., 1954-55, *Kālidāsa kā Bhārata*, vols I & II, Kashi: Bharatiya Jnanapith.

———, 1959, *Gupta Sāmrājya ka Itihasa*, vols I & II, Allahabad: Indian Press.

Vardachariar, S., 1946, *The Hindu Judicial System*, Lucknow.

Varma, Gayatri, 1963, *Kālidāsa ke Granthoṅ Para Ādhārita Tatkālīna Bhāratīya Saṁskṛti*, Varanasi.

Varma, V.P., 1954, *Studies in Hindu Political Thought and Its Metaphysical Foundations* (3rd revised and enlarged edn, 1974) Benares: Motilal Banarsidass.

Vidyalankar, Satyaketu, 1986, *Prācīna Bhārata kī Śāsana-Saṁsthāyeṅ aur Rājanītika Vicāra*, Mussoorie.

Vyas, S.N., 1967, *India in the Rāmāyaṇa Age*, Delhi.

Journals

Annals of the Bhandarkar Oriental Research Institute, Poona.

Bulletin of the School of Oriental and African Studies, London.

East and West, Rome.

Epigraphica Indica, Calcutta, Delhi.

Indian Antiquary, Bombay.

Indian Culture, Calcutta.

Indian Historical Quarterly, Calcutta.

Journal of the Andhra Historical Research Society, Rajahmundry.

Journal of the Asiatic Society of Bengal, Calcutta.

Journal of Banaras Hindu University, Varanasi.

Journal of the Bihar and Orissa Research Society, Patna.

Journal of the Ganga Nath Jha Research Institute, Allahabad.

Journal of the Orissa Historical Research Society.

Journal of the Royal Asiatic Society of Bengal (*Letters*), Calcutta.

Journal of the Royal Asiatic Society of Great Britain and Ireland, London.

Journal of U.P. Historical Society, Lucknow.

Journal of Indian History, Trivandrum.

Poona Orientalist, Poona.

Research Bulletin of the College of Indology, Banaras Hindu University, Varanasi.

Visvabandhu Vishvesvarananda Indological Journal, Hoshiarpur.

Proceedings

Proceedings of the Indian History Congress.

Proceedings and Transactions of the All India Oriental Conference.

Index